Teaching What Matters

Teaching What Matters

Activating Happiness, Kindness, and Altruism

Steve A. Banno Jr.

ROWMAN & LITTLEFIELD
Lanham • Boulder • New York • London

Published by Rowman & Littlefield
An imprint of The Rowman & Littlefield Publishing Group, Inc.
4501 Forbes Boulevard, Suite 200, Lanham, Maryland 20706
www.rowman.com

86-90 Paul Street, London EC2A 4NE, United Kingdom

Copyright © 2022 by Steve A. Banno Jr.

All rights reserved. No part of this book may be reproduced in any form or by any electronic or mechanical means, including information storage and retrieval systems, without written permission from the publisher, except by a reviewer who may quote passages in a review.

British Library Cataloguing in Publication Information Available

Library of Congress Cataloging-in-Publication Data

Names: Banno, Steve A., 1973- author.
Title: Teaching what matters : activating happiness, kindness, and altruism / Steve A. Banno, Jr..
Description: Lanham, Maryland : Rowman & Littlefield, [2022] | Includes bibliographical references and index. | Summary: "Teaching What Matters is a comprehensive guidebook distilling that course with emerging research in the science of happiness and altruism"—Provided by publisher.
Identifiers: LCCN 2021055277 (print) | LCCN 2021055278 (ebook) | ISBN 9781475860894 (Cloth : acid-free paper) | ISBN 9781475860900 (Paperback : acid-free paper) | ISBN 9781475860917 (ePub)
Subjects: LCSH: Affective education. | Social learning. | Emotional intelligence. | School environment—Social aspects.
Classification: LCC LB1072 .B36 2022 (print) | LCC LB1072 (ebook) | DDC 370.15/34—dc23/eng/20220106
LC record available at https://lccn.loc.gov/2021055277
LC ebook record available at https://lccn.loc.gov/2021055278

*For Karen, Andrew, my family, and friends who
have taught me what matters most in life.*

Contents

Preface	ix
Disclaimer	xiii
Acknowledgments	xv
Introduction	xix
Chapter 1: An Invitation to Teach What Matters	1
Chapter 2: Redefining Success	13
Chapter 3: Happiness as an Inside Job: Developing Emotional Courage, Befriending Difficult Emotions, Cultivating Positive Emotions, Optimism and an Attitude of Gratitude	51
Chapter 4: It's About Time: Giving Some Intention to Our Attention	79
Chapter 5: The Heart of Altruism: Compassion, Human Goodness, and Helping Others	109
Bibliography	177
Notes	183
About the Author	201

Preface

Graduation day is my favorite day of the school year. It is a wonderful day. The outpouring of positivity and pride amongst faculty, administration, parents, and students makes this day special. However, back in the early 2000s, an upsetting trend developed in the messages expressed in student graduation speeches. These speeches became a catalyst to the development of the high school course I created and later this book.

On this particular graduation day, the class valedictorian, an extremely positive individual and successful in so many domains, spoke about the shared experiences of classmates. The speech highlighted fun memories, experiences, and collective accomplishments. Then the message of the speech shifted to the future.

The valedictorian shared various reflections from classmates about their schooling experience. These reflections revealed that the time in high school was marred with stress, anxiety, fatigue, and *surviving* high school. Then came the central premise of the speech. One of the benefits of graduating high school was that students could finally look forward to experiencing something they had been lacking in their four years. There was a pause. Then came the big reveal. What was lacking was *"happiness."*

This similar sentiment was expressed over many years in various student speeches. I was well aware of student stress at our high-performance school. The social and societal problems that affect young people are varied and nuanced.

Across the United States young people are bored in school. The High School Survey of Student Engagement reported recently that 66 percent of high school students say they are bored *every day*. The survey also noted that 82 percent of students reported that the material being taught wasn't interesting or relevant to them.

In addition, rates of stress, anxiety, depression, and feeling overwhelmed and chronically stressed are increasing for high school aged youth. According to the Anna Freud National Centre in the U.K., the coronavirus pandemic has contributed to increasing global mental health challenges for children. Young people are experiencing increased rates of anxiety and loneliness along with decreased satisfaction with their lives.

These mental health concerns are also evident across U.S. colleges. According to the American Council on Education, more than 80 percent of top university executives say that mental health has become a central priority on college campuses. More funding has been allocated to meet these increased mental health needs.

Teachers, parents, and administrators have talked about these trends for over two decades. Most adults see adolescents successfully balance the many demands of a stressful high school life: work, caring for younger siblings, sports, clubs, theatre, dance, friends, family, health, SAT prep, college preparation, etc. They also see young people excel at athletics, music, mock-trial, debates, chess, math, theatric performances, and many club endeavors.

Young people today aren't broken. They are compassionate, generous, fun, inclusive, industrious, resilient, empathic, goal-oriented, and ambitious. Unfortunately, at different points of the year, many of these young people also happen to be miserable. In the hallways, these young people who begin the year with a spark in their eyes, instead frequently have worry, stress, frustration, and fatigue in those same eyes.

Many students feel they are engaged in a Darwinian struggle for achievement and "success." As a result, many teens believe that they need to do anything to compete with each other. They admit to frequently lying, cheating, and finding ways to simply do school to get a "good" grade.

Conversations with students have often been filled with condemnations about assessments, grades, homework, incidents involving microaggressions, inequities, lack of connections, problems with friends, problems with families, scarcity of leisure, fear of failure, lack of attainment of perfection in their lives, and all too high expectations for how life is supposed to be. Living during a global pandemic has only added to the list of concerns for young people.

Also in the mid 2000s, while I was teaching modern World History and AP U.S. History, I began realizing that my class lessons were transforming adolescents into misanthropes. The history of the modern world was generally described by students as an "awful history." From their perspective, modern world history was a progression of centuries where war-war-revolution-genocide-war-imperialism-war-genocide-revolution-war-colonialism-oppression-economic underdevelopment-famine-war-human suffering were recurring themes.

These are upsetting realities, but necessary case studies. This history provides insights and backstories to understanding the world and where we are today. My concern was young people were leaving at the end of the year with a myopic understanding of human nature and the positive possibilities of the present and the future.

Dwight Eisenhower warned us in his Presidential Farewell Address in 1959, about his concern over the fusion of informal and formal coalitions of groups, governments, scientists, universities, and private corporations who were working to create a military-industrial complex which endangered the very fabric and heart of American democracy.

With standardization dictates and a devotion to an intangible cult of achievement, schools have been working to create, consciously or not, an *academic industrial complex*. A coalition of forces and unwarranted influences which have led to a disastrous rise of misplaced priorities, actions, and behaviors. Schooling has gradually shifted to survival of the academically fittest. This often comes at the expense of individual needs, differences, and well-being. It is apparent to many other teachers, parents, and administrators that students have been losing a sense of themselves.

Real world learning, nurturing the developmental needs of children, having fun, generating community, fostering agency and efficacy in school, academic experimentation, and fostering leisure and meaningful experiences have been pushed aside in favor of multitasking, treadmill consumption of information. This is compounded with increased amounts of nightly homework. In fact, for some students, homework has become a Faustian bargain: not what students had to do, but rather a decision late at night about what "I can get away with not doing for tomorrow."

The fact is everyone wants children to be happy. As adults, we also hope young people choose to make a difference in the lives of others. We hope young people will put their education toward a purpose higher than just themselves. I chose to teach because I believed this. I've got a sneaky suspicion you believe this too.

After many years of graduation laments, listening to parents, peers, and talking with colleagues about this academic industrial complex, the idea for a class about happiness, kindness, and altruism was born. I named this class *The Love Course: Exploring the Art of Living*. I hoped this class would inspire and engross young people in a counternarrative of human nature. I also wanted to provide the means for young people to explore the complexities and possibilities of living a good and meaningful life.

For over fifteen years students have often asked me, "Do you practice what you teach?" The short answer is yes and no. While I am careful to maintain professional and personal boundaries, I often share my own personal anecdotes and engage in debriefing discussions within our classroom community. I point out various research-based interventions and theories that have had the greatest impact on my life and thinking.

I still fall prey to my old habits of thinking and behavior. These habits prove pernicious to my well-being, often creating inertia in my life. I am happy to say that I know which direction I'd like to point my life compass. This direction is toward joy and erring on being kind.

I understand there isn't a finish line. I often lose my way. At the very least, I know what I want for my life. If sharing my experiences with young people inspires or encourages them to do the same, then I am happy to model that in the classroom. I trust you will as well.

Disclaimer

This publication is designed as a source of information only and is not intended as a substitute for psychological treatment or professional services of any kind. The author and publisher expressly disclaim any responsibility for any adverse effects from the use or application of the information contained herein. If mental health treatment is required, readers should seek individual help and services from licensed mental health professionals. Mental health related information changes frequently and therefore information can become outdated, incomplete, or incorrect.

Acknowledgments

No one writes and publishes a book without a lot of help. There were so many people that helped me directly or indirectly make this book a reality. I am very grateful and fortunate to have them in my life.

A special thanks to one of my close friends Earl Walton. When the idea for this book was just an idea, his support, encouragement, and active engagement helped me to believe that this book was possible and was needed in the world. I'm grateful for your support, three decades of friendship, and coaching me up.

I want to acknowledge the support of those who have shared their time, expertise, and experience. I could have never developed a final form of this book without their help.

A big thank you to Chris Brande for his early reads of multiple drafts, corrections, and line-item commentary that helped me find some golden nuggets for this book.

I would like to express similar gratitude to John Brande, Gregg Bruno, Patrick Kelly, and Sean O'Reilly for their friendship, support, and expertise in shaping early drafts into substantive chapters and helping to facilitate connections with researchers. I am grateful for the hours you have given to this project. Your constant encouragement kept pushing me forward. Great teachers are a gift. I am fortunate to have John, Gregg, Pat, and Sean as friends and colleagues who inspire me.

Chris, John, Gregg, Patrick, and Sean, I could have never developed a final form of this book without your help. Your comments, insights, validations, suggestions, corrections, and constructive criticism all helped. I owe a debt of gratitude to each of you.

I would like to thank my friends John Devaney and Jason Butchko for keeping me grounded while also celebrating this book endeavor. I am grateful for our shared experiences, continued laughter, and fun over our three decades of friendship.

I was lucky early in this process connecting with Dave and Shelley Burgess. They helped motivate me to better understand the nuts and bolts of writing and publishing. Thank you for your support, encouragement, and education early in this process.

A big thank you to my editor Tom Koerner at Rowman & Littlefield for validating and believing in this book and making numerous suggestions that have greatly improved this book. I would also like to thank Carlie Wall and everyone at Rowman & Littlefield for helping to bring this book to fruition.

I would like to express my appreciation for the work of the following individuals that have inspired me and guided my knowledge development during the course of two decades. Thank you to Martin Seligman, Sonja Lyubormirsky, Ilona Boniwell, Emma Seppala, Vanessa King, Richard Davidson, Mathieu Riccard, Tal-Ben Shahar, Barbara Fredrickson, Robert Sapolsky, Jon Kabat-Zinn, Dacher Keltner, Rick Hanson, everyone at Mindful Schools, the late Ed Diener and Chris Peterson, George Mumford, Sharon Salzberg, Laurie Santos, and so many others for letting me stand on your monumental shoulders.

I would like to thank my family and friends for their love, support, and infectious excitement throughout this process. My Dad and Stepmother Rose, my other parents Dave (Vavo) and Alice (Z), my brothers and yogis Jeff and Howard, my favorite nephew Tighe and my favorite niece Allie, Rick and Joyce, and the Cote clan. A big thank you to Rich and Renee, Gay Vernon, Jeff and Lara, and Deepika and Calvin for your support and encouragement.

A big thanks to the support of the Town of Sharon School Committee, with special thanks to the support and work of Jonathan Hitter, Marcy Kaplan, and Emily Smith-Lee.

I would also like to thank my former Superintendents Tim Farmer and Dr. Victoria Greer. Also, a big thank to Bernadette Murphy for her help in the early stages of this writing process.

I'd also like to express heartfelt gratitude and appreciation to all my students in my Love Course and Happiness and Altruism classes. For almost two decades, your feedback and willingness to experiment in the art of living and being anchors for goodness has validated this book. I hope and trust you find greater well-being in your lives and continue to send forth tiny ripples of hope.

A special thank you to my department heads, John Brande, Laura Smolcha, and Chuck Fazzio for their support of my course and also this book. I also want to thank Kee Arguimbau for always helping to support the Love Course and believing in teaching what matters. Thank you for your willingness to help support me and my endeavors but also your work in helping to make the lives of young people better.

I also want to thank friends, colleagues, and staff in my department and in the other departments for their support and encouragement. Thank you to Tom, Courtnay, Nina, Mara, Tanya, Jen, Dorothy, Emily, Glenn, Jill, Hannah, Anne, Peter, and Catherine. Your compliments and encouragement about my class, sharing of resources, and teaching ideas over the years has always been appreciated. Thank you for your hard work in and out of the classroom. You are making the world a little bit better each day.

Thank you to my current and former teaching colleagues at SHS and the current administrative team of Beth and Joe. Your daily commitment to the well-being of young people has been and continues to be an inspiration to me.

Thank you to all retired colleagues and friends, including Esther and especially Janet Picheny for her support and mentoring early in my career.

I would also like to thank one of the biggest sources of my happiness and inspiration, my son Andrew. Thank you for helping me disconnect from long days of writing with encouragement, bike rides, spontaneous laughter, ice cream, good music, and sunset chasing. Being your Dad is one of the things that matters most to me.

I'd like to express my heartfelt gratitude to my wife Karen. I couldn't have written this book without you. You have worn different hats during this process, being the biggest supporter of this book, sounding board on long walks or bike rides, and exemplifying the contents of this book with your own students. I know it wasn't easy watching me sequestering myself, head buried in books or at a computer screen for hours and days during many summers. Your belief in this book, love, and support encouraged me to continually write the chapters of this book. I feel very lucky and grateful that you have chosen to live the various chapters of your life with me.

Introduction

This book is a labor of love. It is an outgrowth of a high school course that has been taught for almost two decades that has encouraged teenagers to explore the philosophy and science of happiness and altruism. This book is a means to share the workings of this course. *Teaching What Matters* attempts to activate happiness, kindness, and altruistic tendencies not only for adolescents but also for anyone that works with young people.

When you explain that you are teaching happiness and kindness, you are usually met with cynicism and skepticism from others. That's okay. Many people have been conditioned to believe that *"If you love, you are considered frivolous and simple. If generous, and altruistic, you are considered suspect. If forgiving, you are considered weak. If trusting, you are considered a fool. If you try to be all of those things, people are sure you are phony."*[1]

Just remember, teaching and modeling behavior that encourages children to open their hearts to the world, to others, and to themselves is the most worthy and important endeavor we can provide to them as adults. An education should connect one's intellect with their heart.

Adolescents want to learn about things that matter. Young people want to know the secrets of living a good life. Everyone wants this. The desire to be happy has been a constant throughout history. Saint Augustine believed that happiness was essential and motivated all our actions. Happiness continues to be what matters most. Wanting to live a good and meaningful life does not make you a naive idealist or a biased optimist. It makes you human.

The lessons enjoined throughout this book attempt to empower adolescents to create changes in themselves that we all wish to see in the world: optimism over cynicism, contentment over stress, compassion over indifference, connection over isolation, resiliency over floundering, and kindness over cruelty. Now more than ever, young people want an education that helps them to improve their internal worlds while promoting opportunities to better the external world. They want to learn how love and goodness win over hatred and malevolence in the world. Teenagers smartly realize what Walker Percy wrote, "You can get all A's and still flunk life."[2]

Take a moment and envision the future. What is the best possible future you could hope for our communities, our nation, the world, and our planet? As writer Marc Ian Barasch reminds us, *"It's amazing what one seed can grow. Sown in the ground, planted in the heart, each day it seems to grow a little more true."*[3] Plant the seeds of benevolence and well-being and watch those seeds grow.

BOOK OVERVIEW

Chapter 1, An Invitation to Teach What Matters provides an invitation for teaching happiness, kindness, and compassion. The chapter provides an overview on what is known about the science of happiness, what happiness is and what it is not. It also provides a summation of recent developments in various academic disciplines to understand the roots of human happiness and the positive side to human nature. Lastly the chapter provides insights into the social-emotional renaissance that is taking place in schools and colleges around the world.

Chapters 2 through 5 encompass recommended user-friendly lesson ideas or *Playbooks*, containing teaching strategies and assessment ideas. These lessons are opportunities for young people to experiment with the art of living. These chapters are designed to explore the components of well-being. Each chapter attempts to demystify the properties of well-being using Martin Seligman's PERMA model.[4] Each of the properties of well-being are integrated in chapters 2–5.

One of the elements of well-being consists of experiencing positive emotions, that is feeling good with an internal sense of control, engaging in activities and pursuits that are enjoyable. Strong and supportive relationships with others is great source of happiness. Cultivating close and meaningful relationships with peers, parents, family, and friends contributes to well-being. Having meaning in one's life rather than pursuit of pleasure or materialism also is an element of flourishing. Doing things for others rather than oneself often promotes a deeper sense of well-being. Lastly, achievement provides a sense of accomplishment and increased self-esteem through agency. Creating goals and dedicating oneself to obtaining intrinsically satisfying pursuits creates a sense of competence and fulfillment.

To investigate these elements and galvanize engagement, guiding questions are embedded. These questions are often parred with thought-experiments and inquiry starters. Opportunities for reflection and journaling are frequent. The content and context of research are explained with recommended readings to help advance understanding. These teaching points are designed to be conversational rather than passively received by students.

Lesson procedures are scaffolded with daily lesson ideas. This means that lessons blend together to build meaning and proficiency. They provide the means to present ideas and facilitate reflection, conversations, discussions and debates, and application. Each lesson contains guiding questions, lesson objectives, activities, workshops, materials, resources, and assessments. Resources for each lesson are provided. Each of the lesson sequences take a broad view of research from positive psychology and other academic disciplines.

Chapter 2, Redefining Success begins by deconstructing conventional notions of success, then constructing individualized broadened notions of success living. In precept #2, the relationship between money, materialism, and happiness is explored. Precept #3 attempts to analyze the illusion of perfectionism, normalizing failure and failing better, while also investigating authenticity and vulnerability. The identification and application of individual signature strengths are also examined. In precept #4, pursuing meaningful life goals is introduced to assess and apply.

In chapter 3, Happiness as an Inside Job, precept #5 introduces emotions, developing emotional intelligence and awareness, and examines cognitive distortions and negative emotions. Recommendations for managing difficult emotions and reframing adversity are offered. Precept #6 studies the benefits of positive emotions, positivity, looking on the bright side, and gratitude.

In chapter 4, It's About Time, precept #7 urges reflecting on one's relationship to time while considering one's time perspective. Precept #8 explores mindfulness and mindfulness meditation to help better understand the anatomy of being present and calm within the moments of our lives. Precepts #9 and #10 introduce ways to improve one's relationship with time by savoring, slowing down, and rediscovering playfulness and flow.

Chapter 5 shifts to understanding the roots of altruism and the positive, benevolent side of human nature. One of the foundational pillars of well-being is the connection people have with others. Not only that, doing for others can be as important to personal happiness as doing for ourselves.

This chapter attempts to make the case for cultivating those elements in human nature that incline us to goodness, compassion, and kindness. Precept #11 begins with gathering perceptions of the state of the world, human nature, and one's responsibilities, if any, to others. The bystander effect is explored to examine why some people help others and why some people may not. The more someone understands the social psychology forces that lead to the bystander effect, the less likely they are to succumb to them in the future. Precept #12 delves into stories and research on the motivations behind heroic action and recognized altruists.

Precept #13 introduces the antecedents of altruism and human goodness in nature and the evolutionary history of animals and humans. The precept illustrates what Charles Darwin believed, that is cooperation and compassion were essential to the evolutionary process. In addition, the origins of human morality are explored, focusing on cognition and helping tendencies in infants and toddlers. Precept #14 highlights the theories that illustrate the origins of altruism. Activities and investigations into kin-selection theory, reciprocal altruism theory, and empathy-altruism theory all help to foster understanding of the origins of altruism.

SOME GUIDING PRINCIPLES FOR TEACHING WELL-BEING IN THE CLASSROOM

Each precept is infused with a playbook or tools in the form of lesson steps. There is flexibility and choice in deciding how long to spend on various lessons and precepts. There is no need to follow a dogmatic adherence to the procedures.

The lesson steps are designed so you can work with students; your own curriculum requirements; and any demands set forth by state standards, your district, or administrators to determine which lessons you will employ. You will also be able to assess how much *you* will model and which to leave to student inquiry.

Since there isn't a one size fits all approach to human flourishing, it would be irresponsible to teach prescriptive notions of well-being. What might be beneficial for one person may not be for another. That is why throughout many lesson steps there is a strong emphasis on trying out what is being learned. Students can experiment outside of school, testing habits of living that research suggests might contribute to increased life satisfaction. Healthy skepticism and scrutiny are encouraged as students test and assess the research and their experiences.

There are multiple pathways to improving well-being. However, various happiness practices may not work universally. Personal traits, life circumstances, how happy you are at a given moment, suitability, personal preferences, motivation, effort, duration, and variety all play a role in the effectiveness of any happiness boosting activity.[5] The best strategy is usually the simplest. Often times just persuading young people to act on what they already know about their well-being is the most effective.

This book is not a self-help course, nor are class discussions meant to be therapy sessions for students. Some students might share things in class discussions that are inappropriate or too personal. What discussions attempt to do is to guide knowledge and foster comprehension. It is important to establish boundaries for class discussions. Within these boundaries adolescents will come to know what is appropriate to share. Providing opportunities for students to self-reflect, to talk with their peers, and to pose questions are all important elements of the learning process.

Presenting various lessons may require a departure from the way one usually teaches. This course requires multiple roles for any adult which are both liberating and demanding. Students can be trusted to work independently. It is important that learners recognize their understanding in whatever form it takes. This comprehension will result in the emergence of self-knowledge, content knowledge, experiential knowledge, and the formation of habits of Eudaimonic well-being. Assessments are loosely designed to provide evidence of achievement within each of the precepts.

With all this in mind, the following foundational principles can be helpful when thinking about creating a learning environment

- **Big questions** frame the units and lessons of the course daily.
- **Reflection, reflection, reflection** . . . students are given ample opportunity to reflect on content.
- Students are given opportunities to **apply the ideas** taught in the course to their lives.
- Students **experiment** with various concepts, theories, ideas, and philosophies in micro-experiments in living.
- **Bridge wisdom** of the past (philosophy, and/or religion, literature) with recent discoveries in various sciences that allow students to construct meanings and answers to the big questions of one's life.
- The job of the teacher is to help facilitate student responses to **big questions.** At times you are to support their inquiry, rather than trying to control it. Value their autonomy over your adult authority.
- The classroom experience **connects the intellect with the heart.** It is cool to care and speak to those things that are intrinsically meaningful.
- **Discussion** more than direct instruction is emphasized.
- There is no right answer, there is no right way to think about these questions of living a good life. Happiness like learning is a **discovery,** a **process,** a **journey** . . . not necessarily an end destination.
- Use the **Socratic method** to arrive at answers instead of an answer key or a didactic approach to teaching.
- Teacher "talks" (lectures) in class are meant to be **conversational, applicable, and interactive.**
- Homework is personal—the "work" is **intra-personal and interpersonal** learning.

- Assessment is about **understanding**—do students understand the theories, science, and philosophy of ideas by which they are experimenting and/or applying to their lives? Do they make meaning?
- Classes are **variable**—some classes emphasize **Life Labs or Workshops** (active doing classes), cooperative-based learning (small-group activities), whole class learning, differentiated problem-based learning activities, solution-projects, and individual reflections/assessment.
- The lessons can be **adapted** to any type of school (private, public, Catholic, charter) and any grade level from middle school through high school.
- **R-E-S-P-E-C-T!** Develop a safe and inclusive classroom environment where students feel that they can be authentic and respected.
- Within the classroom **agency is actively developed.** Students feel empowered as they take responsibility for their decisions, their actions, and their lives that are developmentally appropriate.

For many students, studying human flourishing will validate many habits of thinking and behaviors that have contributed to their well-being. While mental health is a very serious topic to be discussed and explored with real data, it is important to note that a mental health diagnosis be left to professionals.

Depression and anxiety are serious diseases that affect young people. However, misdiagnosing young people or ascribing symptoms in ways that are not valid, can be harmful. Remember that licensed mental health professionals are the only ones qualified to diagnose mental illness in young people.

Evidence indicates that mental health is a very serious public health problem today. But not all young people are depressed or anxious. Hyperbolic headlines in the media certainly do not help. When a child experiences major clinical diagnoses, it is important they receive clinical and professional help and support.

While you are busy giving to young people, it is important to remember to tend to yourself. Carve out time to do this. Remember the oxygen-mask metaphor. As instructed on flights, passengers are reminded to place the oxygen mask over their faces first, before tending to someone else. People have to help themselves, so they can help others. Like many things, one is better equipped to teach happiness and kindness when one practices and experiences it for themselves.

Chapter 1

An Invitation to Teach What Matters

Everyone wants children to be happy. Anyone who works with children hopes they thrive as adults within the many provinces of their lives. Teenagers are frequently asked what they want to do with their lives. Rarely are they asked *how they want to live* their lives.

Beginning in 1938 and continuing into the twenty-first century, Harvard University conducted one of the longest running studies of adult male life (Harvard only admitted male students at that time when it began this study). A Harvard dean selected at random a couple of hundred undergraduates. They were studied for the duration of their lives. The data collected illustrated interesting lessons about not only living a healthy life but a good life.

Researchers identified factors that equated to healthy and happy aging throughout one's lifespan. Before age 50, these were the attributes for these men:

- They didn't smoke
- Limited alcohol use
- Plenty of exercise
- Maintained healthy body weight
- Strong close, social connections
- Happy, loving, and stable marriages
- Being respected and needed in their old age.[1]

The choices these men made in their lives, especially their connections with others, were the most important predicators of healthy and happy living. One of the conclusions that researchers emphasized was that people should be mindful of how they live at every stage of their lives.[2] This study reveals that living well isn't a passive endeavor.

A good life isn't something that needs to be left to chance. One of the main lessons from studying people through the duration of their lives is to pay attention to life and lean into the things that matter.[3]

Research from psychologist and author Sonja Lyubomirsky and colleagues, in their meta-analysis of over 300 studies, show that happiness and success are linked.[4] No matter how an individual determines a successful life—financial success, strong relationships, healthy living, or helping others—it is apparent that some combination of happiness, positivity, compassion, and social connections matter.

Happiness is a skill that can be learned not unlike learning to play an instrument or a sport. However, the formula for flourishing isn't prescriptive. When it comes to happiness and living a good life, there is no one size fits all approach. Teaching the science and ontology of well-being affords young people the opportunity to explore, experiment, and evaluate the building blocks of living good, meaningful, and pleasant lives.

The word ethics comes from the Greek word *ethos*, meaning habit. Aristotle urged us to spend each day in discussion about the good. This meant spending time developing a personal set of ethics and values that would help guide our choices and actions to incline us to live well. Cultivating self-understanding is a wonderful way to rekindle a passion for all learning.[5]

For some, happiness comes easy. It is a natural state. For others the elements of human flourishing require knowledge, practice, and continued commitment. Personal development is a process. Noted psychologist Abraham Maslow developed the term self-actualization to explain how personal growth develops when one's basic needs are fulfilled. Meeting one's fundamental needs in order to flourish is a self-regulated process. Young people are in fact, the only experts of their lives. As adults we can only guide and encourage this process.

Ancient wisdom teaches that learning to live well is one of the truest measures of success. Every study of success illustrates that loving what you do is essential. Knowing yourself and what matters to you is also important.

Researchers at Harvard University conducted a long-term study called the Dark House Project. It explored how men and women (dark horse individuals whose successes no one saw coming) were able to achieve success and fulfillment. The research revealed that these Dark Horses were guided by intrinsic motivation. Success was the byproduct of their unique individuality.[6] This resulted in developed mindsets that helped to cultivate their own paths to success despite the obstacles and doubters.

A recent decade long research study synthesized that prosocial modeling and witnessing others' helpful acts encourages helpful behavior through contagion.[7] Studying goodness and altruistic exemplars fuel young people's optimism. When we observe people doing good things for others, it can inspire us to want to do the same. We are wired to be inspired.

Happiness cannot exist without acknowledging the pathos that exists in the world. However, this can be discerned by urging adolescents to cultivate their altruistic proclivities. It cheapens our humanity to suggest to young people that the human condition is fixed and inherently destructive.

Research indicates that when we act compassionately, help others, and behave altruistically, the more satisfied we can become with our lives. Humans are social creatures. Without a doubt, happiness is interwoven with our connections with others.

The Aspen Institute issued a report recently affirming the promotion of social, emotional, and academic learning. As the report noted, social-emotional learning is not simply another educational fad, but the substance of education itself.[8]

WE ARE AT THE RIGHT PLACE AT THE RIGHT TIME: A RENAISSANCE FOR SOCIAL-EMOTIONAL LEARNING

Social-emotional learning (SEL) along with teaching to the whole child has seen an increased interest from parents, educators, principals, corporations, the public, and even government agencies. CASEL (The Collaborative for Academic, Social, and Emotional Learning) defines SEL as the process though which children and adults understand and manage emotions, set and achieve positive goals, feel and show empathy for others, establish and maintain positive relationships, and make responsible decisions.[9]

Around the world, on every continent, countries like Australia, the United Kingdom, Bhutan, the United Arab Emirates (Dubai), Israel, Jordan, Ireland, China, India, Mexico, Peru, and the United States are implementing some form of positive education programs and social-emotional learning. Happiness classes are ubiquitous on colleges campuses throughout the United States.

In primary and secondary school settings, positive education blends academic learning with learning life skills that attempt to foster personal well-being. Research suggests that teaching well-being in schools helps adolescents perform better not only in school but also outside of it.[10]

Increased levels of happiness have been linked with many positive outcomes. It is true that children learn best when they are happy. Also, happy people have happier marriages, happier relationships, are more creative, live longer, tend to be more altruistic and other-centered, have better friendships, and tend to earn more income.[11] Happiness isn't just an end in itself. Happiness helps us to acquire all the other good things in life.

SEL programs can lead to tangible benefits now and into the future. SEL programs can improve academic performance, emotional well-being of young people, social behaviors, and help reduce poverty and improve economic mobility through the teaching of soft skills.[12]

Also teaching adolescents the science of well-being can help reduce the risk of mental and physical health problems. The happiness class at Yale University taught by Laurie Santos has demonstrated that positive psychology taught in academic settings which encourage young people to engage in evidence-based practices can increase their subjective well-being.[13]

The United Nations Educational Scientific and Cultural Organization (UNESCO) Mahatma Gandhi Institute of Education for Peace and Sustainable Development (MGIEP) are developing programs to mainstream SEL to meet its mission to transform education globally. Its mission entails infusing SEL programs that will empower young people around the world to successfully thrive in the twenty-first century with its rapid changes and unique set of challenges.[14]

The McKinsey Global Institute issued a report titled *Jobs Lost, Jobs Gained: Workforce Transitions in A Time of Automation* in December of 2017. The report illustrated the economy of now and the economy of the future. The jobs of the future will require individuals to be equipped with soft skills.

These soft skills entail more human skills or people skills (like empathic intelligence, communication, industriousness, critical thinking, problem-solving, and teamwork). There will be a noted difference between jobs that will be heuristic (you have to experiment with possibilities and devise novel solutions) versus logarithmic (you follow a set of established instructions down a single pathway to one conclusion to do the job).

Estimates are that in the United States a minority of job growth will come from algorithmic work (think routine-oriented tasks like working at a fast-food restaurant), while the majority will come from heuristic work (which require inventiveness and application of knowledge to complete tasks.)

These jobs of the future, where humans still have the advantage over AI (artificial intelligence) computing, will require a multitude of intelligences—social and emotional intelligence and also creative intelligence. This transformation in the workplace and society is a reality requiring a different set of skills to thrive in this fluid economy.[15]

One of the continued challenges for any educator in the twenty-first century is meeting the needs of students with different levels, abilities, and motivations; differing socio-economic means; and who are culturally and racially diverse. The importance of education to improve significant inequalities has been quantified. As the recent report: *From Nation at Risk to a Nation at*

Hope recently recommended that acquiring SEL skills is important for all students, but equity means acknowledging that not all students are the same.[16]

One of the identifiable obstacles undermining student achievement is whether students feel connected to school and their communities. Researchers have shown that when students feel less connection to school it negatively affects grades, behavior, and even health.

According to one study, by high school, as many as 40 percent to 60 percent of students are chronically disengaged from school.[17] Emotional and social connections are essential elements to fostering environments that can facilitate children's academic success.[18] Social and emotional learning integrated into educational programs lead to positive outcomes like attitudes about school, self, and others. All adults, whether they realize it or not, affect a child's development.

It is obvious that some teenagers are making good decisions for themselves. Some, in fact, are thriving. Some are doing just fine.[19] Continuing to infuse SEL into schooling can shine light, hope, and optimism, and nurture their integrity and character. In doing so, we come to honor young people as well as honoring each other. Unlike the parents of the recent college admissions scandal, young people can be trusted with the important decisions of their lives.

WHAT IS HAPPINESS?

Within the last thirty years, science has revealed much about human well-being. Pioneers in the field of positive psychology Martin Seligman and Mihalyi Csikszentmihalyi identified that the fundamental goal of this field of research was to see individuals thrive. Positive psychology is the scientific study of what makes human beings thrive, flourish, and function optimally throughout most of their lives. It is a branch of psychology that studies how our actions and thinking affect how we feel.[20] As an academic discipline, the goal of positive psychology is to make yourself and the world a little bit better.[21]

Real happiness is a broad notion that appears simple to understand, but in fact can be complex. Happiness, contentment, and living a life of meaning takes hard work and commitment. We act and think in accordance with our authentic selves, enjoying the moments of our lives, and the world around us more fully.

Happiness isn't about feeling good all the time. Happy people experience adversity and hardship. The ancient Romans stressed that one of the secrets to living well was *amor fati*, accepting and embracing the good and the bad that life brings. This mindset requires leaning into these experiences and making the best out of them. This doesn't mean pursuing empty hedonism (the idea that we have to feel good all the time or get whatever we want).

It is from scientific research that positive psychologists urge people in all fields to apply these findings but with caution. This science provides insights on intentional activities that boost happiness, but not necessarily prescriptive solutions. The data driven theories are more valid than merely relying on unproven good ideas or armchair speculation. There are thousands of research studies, books, and peer-reviewed academic journals that have developed within this field. Positive psychology has provided:[22]

- Scientific rigor and validity
- A range of tested Positive Psychology interventions (PPIs)
- A body of evidence and research on a range of Positive Psychology constructs
- A set of underlying values, assumptions, and theories
- A language to explain and communicate well-being, thriving, and optimal functioning

So, what is happiness? Subjective well-being is often used as a way to define happiness. This type of measured happiness means being very satisfied with our life, experiencing more frequently positive emotions and experiences than negative ones, and having a general contentment with our current life. The combination of positive emotions and evaluating how satisfied we are within the different areas of our lives determines happiness.

Psychologists measure subjective well-being by asking individuals to self-evaluate their happiness. This helps researchers determine what people are doing or not doing to increase their well-being. While it is subjective, the data received is as valid as measuring rates of depression. People are usually asked to rate their lives over a long period of time.

This subjective well-being is usually contrasted with eudaimonic happiness or authentic happiness. The ancient Greeks used eudaimonia to explain happiness. It translates broadly as human flourishing, thriving, and living well independently and with others. Eudaimonic happiness is found within the daily moments of our lives, doing good and striving for goodness. By living a virtuous life, Aristotle claimed we could obtain *summum bonum*, or the highest good.

There are many differences and forms of happiness that exist for people. Eudaimonic happiness is dependent on a number of conditions. Scientific research has defined the elements of eudaimonic well-being to be the following:[23]

- Our sense of life purpose and the contribution we make to the world
- Our relationships with others
- The sense of control we have over our lives
- Our ability to be authentic
- Our opportunities to learn, grow, and be challenged
- Our ability to shape our environment

Conventional wisdom suggests that happiness is simply attained by increasing the good, and subtracting the bad. While pleasure is a component of human flourishing, it is not considered fundamentally necessary. Pleasure is often fleeting. Flourishing is more of a constant state of living. Flourishing is often found in some combination of finding meaning (experiencing a sense of connectedness to a greater whole), fulfillment (experiencing a high level of engagement in satisfying activities), purpose, and serenity both internally and externally. This leads to authentic happiness.

CAN WE BECOME HAPPIER?

The good news is that we can increase our happiness and sustain it. In 2005, psychologists Sonja Lyubomirsky, Kennon Sheldon, and David Schkade published a paper where they theorized that our happiness was determined within a range of three major determinants:

- Our biological set point or genetic personality dispositions
- Life circumstances (for example, occupation, socio-economic status, and where one lives)
- Intentional activities of thinking and behavior[24]

This research suggested that as much as 40 percent of our happiness was dependent on our volition. Happiness was theorized to be dependent on these three variables and within the following domain ranges.

Recent research over last fifteen years, however, has raised some important questions regarding these domain ranges and their independent natures. Lyubomirsky and Ken Sheldon in a recent paper have acknowledged that our intentional activities might not be as statistically significant as they once claimed. However, continued research reveals that how we choose to think and act are still very influential for affecting our happiness levels.[25]

Flourishing involves some combination of our genetic dispositions + life circumstances + how we think and act + environmental influences. In the moments of our lives what we do matters. We can boost our happiness. We can also maintain it over a period of time.[26]

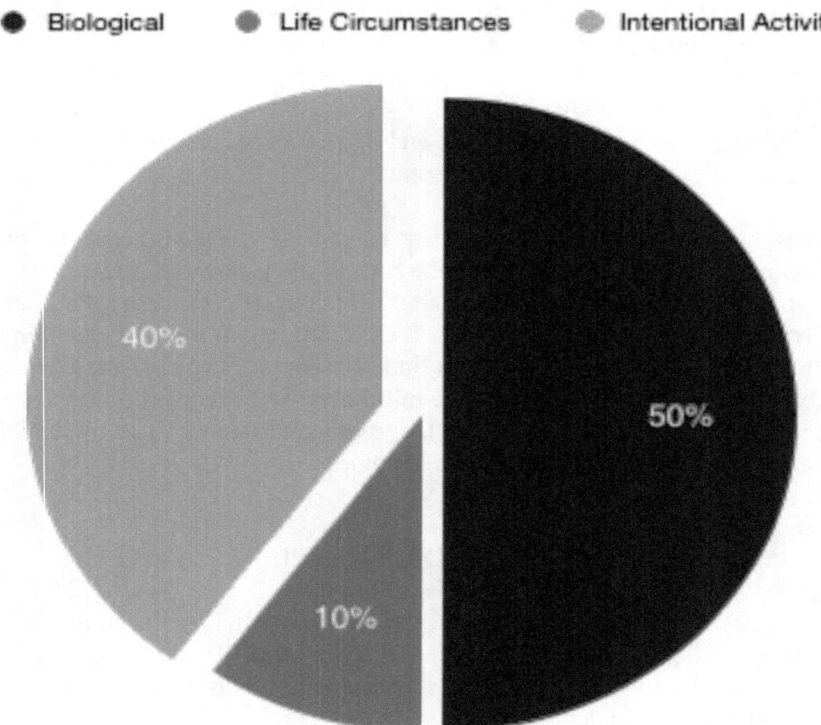

Figure 1.1. Placeholder Caption

Researchers aren't certain yet how much, and to what extent, what activities we should do. It is finding the right combination between duration, dosage, and variety. As Lyubomirsky has stated recently, *"it might be more accurate to say that people have a range of potential well-being rather than a set point of well-being."*[27]

Change is difficult. Improving subjective well-being takes commitment, work, and time. It takes effort. What works for one person to flourish may not work for another. In meta-analysis research analyzing the effectiveness of social-emotional learning programs, students who participate in them show short term improvements in their personal, social, and academic lives.[28]

HOW DO GENES AFFECT OUR HAPPINESS?

The biggest part of our happiness involves our biology. We inherit certain traits that incline us toward happiness or unhappiness. We all have a basic starting point for our personal happiness.

Researcher David Lykken noted, *"Everyone is born with a certain 'set point' for happiness in the same way that your household thermostat is set to maintain a certain temperature in your home. Tragedies and pleasures might affect your level of happiness. But eventually you will return to your genetic set point, just as the temperature of your home will return to your thermostat's set point after you have let in cold air by opening a door or window."*[29]

This is often referred to as our genetic set-point. However, inherited dispositions don't solely determine whether we will have a good life. For many, it is a relief to know that our happiness doesn't only derive from the roulette wheel of genetics. We can live more fruitful lives. Even the most heritable traits can be modified by environmental and behavioral changes. Our environments often influence our well-being. Our inherited genes don't decide what makes life meaningful.

HOW DO LIFE CIRCUMSTANCES AFFECT OUR HAPPINESS?

Does a new hairstyle make us feel differently about ourselves? What if we move to a new beautiful location like Lisbon, Portugal? Recent research has shown that changing one's life circumstances, where you live, what you do for a living, whether you are married or single, a new hairstyle, buying a new car, moving into a new house, or moving to a new state actually has a mixed impact on our happiness.

Early research revealed that generally, changing our lifestyles doesn't significantly affect our happiness. Life circumstances were subject to adaptation. We are wired to adapt to new circumstances as our brains alter our emotional and physiological states. Changes in circumstances may get us excited. These positive changes are often short-lived.

Our brains are wired to adapt or habituate to these changes. This results in a return to our biological set points. Over time, we get used to our new lives in Portugal adapting to the conditions that led to the positive emotional boost.

We adapt or habituate to all kinds of changes. Adaptation allows us to get used to the good and bad things that happen to us. There is good news about adaptation. When something terrible happens, we typically feel bad, but then tend to recover from that emotional state. This is why people generally overcome painful break-ups, failures, and other hardships. That is the good news. When life throws us lemons, we are generally pretty good at turning them into lemonade.

The same is true, unfortunately, for good things that happen to us. Adaptation is often cited as an enemy of happiness. People tend to overestimate the impact that wealth, income, and possessions have. Things we buy are most likely to fall prey to adaptation. The emotional high we get from these purchases or possessions simply wears off with time. That's why we often donate clothing that at one time made us feel good about ourselves.

What do people do to increase their happiness? The simple answer is that everything matters. How we think and how we choose to respond to life on a daily basis is a path toward greater well-being.[30] Positive psychology reveals that happiness exercises or cognitive practices can enhance our well-being. These exercises involve proactive thinking and actions that can be taught explicitly to almost anyone.

These practices have been shared with professional athletes, corporate executives, and young people in schools around the world. Like anything, improving well-being takes daily attention. The effectiveness of these practices is based on a multitude of factors and chiefly dependent on the individuals employing them. Quite possibly we might have everything we need to live a good life.

HOW OUR BRAINS INCLINE US TO HAPPINESS AND UNHAPPINESS

For many years, researchers believed that our brain structures were fixed and stayed that way throughout our lives. We can alter many habits and actually change our brains. Our brain neurochemistry can be affected by how we think and behave. This is known as neuroplasticity. The brain is constantly adapting and changing depending on our experiences by producing new neural connections or neurons themselves. And this happens throughout our lives. If our brains are the old dogs in the adage, then it can learn new tricks. Or as a neuroscientist might say, we can grow more gray matter.

Noted researchers Richard Davidson and Rick Hanson have shown that when we make changes in our lives, these changes become apparent in our brains. Dr. Hanson reveals, "What flows through your mind sculpts your brain. Thus, you can you use your mind to change your brain for the better."[31]

In his book, *Buddha's Brain*, Hanson demonstrates that those neurons that fire together, wire together. We can strengthen those mechanisms that positively affect our brains and incline us to joy like a muscle.

Adolescent brains are incredibly malleable and plastic. Teenage brains are growing and developing all the time.[32] Since most teenage brains aren't fully matured until their mid-twenties, this is an important stage in their development.

Our brains lead us astray when we gauge what will bring us happiness in the future. We are really good at thinking and behaving in ways that are counterproductive to our own well-being.

We aren't adept at predicting the future. We are also loss aversive. Our brains tend to be more aware of what is going wrong or could go wrong more than what is going well. We have a built-in negativity bias or selective attention to the negative.

As a result, negativity makes a greater impression. Dr. Rick Hanson explains that our brains are like Velcro for negativity and like Teflon for positivity. Negative experiences tend to stick with us, while positive experiences tend to slide right out of our consciousness.

Researchers estimate that we have thousands of thoughts a day. Our minds are always on with thoughts and self-talk that shape behavior. What is even more startling is that the majority of those thoughts are repeated day after day. And they happen to be overwhelmingly negative.[33]

Thanks in part to evolution our brains are differentiated engines constantly scanning for changes in our environment that may affect our survival. Our brain tells us to focus attention on aversive differences externally and internally. This helped to keep our early hominid ancestors alive. The amygdala is the part of the brain charged with keeping us alive. We when are faced with a threat, perceived or actual, we succumb to amygdala hijacks that lead to fight-or-flight-or-freeze responses. Any stress response can trigger the amygdala leading to brain changes.[34]

As Stanford University biologist Robert Sapolsky chronicled in his book *Why Zebras Don't Get Ulcers*,[35] other mammals experience the same physiological changes we experience when the amygdala is activated. Animals can shut it off, but we cannot. The moment other mammals recognize that danger is averted and deem themselves safe, they reset and return to homeostasis without long-term rumination. Humans have the capacity to ruminate.

Yet, we can control what we pay attention to, how to manage our stress and difficult emotions. We can learn how to engage with the world that inclines us to positivity, optimism, and joy.

Since we are often wrong about what we think will make us happy or unhappy, we should reevaluate the narratives that culture, advertising, and other forces suggest about living. Harvard psychologist and author Dan Gilbert and colleagues note that what we think we want isn't what we always experience. This often leads to a "*naive psychology of happiness . . . we want, we try, we get, we like. And then with the help of commercials, we want some* more ... *Most of us feel certain that if we could experience all the events and only the events we want to experience, happiness would inevitably follow.*"[36]

There has been a specific piece of Native American wisdom that circulated around the web. It is instructive in understanding the importance of our habits and the choices we make. The wisdom reveals the following:

One evening a Cherokee elder told his grandson about the battle that goes on inside of people. He said, "My son, the battle is between the two 'wolves' that live inside us all. One is Unhappiness. It is fear, worry, anger, jealously, sorrow, self-pity, resentment, and inferiority. The other is Happiness. It is joy, love, hope, serenity, kindness, generosity, truth, and compassion.'"The grandson thought about it for a minute and then asked his grandfather, "Which wolf wins?'"The Cherokee elder simply replied, "The one you feed."

Aristotle taught we are what we repeatedly do. What we tell ourselves and how we act ultimately help determine what we become. Since we have negative propensities, it is important to examine ourselves and shape our minds toward a good life. As Gandhi remarked,

> Your beliefs become your thoughts,
> Your thoughts become your words,
> Your words become your actions,
> Your actions become your habits,
> Your habits become your values,
> Your values become your destiny.

Chapter 2

Redefining Success

In more than two decades of teaching, young people have shared that they rely on a simplified formula for success. The formula in usually expressed in this way: "Graduate high school, get into a 'good' college, or get a good paying job, this will then equal a good life. Everything else, 'will just fall into place.'"

This chapter contains precepts that encourage expanding any formula for success. Success can include the ability to be fulfilled, ethical, decent, successful, productive, independent, resilient and self-reliant, compassionate, confident, curious, creative, being a critical thinker, and a good communicator. Success can encompass encouraging young people to achieve their fullest potential as individuals.

Kintsugi is the Japanese art of repairing broken pottery by mending the areas of breakage with gold, silver, or platinum. This tradition teaches that we should celebrate each artifact's unique history with its breaks and fissures. Each artifact should be displayed with pride instead of hiding or disguising them. A successful life is never an upward, linear trajectory. Often it is full of experiences that leave dents, marks, and cracks.

Kintsugi is sound practice that teaches us how to be the best versions that we want to be, regardless of our imperfections. It teaches that life challenges, complications, and our imperfections are occasions for revitalization. As Sonja Lyubomirsky writes, "instead of being frightening or depressing, your crisis points can be opportunities for renewal, growth, or meaningful change."[1]

Too often young people view success as a mountain to climb. The perception of success in this way can be daunting. Success is too often based on social comparison, acquisition of material items, prestige, or status. While it is natural to base how well we are doing in relation to others, this can be toxic to well-being. Envy is an enemy of happiness. Social comparison can make us feel inadequate, anxious, or guilty.

Any great success story developed by living in concert not in opposition to one's values, goals, and authentic natures. Success, like happiness, has to be earned. It is vital to hold a strong sense of self, living by our values, and knowing our aspirations to feel successful. When these are congruent, we feel that we are not lost in our lives, but at the helm of meaningfulness and purposefulness.

People who are flourishing, research tells us, are embroiled in meaningful and purposeful pursuits. They act on their signature strengths. These strengths or virtues validate oneself while repudiating the need to keep up with the Joneses. People who are flourishing in their lives also set and work to achieve intrinsic goals. Research from Carol Dweck on growth mindsets reveal that what we believe about our ability to grow, develop agency, fail, and succeed is important.

Students can be encouraged to identify their signature strengths by taking the VIA Signature Strengths Survey. Research on signature strengths indicate a strong empirical record of success across varied populations of people regardless of age. Knowing and utilizing our character strengths allows us to be authentically ourselves and feel more engaged with life.

Students will also explore their relationships to money. While exploring two ingredients that are toxic to well-being, envy and "status anxiety," students will examine cultural messages pertaining to success. This section of work will allow students to do some introspection about their beliefs, values, and future wants. Redefining success in non-materialistic ways helps us realize that money can buy happiness but not in the ways that consumerism propagates.

Precept #1: *In order to live a successful life, we must figure out what it means to get a life.*

TEACHING WHAT MATTERS PLAYBOOK: TOOLS FOR EXPLORING THE ART OF LIVING

Playbook Lesson Sequence 1: What does it mean to be a success? Is there a template? What are the ingredients of a successful life?

Lesson objective: Compare and contrast your definition of success with society's definition of success.

Step 1-Class conversation, ask the following and make a class list: How do you define success? What are the elements of success, now and in the future? How do you obtain a successful life?

What is a successful life? What is society's message of success? Are there different kinds of success? Which messages does your community convey about what success might be? What are those markers, habits, norms, beliefs, and ways of living that society have taught that lead to success? Evaluate them. Are they valid?

Step 2-Create a work of art (this can be a painting, drawing, photography, collage, etc.) that illustrates how you perceive that our society defines success. Create a visual template. Provide a brief, one page description/interpretation of your art. Help the viewer translate and understand your work. What are you hoping is seen and understood?

Playbook Lesson Sequence 2: Redefining Success in a Kinder and Broader Way.

Lesson objective: Conventional wisdom suggests that if one follows their passion, success will follow. Analyze the extent to which this may or may not be true.

Step 1-Guiding Question: What do each **of the following** reveal **about** what success may or may not be?

- Read about Tiger Woods from Ryan Holiday's *Stillness is the Key* (Part 2: The Domain of the Soul, p. 85–94).
- Watch Allain de Botton's TedTalk, *A Kinder, Gentler Philosophy of Success*.
- Read *How purpose changes over our lifetime-by Kira Newman* (available via Greater Good Center).
- Read Australian nurse and writer Bronnie Ware's *The Top Five Regrets of the Dying*.
- Read *A Life Worth Living: A new book explores why it's so hard to resist speculating about the steps we didn't take* by Gary Devitch. (available via Psychology Today).

Step 2-NB-Journal: What did you learn/discover? What insights are valuable?

What can be taught & learned about *Happiness?*

Research from psychologist and author Sonja Lyubomirsky and colleagues, in their meta-analysis of over 300 studies, have shown that happiness and success are linked. No matter how an individual determines a successful life—financial success, strong relationships, healthy living, or helping others—it is apparent that some combination of happiness, positivity, compassion, and social connections are important.

Is success measured in zero-sum ways? False notions of success can frustrate us and lead to actually being unhappy. Like the compensation for the work we do, or the grades young people receive for the effort they put into their learning, success does not come at some conceived finish line. Success is more than just winning. Success doesn't have to be a zero-sum game, as psychologist and author Adam Grant noted. Success is often a byproduct of collaboration.

Playbook Lesson Sequence 3: Life Lab Activity.
Journaling Your Best Possible Future Self Exercise[2]

Lesson objective: The first step in creating anything, is to imagine it.

Step 1: Provide about 15–20 minutes of uninterrupted journal writing. Students journal on imaging the best possible future selves in the various domains of their lives. Encourage students to be imaginative and not to worry about grammar or spelling.

Step 2-Students take 5 minutes to examine the nature of what was written.

NB-Journal (notebook/journal reflection): How would you characterize what you wrote? Is it positive? Achievable? Practical? Pleasing? Or Negative?

What can be taught & learned about *Happiness*?

Why is happiness more like a journey rather than a destination? Happiness is not a destination but it is a journey. Being happy can simply be choosing how to live. This can be done by creating direction and purpose. Happiness is about living in accordance with goals and values. To better construct the conditions for better lives, we should consider a direction, a meaning, and determine goals to help do so.

Why is purposefulness a necessary ingredient for happiness? People who are flourishing, research tells us, are embroiled in purposefulness. They integrate their signature strengths or virtues that validate their sense of self. Happiness is earned by planning, thinking, and vigilant pursuit.[3]

Playbook Lesson Sequence 4: Visualizing the Days of Our Lives.

Lesson objective: Understand the end of history illusion, affective forecasting, and how to reevaluate what will bring us future happiness.

Step 1-Discuss what Annie Dillard wrote, "How we spend our days is of course how we spend our lives. What we do with this hour and that one is what we are doing." What are you doing with your days and weeks of your lives?

- Examine a 90-year life span on paper via a page full of boxes. Ninety-year grids can be obtained online. Horizontally, in each row, there are 52 boxes, representing one year of life. Vertically, there are 90 rows or years. Ask students what they think this represents before telling them.
- Next have students hold out their life grids and close their eyes. Observe their faces as they open their eyes and examine their grids. Then ask, *What is your knee-jerk reaction to looking at your grid*? (Note how many students actually smile looking at their grids.) Ask them: why did or did not a smile emerge? What do you see when you look at your life in boxes? Discuss this as a whole class.
- Watch *The Time You Have in Jellybeans* (available via YouTube)
- Watch *A Valuable Lesson for a Happier Life* (available via YouTube)

Step 2-Guiding Question: What is Plutarch's thought experiment and what does it suggest about the nature of change and time throughout our lives?

- Watch Amy Adkins (TEDEd) *Who am I? A philosophical inquiry*—Ship of Theseus thought experiment explained.
- The ship that Theseus and the youth of Athens returned had thirty oars, and was preserved by the Athenians. They tore up and took away the old, decaying planks of wood from the ship and replaced them as they did with newer and stronger wood. By the time the ship arrives at port again, it is a ship made up of new wood.
Ultimately, there was not a single plank left of the original ship. The thought experiment is this: Is it the same ship? Did the Athenians still have the same ship that used to belong to Theseus? One side argues that the ship remained the same, and the other contends that it was not the same because all the original wood was removed.

Ask students to consider applying the thought experiment to their lives. How do things grow and change? How much of yourself can you change while remaining true to yourself? What aspects of your life should remain fixed, that are unique, original, and are your strengths? What happens if we change and strip away old habits and replace them with new ones? Will you still be authentically you, similar to the Ship of Theseus?

Step 3-Guiding Question: What is the personal significance of change?

- Read *The Nature of Change* by Abigail Brenner (available via Psychology Today).

Step 4-Allow students to debate, then discuss among themselves. Students can write a response in the journals. How should one respond to Plutarch's question of change?

Step 5-Guiding Question: Why are we bad **at** predicting **the** future?

- Watch *How much will you change in the future? More than you think* by Bence Nanay (available via TED-Ed)
- Read *Why You Won't Be the Person You Expect to Be* by John Tierney, 2013 (via *The New York Times*)
- Discuss and analyze the end of history illusion. Ask family members and others the extent to which they changed. Have their personalities, preferences, habits, etc. changed throughout their lives?
- NB-Journal: To what extent would you consider yourself a work in progress?

What can be taught & learned about *Happiness?*

Why are we more like works in progress rather than finished products? The end of history illusion defined by Dan Gilbert and colleagues suggests we imagine that the person we are right now is the person we will be for the rest of time.[4] This is not the case. This phenomenon leads to underestimating our ability to change over time in many different facets of our lives. Our preferences throughout life often change.

We often create illusions about what will make us happy in our lives, both in the present and the future. This often leads to miswanting or overemphasizing milestone events in the future that don't usually lead to any greater life satisfaction once we reach them. It can be difficult to begin thinking about who we are and what we want to do upon entering adulthood. Experience certainly at times is the best teacher. However, we are not obviously static, but fluid.

We are usually incorrect in predicting what will make us fulfilled or unsatisfied in the future. In our daily lives, we generally work toward getting what we think will make us happy and avoid outcomes that will make us unhappy.[5] However, we are really good at thinking and behaving in ways that are counterproductive to our own well-being. We are really bad at gauging what will bring us happiness. We tend to overestimate the negative and positive effects of life circumstances.

What is affective forecasting? Affective forecasting is the prediction of one's affect (emotional state) in the future. Dramatic life events, divorce, or loss of job or a move to San Diego, have much less long-lasting impact on our happiness than we think. We think that negative things that happen to us will be devastating. They might be, but in the short term and for not as long as we think.

Experiencing a painful break up with a partner, we adapt and move on. The same is true of positive events, like getting a promotion or even winning the lottery. We receive a happiness boost, but it does not last as long as we think.

Why is it more difficult to be happy than it is to be unhappy? The pursuit of the good life takes effort. It takes commitment to not only make changes in one's life but the will to sustain them. Changes in our well-being can be affected by how much effort we apply.

Also, the variety, dosage, social support, motivation, our demographics, personalities, and our beliefs in the positive effects of the changes we make will contribute to our ability to increase our well-being. In addition, research suggests changing daily activities, how we think and act, more than our circumstances produce more bang for the buck and over a longer period of time.[6]

Why is a growth mindset important for living our lives? Stanford University researcher Carol Dweck has studied people's sense of self-efficacy. She contrasts two different types of mindsets. One that is positive, a growth mindset, while contrasting that with a fixed mindset. Her research reveals that when we develop a growth mindset, we can obtain short term achievement but also long-term success.

People who cultivate a fixed mindset believe that certain traits are fixed, are unable to be altered. This is a flawed thinking especially if we relate it to our beliefs about our intelligence, or the quality of our lives.

Why is being hopeful an important element of human flourishing? Hope Theory was developed by psychologist Rick Snyder. Hope is an important element of flourishing. Snyder has defined hope as the process of thinking about our desired goals for our lives. Hope also encompasses thinking about the different ways to achieve our goals and how firmly we believe we have the ability to do so. When we are hopeful about the future, we are more likely to be happier. Hope is a motivational state, where we develop agency, resiliency, and perspective for what we would like to attain or achieve.

Synder's research has shown that people with higher levels of hope see improved outcomes in academics, athletics, physical health, and balancing conflicting needs, and challenges by obstacles in one's environment. Hope is different from optimism. Although they often go hand in hand, hope provides confidence and agency. Optimism provides a general positive feeling in the absence of control about our situation. Hope usually demands that we think about our goals and act to build our lives accordingly.

Playbook Lesson Sequence 4: Introduction to the Hedonic Treadmill

Lesson objective: Identify and explain how short-term markers of success are subject to adaptation and are unsustainable for our long-term happiness.

   Step 1-Guiding Question: **What is the hedonic treadmill and adaptation?**

- Explain and illustrate the Hedonic Treadmill and Adaptation. Read *The Hedonic Treadmill* (available via Psychology Today)

What can be taught & learned about *Happiness?*

What is the hedonic treadmill? Part of the reason that things cannot satisfy us for very long (or not at all) is because of what psychologists call the Hedonic Treadmill. Hedonic, meaning hedonism, or the pursuit of pleasurable things. Every time we buy something or obtain something and we get a little positive boost in mood, elevated positive emotions, or dopamine reward, we quickly adapt to that, then return to our prior baseline, emotional levels. We might then buy something else only to adapt to that. Perhaps it was a sweater, or a new song, that just does not seem to get you jazzed up. The sweater gets donated and you find new music.

   It is like being on a happiness consumption treadmill. We tend to purchase more, perhaps working more, but our happiness levels remain in place. Rarely do we seem to gain sustained, long-term satisfaction from the objects that we have purchased. More of anything, but especially money, typically only raise our expectations. Getting more stuff leaves us no better than we were before. Our relationship to things changes. It takes quite a bit of effort in today's world to be satisfied with what we have.

   What is adaptation? Adaptation is a natural psychological process. The bad news is when life is going really well and we are experiencing positive emotions, we will adapt to that emotional state and return to our baseline. We will lose that joyful feel-good connection. The good news is that when life throws us lemons, and depending on the severity of the experience, we will adapt to that emotional state and recover. We will feel and get better.

Playbook Lesson Sequence 5: The Ability to Maintain and Sustain Happiness.

Lesson objective: Evaluate the **PERMA** model in relation to your life.

   Step 1-Guiding Question: **What are things that we take for granted that have helped or continue to help us be happy?**

Understand that we are already making ourselves happier. Make a list of 50 things that you might have or are taking for granted that are contributing to your life being good, and setting you up for obtaining a great life/your best possible future self.

Step 2-Guiding Question: What is the PERMA model of human flourishing?

- Identify the aspects of PERMA in your life. NB-Journal reflection.

One of the pioneers of positive psychology, Martin Seligman, defines authentic happiness in three ways: the obtaining of pleasure regularly (hedonism), experiencing high levels of engagement with and in life, and experiencing a sense of connectedness to a greater whole or something bigger than just ourselves.

In his book *Flourish* he explains a broadened notion well-being. His PERMA model consists of both objective and subjective elements of well-being:

P=positive emotions and the experiences of positive mood and feelings. These positive emotions help us to flourish as they allow us to engage with life and with others more fully. Negative emotions tend to close us off from life and others and lead to myopic focus of daily living.

E=engagement or development of Flow experiences are sources of continued well-being. Flow refers to the positive feelings obtained from being so engrossed in a task, you lose sense of time, sensations, etc. all while your mind is actively engaged.

R=as seen in Harvard's longitudinal study, relationships that are close, supportive, and loving are essential to our well-being. Having and maintaining not only strong friendships, but positive relationships with other people in our lives are one of the essential ingredients to well-being.

M=finding meaning in our lives gives us a sense of purpose and direction. Rather than striving from one pleasurable experience to another, we should look to develop experiences that transcend our own selfish, transitory needs. Connecting with a purpose higher than just ourselves has been shown to be pillar of well-being.

A=striving toward accomplishments in our lives is the last pillar of Seligman's model. Improving ourselves through mastery of skills, working to achieve intrinsic goals, or experiencing success in areas of our life that are valued correlates with well-being.

Step 3-Guiding Question: What are fundamental human needs that all humans need to actualize in order to flourish or reach transcendence?

- Read and identify Maslow's hierarchy of needs or the sailboat metaphor from Scott Barry Kaufman https://scottbarrykaufman.com/sailboat-metaphor/

Step 4-NB-Journal: Evaluate what you learned and evaluate how to apply it to your life.

What can be taught & learned about *Happiness?*

What is the PERMA model of human flourishing and why is it important? Figuring out how to apply this PERMA model can increase well-being in our lives. These habits and skills become the subject matter. Seligman consistently stresses that the goal is not to teach happiness. The goal is to teach habits and skills that, from moment to moment, culminate in living more fully. Seligman writes that *"happiness, flow, meaning, love, gratitude, accomplishment, growth, better relationships-constitutes human flourishing. Learning that you can have more of these things is life changing."*[7]

What does Abraham Maslow reveal about our ability to reach our full potential? In his distinguished and renowned 1943 paper *A Theory of Human Motivation* Maslow stated that all healthy human beings have fundamental needs that must be satisfied before one is able to fully realize their individual potential. While the common pyramid model serves as the most common illustration of these needs, Maslow actually never emphasized a strict hierarchy.[8]

Maslow argued that once these basic needs are met, an individual is free to focus on one's self-actualization needs. If not, people can experience anxiety and deficiencies in their lives. The main point is that it is extremely difficult or even prohibitive to do anything, including achieving one's goals when you are battling to get your basic needs met. Effort will be directed toward meeting our most basic needs.

Why is intrinsic more than extrinsic motivation an important component of living well? Based on the research of Edward Deci and Richard Ryan, self-determination theory (SDT) attempts to help clarify the difference between behavior that is self-determined and behavior that is controlled externally. SDT determines those forces that undermine versus help develop our sense of agency to cultivate well-being.

People are happiest when acting and doing things that are intrinsically rewarding. We take control and responsibility for our lives more than being influenced by the opinions of others. That is when we become self-actualized. Having this internalized locus of control motivates us to determine the course of our lives.

Research reveals that people whose lives are dominated by activities outside of our locus (location) of control are less healthy and happy. When we become who we yearn to be, we become actualized. We then grow into being the best versions of ourselves.

Playbook Lesson Sequence 6: The Power of Expectation-Getting a Life

Lesson objectives: Understand that getting a life is really an exercise in perseverance, grit, industriousness, positivity, optimism, growth, motivation, commitment, achievement, meaning, and developing purpose for our lives. Identify the elements of an internal locus of control and intrinsic motivation.

Step 1-Guiding question: How do you explain your successes or your failures?

- Engage in whole class conversation.

Step 2-Guiding Question: What effect do self-filling prophecies create?

- Students research Pygmalion Effect vs. the Golem Effect. How might each impact us?

Step 3-Guiding Question: What good might you want to do with the days of your life to make a difference not only in your life but in the lives of others?

- Watch *30,000 Days* Directed by Tiffany Shlain (available via Vimeo) The film explores the 3,000-year history of humans wrestling with the question of how to live life with meaning and purpose.
- Read *"To change your life, learn how to trust your future self"* by Jeff Wise (available via *The Cut*)

What can be taught & learned about *Happiness?*

What motivates us to engage with life and ourselves in finding happiness and meaningful success? The answer is largely explained by SDT.[9] SDT posits that when people's basic psychological needs are routinely satisfied, namely autonomy, competence, and relatedness, people will develop and experience wellness and optimal functioning.

Playbook Lesson Sequence 7: Happiness Around the World Learning How Other Cultures Live Well.

Lesson objective: Identify and explain what it means to live well around the world.

Use the book *Atlas of Happiness: The Global Secrets of How to Be Happy* by Helen Russell. Students should select one concept or cultural premise from a country and complete the following project. Prepare a piece of art that compares the elements of success around the world with your community/society's definition and/or notion of success. No country or culture is perfect, but explain the cultural concept. How does it equate to happiness or enjoyment of life? How might one apply it to their own life?

Precept #2: Money, as a marker of success, buys happiness just not in the ways we think it does.

TEACHING WHAT MATTERS PLAYBOOK: TOOLS FOR EXPLORING THE ART OF LIVING

Playbook Lesson Sequence 1: What is the value of money?

Lesson objective: Understand and identify how we develop a relationship to money. Identify the ways in which we believe money buys happiness.

Step 1-Guiding Question: What is the relationship between money and success?

- Begin by asking: *How much money do you think you need to earn in annual salary to be happy [before taxes]? Consider your future age, whether with a life partner, children, your quality of life, standard of living, where you live, etc.* Ask students to consider what their imagined quality of life is like, what they own, what did they do, do they have disposable income. What is it that money is buying that is providing you the best life?
- Then students share the annual salary amounts. Catalog them for the whole class to see. Keep a running list of all incomes, without judgement and commentary.
- Next, students turn and talk with each other based on the following prompts: Explain why you chose this income amount? Help your partner understand the kind of life this income buys. What are those income generated indicators of success? They can first draw images, or names

of things that they envision money affording them that leads to a good life. Ask the specific students who had the highest and lowest amounts of income to share with the class why they chose these incomes.

Step 2-Guiding Question: What do people earn in the United States? Next, share with students the following socio-economic realities. In 2019, median household income was $68,703.[10] That means that half of American households earn *above* that amount. However, half of American households earn *below* that. This can consist of multiple income earners. As a way to frame median income realities, compare the cost of attending Harvard University, tuition plus room and board, which adds up to $78,000 for one year for 2019–2020! One year of attending Harvard costs more than what half of American households earn in a year.

Step 3-Guiding Question: How does your school district compare **to others in the United States?**

- *The New York Times* has an excellent infographic, *Money, Race, and Success. How Your School District Compares* illustrating the vast socio-economic realities and inequalities. This information serves as both affirming and alarming for many students. Earning high incomes to obtain a certain lifestyle comes with certain costs and obstacles.

Step 4-**Guiding question: What is the paradox found in the Easterlin Paradox?**

- Share economist Richard Easterlin's paradox he posited in 1974. (Any search will show you a graph of income vs. subjective well-being or happiness over time.) Ask, what explains this data? What is the paradox? If money buys happiness, why isn't it? As individuals become richer since 1950s (adjusted for inflation), self-reported happiness levels have remained constant.

What can be taught & learned about *Happiness?*

What is the Easterlin Paradox? The Easterlin Paradox (1974) illustrates that happiness seems to rise with income to a point, but not beyond it. Meaning income matters to happiness, but after a certain point more money does not create more happiness. The Easterlin Paradox has shown that since the 1950s average household income has been steadily increasing, while the percentage of people self-reporting happiness has remained relatively constant. This is the paradox.

Happiness levels have not increased with income. If we have gradually become wealthier and have more than any other generation, why have happiness levels stayed consistent? This paradox is better understood by what psychologists call the hedonic treadmill.

Are we living through a period of satisfied expectations? Nobel prize economist, Daniel Kahneman has noted that we are living through a revolution of satisfied expectations. Relatively speaking, because people have so much more now than what people possessed in prior years, it is difficult to expect that in the future we can get even more. This is can skew our satisfaction with life.

There has never been a time in history where the average American has more wealth, better health, prosperity, and stuff. That is not to say there is not inequality or inequity in the world today. In the United States we are all too familiar with communities who are plagued with problems exacerbated by poverty and inequity.

According to the World Happiness Report in 2019, happiness levels around the world have been decreasing. This might be due to higher expectations, especially in wealthier countries, where the standard of living as been increasingly steadily over the last fifty years. Since we have more, we keep wanting more. When we get more, we simply adapt to what we have obtained, and simply want more. While we are busy acquiring more things, our happiness levels ebb and flow.

Who determines what we want or need? In any introductory economics class, the fundamental problem studied is scarcity. How to satisfy unlimited human wants with limited resources. The *problem* of any economic system is to meet the basic needs of its citizens and theoretically their unlimited wants. In 2018, the media advertising industry spent over $240 billion to persuade us to purchase stuff.[11] This helps to artificially create a want. Earning high incomes to obtain a certain lifestyle comes with certain costs and obstacles. Economists call these opportunity costs or the trade-off between choices.

What are differences in deprivations caused by poverty? There is a difference between relative and absolute poverty. For the average person in wealthier countries, it is difficult to argue against the feeling of having more in material terms than our parents or grandparents. Despite rising rates of inequality[12] of income, wealth, and consumption there is a larger geographic inequality of income.

When one compares themselves to others living around the world today, we are often surprised. The median household annual income in the U.S. in 2018 was $62,000. If you earned an income of $59,000, you were in the richest 10 percent globally.[13] For most of us, in relative terms, we have hit the economic jackpot based on where and when we have been born.

Playbook Lesson Sequence 2: Veruca Salt's relationship to money and miswanting.

Lesson objective: Defend or refute Veruca Salt's approach to life (as she explains it in the song "I Want it Now")

Step 1-Guiding Question: Does Veruca Salt's relationship **to money and wanting whatever we want equate to a good life?**

- Watch video of scene with Veruca Salt–*I Want It Now* (from Willy Wonka and the Chocolate Factory)
- Students turn and talk: What, if anything, is wrong with Salt's approach to life? What, if anything, is wrong with materialism (the importance that people place on their possessions either for self-enhancement or in an effort to define themselves)? What explains why we spend money the way we do? Why do we believe wanting and having it all will provide lasting happiness? Does it? How are you similar to and/or different from Veruca Salt?

Step 2-Guiding Question: Would winning the lottery change your life for the better?
After discussions, share with them John Falcone's experiences of winning the New York state's lottery. Watch his story in the video *This Emotional Life with Dan Gilbert* (DVD). Evaluate John Falcone (he was New York state's single biggest lottery winner.) He literally went from rages to riches—from a struggling artist to living in "uber luxury."

- After watching, ask the class: Falcone appeared to be able to have anything he wanted when he wanted, was this a recipe for a good life? Did money improve his life? What did he cite about the ways that he spent his money that seemed to make him happy? What other ideas resonated with you?
- Read "*Would Winning the Lottery Really Change Your Life? Research reveals some surprising truths about lottery winners*" by Wendy Patrick, Oct, 2018 (Psychology Today)
- Watch and read about Luke Pittard: He became a millionaire after winning the lottery. After a lavish wedding, honeymoon, and new home, he went back to work. https://www.standard.co.uk/news/

millionaire-lottery-winner-goes-back-to-job-at-mcdonalds-because-he-misses-his-workmates-6688295.html

Step 3-Guiding Question: How much stuff do we actually own?
Examine the following statistics from Joshua Becker's Becoming Minimalist blog: *21 Surprising Statistics That Reveal How Much Stuff We Actually Own.*

Step 4-Students complete a five-minute NB-journal: Why do you care so much about money? Why do you buy stuff? If you had all the money you wanted, how would you change your life? Would life change make your more satisfied with life? Why? When you spend money, what makes you happy? Does the happiness sustain?

What can be taught & learned about *Happiness?*

How much money is needed in order to be happy? In a now ubiquitous study done by Nobel Prize winners in economics, Angus Deaton and Daniel Kahneman found a link between happiness and income but only up to $75,000. After that, more income does not lead to an increase in emotional well-being.[14]

The $75,000 illustrated a range. It is variable based on where you live. It also is not a hard limit. If you earn $5 more than $75,000 you will not fall off an emotional cliff. More money does seem to increase expectations and social comparisons which are toxic to well-being. As the study illustrated, once money buys you out of the stresses and deprivation that comes with poverty, more money leads to diminishing returns.

Another conclusion raised in the study was the cost-of-living adjustment. Earning $45,000 a year in one country might be enough to have your basic needs met. Where you begin socio-economically matters too.

One research study found that for over 32 years (1972–2004) in the United States where you start and/or end up in terms of socio-economic status matters. If you are able to experience upward social mobility then money matters. However, if you are born into a lower socio-economic status, and are unable to rise in classes, then money matters too.

Also, living in a nation with greater economic inequality contributes to less happy people. On average, people are less happy living in a nation with significant income inequality. This isn't necessarily due to having less money but because inequality exacerbates an erosion of trust and a perceived systemic unfairness.[15]

Does more money actually buy more happiness? Recently a study released by Matthew Killingsworth made some headlines nationwide when it appeared that the $75,000 happiness earning benchmark may no longer be accurate. He found that happiness does indeed increase with income, well past the $75,000 threshold. The data seemed to confirm that money does in fact buy happiness.

However, Killingsworth's research supports the idea that where you begin matters a lot. Every extra dollar that moves you out of the deprivations of poverty brings a bit more life satisfaction.[16] But, with each dollar earned, the less that dollar matters. There is a difference in life satisfaction increasing earnings from $30,000 to $60,000 a year.

But the difference between earning $100,000 to $200,000 isn't proportional to that. Two times the amount of money does not equal two times the happiness similarly for every person. Generally, every extra dollar earned significantly helps poorer individuals, more than rich ones.

Secondly, materialism is a strong predictor of unhappiness. He found that people who equated money with success were less happy than those who didn't. Higher income individuals also tended to be more stressed and time starved. The biggest conclusion from the study was that people who reported that money did increase life satisfaction revealed that money provided a greater sense of control in their lives.

When did shopping become equated as a way to spend leisure time? Shopping as a form of leisure is a fairly recent development in human history. Roughly 1 in 10 Americans are addicted to shopping or have a compulsive buying disorder.[17] Fast fashion has created the idea that clothing is disposable.

Advertising has sold the idea of four-season clothes shopping. It has resulted in 80 billion items of clothing each year being consumed by people around the world. This clothing doesn't seem to make us happy over the long term. The average American tosses 82 pounds of textile waste each year, which adds up to 11 million tons of the stuff from our country alone. For the most part, these textiles are not biodegradable. The clothing sits in landfills for at least 200 years.[18]

Estimates are about 5 to 15 percent of the population is addicted to shopping.[19] And 3.5 percent of high school aged adolescents have a shopping addiction.[20] Research indicates materialism is a strong predictor of unhappiness.[21]

Playbook Lesson Sequence 3: Why is success based on comparing ourselves to others or trying to keep up with the Joneses (effect)?

Lesson objectives: (A) Examine status anxiety, social comparison, and trying to keep up with others and its negative effects on well-being. (B) Describe the history of consumerism and shopping and how it has evolved culturally to influence how we think and act.

Step 1-Guiding Question: How might consumerism (the preoccupation of the accumulation of consumer goods) be a product of status anxiety

(the constant tension or fear of being perceived as unsuccessful by society in materialistic terms)?

- Watch the video *Consumerism* (available via *The School of Life*). Can understanding the history of consumption guide us to a wiser future?
- Read *Consumer culture has found its perfect match in our mobile-first, fast-fashion lifestyles* by Marc Bain. (Available via Quartz.com)
- Watch *What Are You Worth? Getting Past Status Anxiety* by Alain De Botton (available via Big Think)

Step 2-Guiding Question: Did you ever wonder where all our stuff comes from?

- Watch the "The Story of Stuff" (available at www.storyofstuff.org)

Step 3-Guiding Question: When it comes to our lives, is there a paradox between how you are living and how you want to live?

- Evaluate the poem *The Paradox of Our Time*. To what extent is this paradox valid? What, if anything, can be done?

Step 5-NB-Journal, students spend 5 minutes chronicling their thoughts.

What can be taught & learned about *Happiness*?

Why is social comparison or keeping up with the Joneses toxic to well-being? Social comparison and envy are toxic to well-being. We have a strong desire to evaluate ourselves in relation to others. In order to know how well we are doing we engage in social comparison, or keeping up with the Joneses.

How satisfied we are with how much money we earn for example, is largely determined by points of reference, people to whom we compare ourselves. This is a dual-edged sword. Comparison can make us feel better or it can as easily make us feel worse about ourselves when we don't stack up with others. How we think about money, our spending and saving tendencies, largely determines how much satisfaction we feel. People tend to overestimate the impact that wealth, required income, and possessions will have on their well-being.[22]

How do consumer products tend to separate us from others? Daniel Pink, the author of the *Drive: The Surprising Truth of What Motivates Us*, stated that money gives us less of what we want and more of what we don't want. Conspicuous consumption is a zero-sum game. When people buy perceived luxurious things that are visible to others it helps form the basis of judgement of a person's relative success. Acquisition of things separate us from others by intentionally or unintentionally devaluing the possessions of others.

Why might too many choices sometimes diminish our satisfaction with our purchases? Barry Schwartz's research on the paradox of choice has indicated that people can feel regret because of the overwhelming amount of consumer choices available. We value choice but are undermined by the number of choices. This often puts a dent in our happiness because we never quite feel we purchased the right item, making people feel less satisfied with their decisions.

Societal messages and norms about obtaining money as a marker of success often conflates what it means to live a good life. These messages encourage us to believe that we should express ourselves through our possessions.

Playbook Lesson Sequence 6: Work as a means to happiness.

Lesson objective: Identify the reasons why some people believe their jobs lack meaning or the effect of doing work that they dislike.

Step 1-Guiding Question: Do people's jobs generally make them happy? Read *On The Phenomenon of Bullshit Jobs: A work rant* by David Graeber (Strike Magazine) https://www.strike.coop/bullshit-jobs/.

- Read: *Bullshit jobs: why they exist and why you might have one and why this professor thinks we need a revolution by* Sean Illing (available via Vox.com)
- Read *Feel like you have a socially useless job? You're not alone* by James Adonis (available via the Sydney Morning Herald)

Step 2-Guiding Question: How might a career make you happy?

- Read *Does work make you happy? Evidence From the World Happiness Report* by Jan-Emmanuel De Neve and George Ward (available via Harvard Business Review)

What can be taught & learned about *Happiness?*

Generally, do people believe that their job is useful to society? A recent study was conducted by Robert Dur and Max van Lent with more than 27,000 workers in 37 countries. Each were presented with the statement "my job is useful to society," and asked how strongly they agreed.

Based on anecdotal reporting about 8 percent of workers said their job was "socially useless." Another 17 percent were neutral on whether their job is useful or not, they simply didn't care. The study revealed that nearly all police officers, firefighters, nurses, teachers, and religious professionals described their careers as useful.

Overall, about 75 percent of workers agreed or strongly agreed that their job was useful to society. The research also revealed that having a job that is useful to society is considered an important job characteristic by a vast majority of workers, with nearly 77 percent of workers deeming this important or very important.[23]

Playbook Lesson Sequence 7: Evaluating the advice of following your passion

Lesson objective: Conventional wisdom suggests that if one follows their passion, success will follow. Analyze the extent to which this may or may not be true.

Step 1-Guiding Question: What really drives people to successful living or careers?

- Read *The Fallacy of 'Love What You Do': Why one of the most repeated pieces of career advice is completely bogus* by Jason Fried (available via Inc.com)
- Read *Why Some Dreams Should Not Be Pursued: Society and pop culture often encourage you to follow your dreams with passion and persistence. But what if you have the wrong dream?* by Mark Manson https://markmanson.net/dreams

Step 2-Watch a scene from the documentary film *Happy*[24] by Roko Belic on the story of Andy Wimmer, a volunteer at Mother Teresa's home for the sick and dying in Kolkata, India.

- Watch, NYU professor Scott Galloway's talk *Don't Follow Your Passion* (available via YouTube.)
- Evaluate the messages about following your passion.

What can be taught & learned about *Happiness*?

What do individuals whose success no one saw coming reveal about becoming successful? Researchers Todd Rose and Ogi Ogas at Harvard University conducted a long-term study called the Dark House Project. It explored how men and women (dark horse individuals whose successes no one saw coming) were able to achieve success and personal fulfillment.

The research revealed that these Dark Horses were motivated by what mattered intrinsically. They looked internally for validation rather than externally. They redefined success by determining and shaping their own path to personal fulfillment. These individuals used their personalized ambition to stay motivated and empowered them to ignore detractors. Success was individualized, defined differently by each person.

Playbook Lesson Sequence 8: Redefining Luxury and Wealth in Our Lives

Lesson objective: Evaluate the ideas of minimalism featured within the film.
Step 1-Guiding Question: Would life be better with less?

- Watch the documentary *Minimalism* film (available via Netflix).
- Students should take notes on ideas that the resonate with them because they strongly agree with them or strongly disagree with them. After the film have students discuss with partners their reactions and points that resonated with them the most.

Step 2-Guiding Question: Is minimalism a kind of elitism or practical idea for all?
Students can also examine critiques to certain kinds of minimalism. The central premise being it is easy to minimize when you can afford anything you want.

Read *Minimalism: Another boring product wealthy people can buy* by Chelsea Fagan (available via *The Guardian*)

What can be taught & learned about *Happiness?*

What is minimalism? There are ways to shift our beliefs about the role money should play in our lives. Simplifying our lives is not that difficult. Author Roman Krznaric suggest to not abandon luxury, but simply discover it new places.[25]

Minimalism is a choice to free oneself from materialistic trappings. It is a tool to rid yourself of the superficial. Minimalism can help recast and recommit ourselves to a different type of wealth. This prosperity can be found in meaningful work, strong relationships, laughter, hugs, solitude, sun on our faces, the feel of grass between our toes, good music, and offering a hand up to others. This can be a non-monetary investment, in living fully and with luxury.

Was Thoreau the first minimalist in America? Perhaps the first minimalist was naturalist Henry David Thoreau. He urged himself to simplify, simplify, simplify. As he wondered off to experiment with the art of living at Walden Pond, he was rejecting in some ways the cultural and commercial changes that were taking place in the United States as a result of industrialization and transportation.

The costs that came from the expansion of the railroad concerned Thoreau as well as others in this era. He believed that this technology was changing Americans and American culture in ways that were not conducive to living a good life. He decided to experiment at Walden pond, living deliberately to see what it meant to live more simply.

Playbook Lesson Sequence 9: The other value of money. Thinking about money ethically

Lesson objective: Identify ways in which money can empower someone to be an impactful moral agent.

Step 1-Guiding Question: Is being generous a way to increase our satisfaction with life?

- Examine the following infographic from *Happify: The Science of Giving: Why Being Generous is Good For You.*
- Watch, *Helping Others Makes Us Happier, But It Matters How We Do It*–Elizabeth Dunn TedTalk (2019)

Step 2-Guiding Question: If you feel like engaging in pro-social spending, what tools are available to do good with the money you donate?

- Examine charitable giving: givewell.org. Toby Ord and his friend Will MacAskill in 2011 founded *Giving What We Can.* This organization evaluates charities and members pledge to give 10 percent of their income over the course of their lives to the organizations that will have the greatest impact in the developing world. To date over 4,175 members have donated more than $127 million dollars. Over the course of their lifetimes *Giving What We Can* estimates that this will translate to $1.5 billion dollars.
- Watch, The Story of the Salwens (available via YouTube) and/or read selections from their book *The Power of Half.*
- Watch, Peter Singer's TedTalk on *The Why and How of Effective Altruism.*

What can be taught & learned about *Happiness?*

How does research suggest money buys happiness? Research has broadened the ways in which money seems to buy happiness, but there is a caveat. Money does buy happiness, but typically not in the ways that we think. The relationship between money and happiness is far more individualistic, than universal. Our personalities, preferences, and our beliefs about money largely shape how satisfied we are with our lives and the role money plays.

How we ultimately decide to spend money and even whether we have money to spend affects our happiness. Since the relationship to money and happiness is individualistic these recommendations might not pertain to everyone in the same way.

- Spend money on experiences not things. Experiential purchases (e.g., concerts) are more difficult to emotionally adapt to than material objects (e.g., sunglasses). Generally, experiences are more difficult to compare with others. We don't need to judge the quality of our experiences and fall prey to status anxiety. Whereas material objects are easier to compare. The value of a pair of sunglasses bought for under $5 can easily be determined by comparing them with the number of people we see with designer $200 sunglasses. That is how we succumb to status anxiety.
- Redefine luxury in your life. Wealth can be expressed in laughter as much in dollars, in close friendships as much as cars, as much as the scale of good health, as much as the size of one's home. Luxury can be found in non-materialistic means.
- Spend money on others instead of yourself.
- Save money. Having a financial cushion, that is seeing money saved improves our satisfaction with life.
- Use money as a means to connect you with others, not separate yourself from others. Strong and meaningful social connections are essential to happiness. Purchasing certain objects tend to separate us from others simply because others don't have them.
- If you do spend money on indulgences, try delaying the purchase until a future date. The anticipation could be the benefit. Anticipation can lead to free happiness by savoring the anticipatory positive emotions.
- Think about the amount of your time and energy is required to obtain the money to purchase this item. Does the opportunity cost warrant the expenditure? Buy time instead of things. Invest in time saving devices or services. Time is often viewed as our most precious commodity.

What is the connection between pro-social spending and happiness? Spending money on others is another way that provides greater and lasting well-being. Prosocial spending activates reward centers of our brains. When we give to others neurotransmitters like dopamine (reward), oxytocin (connection), and serotonin (happy feelings) are all produced in our brains. It can feel just as good to use your financial resources to enhance the life of another than using money to benefit yourself.

Either by donating to charities or buying a gift for a friend, the amount of money doesn't matter. Spending twice as much on another gift doesn't give us an increased boost in happiness.[26]

How generous are we? According to The World Bank, there are 800 million people who live on less than US$2 per day. There are many people who want to make a difference in the lives of others. Based on available data on charitable donations, a 2018 Giving USA report, Americans gave a total of $410 billion to charity last year. More than two-thirds of Americans donated to charity in 2000, decreasing to 55.5 percent in 2014 with the average American donating $2,500 annually.[27]

Playbook Lesson Sequence 10: Assess Understanding and Learning

Assessment options: These are intended to be a fun way to connect with and reflect on the ideas, practices, workshops, and their applications to our lives. Student ideas should be based on personal experiences, reflections, and insights. Don't simply summarize what was done in class.

Concept check, quiz-Do you understand the research, the theories, the data, and philosophical considerations behind the various ideas. (Points subject to assessment.) Traditionally designed quizzes along with using scenes from films by which students must demonstrate application of their knowledge based on what is seen in the film. Students can select any film and identify and explain scenes from the film that illustrate each of the assessed concepts.

Reflection journal-students explain what they have learned about the various lesson steps. Explain what they agree with or disagree with. Also how they could incorporate information into their lives and discard other types of thinking and behaving from their lives, if applicable. In the journal students should document (1) the extent to which they have changed as a result of the lessons [this includes habits of thinking, behavior, actions, experiences, epiphanies, insights, philosophies, accomplishments, goals, etc. and (2) their plans for themselves in the future. This includes all that they want to accomplish in terms of goals; aspects of themselves that they want to discard; and practices, ideas, actions, and experiences that they want to add to their lives.

Draw what you've learned-Explain the applicability of the information to your life. Also explain what you have drawn, how it represents what you've learned. Summarize why you chose to express your understanding in this way.

Analogy concept paper-explain how what has been learned is like a _____ (e.g., an acorn). Make specific connections between assessed concepts and whatever the object may be.

Life Maps-A summation of what students learned in a unit, mapped with images, quotes, and multi-page reflection that explains the map and how if followed, helps one to attain a good life. This should also critically analyze rather than merely summarize what students learned or found applicable to understanding well-being.

Precept #3: Keep it real. Develop **an** inner integrity **to** live successfully

TEACHING WHAT MATTERS PLAYBOOK: TOOLS FOR EXPLORING THE ART OF LIVING

Playbook Lesson Sequence 1: Combat the illusion of perfectionism. When good enough is good enough

Lesson objective: Identify perfectionism, its causes, the dangers, and the trends associated with it.

Step 1-Guiding Question: **What are the costs associated with striving for perfectionism?**

- Watch *The Problem of Perfection* (available via *The School of Life*)
- Read *The Dangerous Downsides of Perfection* by Amanda Ruggeri, BBC Future

Step 2-Guiding Question: What are ways in which to thwart perfectionism?

- Read *How to Beat Perfectionism, Make Progress, and Find Happiness* by Ryan Holiday (available via Psychology Today)

Step 3-NB-Journal reflection: What are your best failures? What failures have enriched your life? What does it mean to fail well? What is a risk you took that paid off that enriched your life?

Step 3: Guiding Question: What is failure and how can we embrace failures?

- Discuss the meaning of failure. What is failure? Do you remember when you were younger and failure was encouraged? Watch the following and make conclusions about success from these failures.
- Watch Famous Failures (available via YouTube, from Motivating Success)
- Watch Dwayne Johnson (The Rock) discuss his CFL experiences. (available via YouTube "The Rock shares his love for Vancouver")
- Watch speech from actor Idris Elba "Work Hard Sleep Less" (available via YouTube)

What can be taught & learned about *Happiness?*

Do successful people fail or do they always succeed at their endeavors? Most successful people throughout history have been great failures. From Michael Jordan to Oprah Winfrey to Steve Jobs to Thomas Edison, to many others, they all have come to realize that there is no success without failure. There are small failures and big failures. All of which help us to achieve the level of success we want.

Is perfectionism on the rise? Success isn't about being perfect in the many provinces of one's life. Perfectionism is the need to be or appear to be perfect, or even to believe that it's possible to achieve perfection. Unfortunately, Thomas Curran and Andrew Hill have conducted a recent meta-analysis of rates of perfectionism from 1989 to 2016, the first study to compare perfectionism across generations. They found significant increases among more recent undergraduates in the US, UK, and Canada.

Perfectionism as a negative trait is fueled by unrealistic standards, intense self-criticism, low self-esteem, and a defensiveness which leads to procrastination.[28] Good enough is never believed to be good. Thus, a fear of failure develops which can result in sabotaging oneself.

How might failure actually be good and necessary? Some psychologists, like Jonathan Haidt, has argued that adversity, setbacks, and even trauma may actually be necessary for people to be happy, successful, and fulfilled. As we know some of our failures are great.

Successful people attribute their accomplishments to earlier failures. The reason for this is that failure can teach us more. Failure teaches us about overcoming adversity, learning how to become more flexible with our expectations. When we fail, we generally ask for help. Failure often simplifies what is most important in our lives.

Why does being you require grit, resiliency, stamina and hard work? Angela Duckworth switched careers from a management consultant to teach middle school math to students in the New York City public schools. Based on her experiences she came to the conclusion that intelligence is not the only determinant of learning for children.

Duckworth penned the book, *Grit: The Power of Passion and Perseverance* to illustrate the importance of resiliency, grit, stamina, and industriousness. She also stressed the importance of a growth mindset. Students who have a growth mindset are more likely to not give up if they are unsuccessful because they know that failure is not a fixed condition.

One of the keys to success involves inspiring yourself, fueling your motivation and tapping into your reservoir of passion. Grit is one of the important motivating factors that keeps you on track for long periods of time.

Duckworth tested out the work of Gabrielle Oettingen. Oettingen published a book *Rethinking Positive Thinking*, where she described a process called WOOP (Wish, Outcome, Obstacles, and Plan). Duckworth had her students incorporated the WOOP model every day. After employing WOOP, students improved their grades, their on-time attendance, and class behavior.

Playbook Lesson Sequence 2: Authenticity and vulnerability.

Lesson objectives: Analyze and identify the principles of self-determination theory and authenticity. Explain how happiness is dependent on who we are and what we are in our individuality.

Step 1-Guiding Question: How does one develop **the courage to live authentically?**

- Identify and evaluate Brene Brown's special *"The Call To Courage"* (available on Netflix) or watch her very popular TedTalk, *The Power of Vulnerability.*
- Take notes on the main ideas expressed in her talk. What rang true? What didn't?

Step 2-Guiding Question: How did Taylor Swift develop the courage to live authentically?

- Watch Taylor Swift's *Miss Americana* (available on *Netflix*).
- Identify the factors that allowed Taylor Swift to develop the courage to be authentic.

Step 3-Write a 1–2 page response where you respond to both Brene Brown's talk and Taylor Swift's maturation and political transformation from a self-described girl who smiles and does not say anything to someone who tries to inform others and be true to herself.

Step 4-Guiding questions: What does it mean to be authentic? Is it possible to be too authentic?

- Read *Five Ways to be Fully Authentic* by Christine Carter (available via Greater Good Magazine)
- Read *How to Be Authentically You in Any Situation* by Homaira Kabir (available via Happify.com)
- Read *Unless You're Oprah, 'Be Yourself' Is Terrible Advice* by Adam Grant (available via *The New York Times*)

Step 5-Guiding Question: What makes it a struggle for some people to be authentic and live authentically?

- Watch scene from the film *Mona Lisa Smile* (where Julia Roberts character shows slides of advertisements of women in the 1950s and finally asks "What does this mean?"). In what ways does culture influence us to live inauthentically? Who or what in your life pushes you to be the best version of yourself?
- Watch the beginning of the film *Jerry Maguire*. The first ten minutes illustrate the catharsis that hits Jerry Maguire in his struggle to be authentic.
- Watch Season 2, Episode 6 "Zoey's Extraordinary Reckoning" of NBC's *Zoey's Extraordinary Playlist* (The episode explores the issue of racial bias and the struggle that comes with denying a fundamental part of one's racial identity.)
- Discuss in small groups for about 5–10 minutes: What is authenticity? What is inauthenticity? Why is it not appropriate or practical to be authentic all the time? What is the difference between being authentic and acting differently depending on situations? To what extent does your school, community in which you live, and society promote your authenticity?
- NB-Journal: Catalog what you have learned about authenticity.

Step 6-Guiding Question: What do we sacrifice, if anything, to live a life of meaning and purpose? What is the reward in doing so?

- Watch A. J. Leon's TedTalk *This is Not Your Practice Life.*
- Draft a 1–2 page mission statement for your life.

What can be taught & learned about *Happiness?*

What is the importance of authenticity? In ancient philosophy, the Delphi Oracle taught us to know ourselves. The ability to be true to oneself, to maintain authenticity in one's life is an important element to well-being. Psychologists use the term neurotic or neurosis, although no longer an official diagnosis in the DSM, to describe the maladaptive response to our insecurities, sensitivities, and coping strategies. This is because they hinder our ability to meet our needs and goals.

All of us experience neurotic reactions during the course of our lives. Research demonstrates that true-self behavior, or authenticity, correlates with positive psychological benefits as individuals report higher self-esteem, more positive affect, and more hope for the future.

What does it mean to be authentic? Striving for authenticity involves sincerity. Sincerity is being aware of how we present ourselves to others as we strive to be the person we claim to be. Susan Harter has done extensive research on the relationship between false-sense behavior (inauthenticity), not saying what one thinks or believes, and not expressing one's true opinion.

Authenticity, according to Harter, "involves owning one's personal experiences, be they thoughts, emotions, needs, wants, preferences, or beliefs, processes captured by the injunction to 'know oneself.'"[29] To be happy we have to find our true selves. Who are we, independent of constructs influenced by parents, friends, culture, and our education?

What might it mean to have the courage to live one's life authentically? In the documentary film *Minimalism*, A. J. Leon shared an example of living life authentically. After losing his father as a teenager, and not growing up wealthy, he arrived at college with the hope of working to become wealthy. He chose finance as a focus of study. He admits he was miserable, sacrificing his hopes and wants for fulfilling life in pursuit of more money. He was offered a lucrative promotion.

He walked away from this promotion at an illustrious Wall Street firm. He came to the realization that the life being afforded to him wasn't the life he wanted. He wished to start a life of meaning.

He didn't jettison with a financial cushion. He was broke. He outpaced his earnings by spending extravagantly, often purchasing to maintain the facade of lifestyle. With increased perceptions of success, came increased expectations to sustain it. However, Leon was free for the first time to live his life. Independent of how he came to believe he was supposed to live it.

How authentic might a person be? How authentic you want to be might be determined by a certain personality trait called self-monitoring. People who are high self-monitors have a heightened awareness of others and the environment around them. Being acutely aware, they adjust their behavior to avoid offending, hurting anyone, or experiencing awkward situations.

Low self-monitors are more self-aware of their own personality and inner emotions regardless of their environment or the people around them. They are who they are regardless of where they are or who they are with at that time. The adage "you do you" is applicable for low-self monitors.

Why are courage and bravery necessary to be authentic? Being authentic takes courage and bravery. Brené Brown, author and researcher of shame, tells countless stories of people who step out of their comfort zones. In the attempt to be their real selves, these people are sometimes successful, and other times unsuccessful in different moments of their lives. To be authentically ourselves we usually have to face some combination of vulnerability, fear, disappointment, and possibly shame.

Why is it important to control what we can control? No one has one hundred percent control over their inner and the outer elements of their lives. Having the ability to manage stress, frustration, and disappointment is important. For example, this can begin by realizing that failing to win a tennis match is not because we are a failure.

Nor does it mean that we are not good at tennis. It simply means we were not good enough that match and require more practice. Or that it was a really windy day, and the usual playing conditions upset how we would typically perform. However, we should not deceive ourselves by thinking we can change things that are not changeable. Research reveals that this can lead to frustration, disappointment, and depression.

When things are outside of our control the best way for dealing with this is by externalizing it. Julian Rotter, an influential behavioral psychologist, theorized that people differ significantly in attributing responsibility for what happens to them in life. Some people, with an internal locus of control will justify consequences of their behavior based on their own doing.

When something bad happens, people tend to justify it by externalizing what was done. We often chalk it up to fate or bad luck. Rotter's social learning theory reveals that our personality is a byproduct of the countless interactions between the individual and our environment. The sum of these experiences helps to explain why we behave the way we do.

People have an intrinsic desire toward self-actualization. Self-actualization is the tendency to develop your capabilities, maintain or enhance ourselves. Well-being is the result of the freedom and responsibility for the choices we make. This is seen in school settings. Research shows that intrinsic goals produce deeper engagement, deeper learning, and interest.

Can we be too authentic? Psychologist and author Adam Grant warns we can be too authentic. Not everyone wants to experience our true selves, thoughts, and behaviors at every moment. Authenticity is dependent on a trait called self-monitoring. High self-monitors tend to be vigilant of their surroundings and adjust how they act based on these social cues. As Grant notes, high-self monitors are consciously aware of not offending anyone. They adapt to their surroundings as to not make any waves when socializing with others.

Low-self monitors however, are themselves regardless of their surroundings. No matter the place or who they are with, they don't act differently. Just because we act differently in different environments does not make us inauthentic. It makes us practical and malleable to our surroundings.

Young people who self-report themselves as authentic maintain a number of psychological benefits like intra-personal intelligence, higher self-esteem, have more hope for the future, and more positive affect.

Playbook Lesson Sequence 3: Explain why signature strengths might be tools to live authentically

Lesson objectives: Identify why strengths are critical to managing one's life in the short term and long term. Identify how strengths help us to achieve our goals and be true to ourselves.

Step 1-Guiding Question: What are signature strengths?

- Introduce the Science of Signature Strengths. Strengths are the positive parts of your personality that helps us achieve our goals and live authentically. Strengths are positive parts of your personality. Watch various videos from the VIA Institute (University of Pennsylvania).
- Watch *The Science of Character Strengths* from the VIA Institute.

What can be taught & learned about *Happiness?*

What are signature strengths? Martin Seligman and Chris Peterson identified across nations and cultures 24 character strengths that contribute to living a good life. These 24 core virtues or signature strengths have been recognized because of their highly respected value amongst people around the world and throughout history.

Martin Seligman and Chris Peterson's research indicates that your signature strengths integrated into your personal life, in your relationships, and your professional life, lead to fulfillment and increased satisfaction.[30] These strengths have been found to be consistent in the lives of people over time. Seligman argues that these signature strengths are pathways to each of the five areas of well-being, as described in his PERMA model.

Why are signature strengths important to human flourishing? When you think about people you admire, what are their strengths? What defines you as a person and what aspects of yourself do you share with others? Early pioneers in the field of positive psychology determined that human beings who flourish live consistently with certain virtues. They also implement their signature strengths into their everyday lives. In doing so, people are able to be authentic.

When we live according to our true selves, we are living in concert to those virtues that make us unique. Strengths and virtues allow us to adapt to stressful life events. Helping adolescents to cultivate resiliency, agency, and authenticity helps them to develop psychologically into good people. As research on signature strengths indicate, we are at our best when we are acting in ways that makes us proud.

How are strengths different from talents or skills? Strengths are not the same thing as competencies, talent, or even skills. Current research indicates that you are most likely to value a job or a relationship that not only aligns with your core signature strengths but also require you to regularly utilize them. In fact, research indicates that one of the best ways to boost your long-term happiness is to use your strengths in new ways, rather than solely focusing on your weaknesses.[31]

Playbook Lesson Sequence 4: Take the free and confidential VIA Signature Strengths Survey

Lesson objective: Determine your strengths and interpret the results of the detailed report of your signature strengths.

Step 1-Have students take the VIA Strengths Survey. They will get a detailed report of their signature strengths. You could set up a teacher site to do this: If students are under the age of 13, you will need a parental consent form.

Step 2-A link to the survey: https://www.viacharacter.org/. It is fairly long. Plan to devote 20–30 minutes for students to complete. There is an adult survey for ages 18+ and a youth survey for ages 10–17. For grade 12 students, I usually recommend that they take the adult survey.

Step 3-Class conversation/reflection on the following statement by Todd Kashdan: "Balance in talents and abilities might be less important than possession and mastery in a singular domain."[32]

- Read *Is It a Good Idea To Build on Signature Strengths? The status quo is wrong* by Todd Kashdan (available via *Psychology Today*).

Step 4-After students take the survey, have them complete a journal reflection in their notebooks. To what extent were your strengths a validation or surprise? Why? Note that some strengths might be unrealized strengths. As the VIA institute notes on their website, only 1/3 of people actively know their strengths. In order to live a good life, full of meaning, purpose, and satisfaction, which strengths will be helpful in doing so? What strengths will help you on daily basis, to live life fuller, but also help you to cope with you experience adversity? What would it be like if teaching and learning was designed based on your individual strengths as opposed to your weaknesses? How would classes and/or school be designed to foster this? During an average week, how often do you suppress your strengths versus utilizing your strengths? What is the effect?

What can be taught & learned about *Happiness?*

Once you identify your strengths, what should do with this information? The first step Peterson and Seligman suggest is to discover your signature strengths by taking their free, anonymous signature strengths test. This VIA test or Values in Action Inventory of Signature Strengths test is the most widely used. The next step is to use your character strengths in new and different ways every day for a week.

Ryan Niemiec, author and Education Director at the VIA Institute, notes that knowing your strengths is only part of the equation. You must also cultivate novel ways to incorporate them daily into your life. Much of the time we are told we should work on our weakness and improve our shortcomings. This is beneficial some of the time.

We could also strive to live by our unique strengths. Living by these traits help us to better navigate the world around us. Consider creating a classroom culture that attempts to utilize the collective strengths of your students.

Playbook Lesson Sequence 5: Use your strengths in a new way

Assign as a homework assignment. Use your signature strengths in a new way every day for a week. https://www.viacharacter.org/topics/articles/use-your-strengths-to-boost-happiness

This link also has prompts that help with the implementation of strengths: https://www.actionforhappiness.org/media/52486/340_ways_to_use_character_strengths.pdf.

At the end of the week, students can reflect on their experience.

Playbook Lesson Sequence 6: Creating a class culture of strengths

Lesson objectives: Determine your strengths and create a class culture of strengths. Recognize and celebrate our individual and collective awesomeness.

Step 1-Students arrange themselves in groups. Each student draws a silhouette of a body on a big piece of paper. They write their name on the top as well. Each student creatively lists their top 5 strengths, with a brief summary. In addition, they pick one strength and describe a time when they were at their best using one of their strengths. This should be a written narrative somewhere on the body of the page. Hang the body silhouettes around the room.

- Discuss as a whole class: Despite our different strengths, how are we similar? What are the signature strengths of this class? How can we make class better suited to our strengths?

Playbook Lesson Sequence 7: Apply understanding of signature strengths

Lesson objective: Determine and identify various character strengths and their benefits.

- Assess understanding and application of signature strengths. Students select one film to watch at home. Select a main character from the film and list the top 5 strengths of the character using the VIA-Signature Strength inventory. Provide a 2–4 sentence explanation for each strength, using evidence from the film and your knowledge of the strength itself. How do their strengths benefit society? How do the strengths benefit the character?

-

Precept #4: Creating and committing to meaningful life goals liberate us from the tyranny of passive living.

TEACHING WHAT MATTERS PLAYBOOK: TOOLS FOR EXPLORING THE ART OF LIVING

Playbook Lesson Sequence 1: Setting meaningful life goals

Lesson objective: Understand the process for setting goals, the relationship between meaningful goals and life satisfaction.

Step 1-Guiding Question: What goals do you have for yourself?

- Have students identify at least 3 goals that are most important to them. They can be long-term or short-term. For each goal, encourage students to answer the following questions. What are small steps that can be measured in order to meet this goal? Why these goals? Why are they important to you? Who are sources of support and encouragement? What are

possible obstacles? What are actionable ways to overcome them? How will I measure progress? How will I celebrate any progress?
- Encourage students to achieve a small goal by the end of the week or month. Try to make it non-school related. Keep a jar of awesome. Every time you do something or achieve something during the course of the week, big or small, one thing or many things, by design, write it down and put it in the jar. At the end of the week, reflect on all that you accomplished. Celebrate the awesomeness of what you accomplished.
- Read *How to Let Go of Materialism: Enhance your well-being by focusing on deeper goals* by Tori Rodriguez (available via *Scientific American*).

Step 2-Guiding Question: What are ways to help achieve our goals?

- Watch WOOP-Wish Outcome Obstacle Plan model (available via Character Lab Woop on Vimeo).
- Read *Goal Setting: A Scientific Guide to Setting and Achieving Goal* by James Clear, author of *Atomic Habits* (available via https://jamesclear.com/goal-setting).
- Read *The Science of Achieving Your Goals* by Caroline Adams Miller (available via HappifyDaily).
- Read, *Here's How Science Can Help You Stick to Your Goals*, Happify Infographic.
- Assess: Students write a 1 page journal response to the guiding question.

Step 3-Guiding Question: What does it look and feel like to achieve your goals?
Listed below are suggestions for examples to share.

- Watch surfing film *Step Into Liquid* (available via DVD) and chasing the stoke.
- Watch the film *Hidden Figures*.
- *100 Days of Dance* from Project One Life, https://www.youtube.com/watch?v=6ycn5VmBUYY (I really enjoyed the movie Napoleon Dynamite so I appreciated his commitment to learning this epic dance).
- Watch: *"The 99ers"* about the 1999 United States Women's World Cup Soccer team.
- Read Gretchen Rubin's book *The Happiness Project*. She committed to improving her life by constructing daily and long-term goals that had positive effects on her life.

Step 4: NB-Journal: What does it feel like to achieve a meaningful goal?

What can be taught & learned about *Happiness?*

What are goals and why are they important? A goal, an explicit commitment, focuses our attention on a target. Goals help us to find ways of getting to that desired result. Beliefs, psychology tells us, can be self-fulfilling prophecies.

When we commit to goals, we demonstrate faith in ourselves. We create aspirations rather than accepting outcomes by default. In doing so, there is enjoyment in the little accomplishments that lead you closer toward a goal. This does not mean that we should be filling our days with incessant activities, reducing ourselves from human beings to human doings.

Success in life does not entail the Sixties mantra of "if it feels good, do it." Goals give our lives direction and intention. Ask yourself, what kind of life do you want? What will make you authentically happy in the long term? Thinking carefully about your answers to these questions are easy ways to remove you from simply going with the flow.

Goals can help you find meaning and give your life purpose. Goal setting in many ways involves taking life into one's own hand, instead of abandoning it to tendencies created by habit or mental confusion. Like a sailor on a boat, we have a tendency to let go of the tiller and let our boats drift wherever life takes us. This is drifting.

Goal setting allows us to take hold of the tiller and sail toward a chosen destination. People who strive for something personally significant, whether it is learning how to play an instrument, speak in a different language, or being a good parent and friend are happier than those who don't have valued aspirations.

How do people achieve their goals? Edwin Locke has done extensive research on the importance of goal setting in relation to life satisfaction since the 1960s. His research, along with Gary Latham, has shown that there is a relationship between the difficulty and specificity of a goal in task completion and overall performance of that goal.

Having easy or vague goals led to less completion of the goal. People simply stopped trying to attain them. The lesson is to aim high with our goals and be ambitious. When people believe in their own agency, they are more likely to achieve their goals.

According to Locke people block their own ability to achieve more out of life for a number of reasons. One reason is because a simple lack of effort, both physical and mental. Lastly, people can become deterred from working toward goals because of fear.

There are countless fears and doubts that will deter, block, or separate you from striving toward what gives your life meaning. Things like fear of failure, being rejected, being different, being hurt, loss, inadequacy, and not having anything to offer all can block you from simply striving for more enjoyment or meaning out of life.

Playbook Lesson Sequence 2: The nuts and bolts of different kinds of goals

Lesson objective: Evaluate your goals.

Step 1-Self-assess your goals. Are the goals you set able to be achieved? What kind of goals are they? Are they conflicting with one another? Are they intrinsic? Are they authentic to you and to no one else?[33]

- Read and reflect on the following *Choosing to Free Yourself* by Eric Jorgenson https://www.navalmanack.com/almanack-of-naval-ravikant/choosing-to-free-yourself

What can be taught & learned about *Happiness?*

Are goals like a bucket list? Goal setting is not a bucket list. Setting and committing to goals are not resolutions we make for ourselves for a new year. According to research from K. Anders Ericsson and colleagues, made famous by Malcolm Gladwell in his book *Outliers, it takes a minimum of ten years or 10,000 hours of committed practice to become an expert.*

Working to become an expert at living life more fully or increasing your well-being will involve leaving one's comfort zone. It will also involve maintaining self-motivation and daily commitment. Goal setting is not only a means to an end, but a way to transform our relationship to our everyday lives.

Chapter 3

Happiness as an Inside Job

Developing Emotional Courage, Befriending Difficult Emotions, Cultivating Positive Emotions, Optimism and an Attitude of Gratitude

Philosopher René Descartes famously declared, "I think, therefore I am." Thoughts and emotions can be our best friends but also our worst enemies. The Stoic philosopher Seneca taught in his treatise *On the Tranquility of the Mind* that a happy life is one that requires having a calm mind.

This requires no longer tormenting ourselves by imagining doomsday scenarios that almost always never come to fruition. Seneca believed that those achieving a state of inner tranquility, as Sissela Bok wrote, ". . . *will live in constant cheerfulness and with a joy that is profound and issues from deep within, since they find delight in their own resources and desire no joys greater than their inner joys.*"[1]

Yale University researcher Marc Brackett and colleagues investigated students' feelings in a nation-wide survey of 21,678 US students in two samples.[2] They asked students to respond to open ended questions and fill out ratings scales. In their responses, 75 percent of student feelings reported were negative. The three most frequently mentioned negative feelings about school were fatigue, stress, and boredom.

A recent Pew Research study revealed that anxiety and depression are on the rise among America's youth. About 70 percent of teens see the problematic effects of anxiety and depression on their peers.[3] The National College Health Assessment (NCHA), a nationally recognized research survey, has been revealing that two out of three college students report "overwhelming anxiety." It has been the top concern among college students for seven straight years.[4] The impacts of which affect all aspects of student lives both in the classroom and outside of it.

Stress, in and of itself, is not bad. Chronic stress, however is problematic. The American Psychological Association, in a survey of 1,018 teenagers, found the majority reported feeling "extreme" levels of stress and ineffective coping mechanisms. They also revealed "the negative emotions related to their stress levels: 31% feeling overwhelmed, 30% reported depression, and 36% stated they felt fatigue."[5] The sources and causes of stress and anxiety are varied and are numerous.

Mental health literacy is important for any teenager. Understanding feelings, either negative or positive emotions, is empowering. Emotions are complex responses to our immediate perceptions or appraisals about a situation and/or something that has happened. No one should expect to feel happy all the time. That is impractical and undesirable, frankly.

For many young people and adults, the forces of fatalism triumph. With high profile suicides, mass school shootings, non-stop images of suffering around the world, and living during a global pandemic, the world can appear to be overwhelming broken.[6] This makes anyone feel vanquished. Trust in public institutions that have long provided hope and helped to create community, is at historically low levels.[7]

However, research on today's teenagers also reveal them to be more cautious, making better and healthier decisions, and are more responsible than previous generations. We have seen this recently, as evidenced by the Marjory Stoneman Douglas students turning their school shooting tragedy into a movement against gun violence. These young people have demonstrated attributes and characteristics we applaud as adults: courage, resiliency, intelligence, and hope.

As the New York Times recently noted, *"Today's teenagers drink less than their parents' generation did. They smoke less, and they use fewer hard drugs. They get in fewer car accidents and fewer physical fights. They are less likely to drop out of high school, less likely to have sex, and less likely to become pregnant. They commit fewer crimes. They even wear bike helmets."*[8] In addition, teen driving fatalities have declined, as seatbelt usage has increased.

This is not to suggest that teenagers don't engage in risky behavior. They do. It is evident teenagers are successfully navigating the complexities of life in ways that are worthy of being praised. How have they honed the skills to manage the ups and down of life experiences?

It is possible to change our relationships with emotions. Emotional literacy allows one to choose new approaches and different outcomes. You can't change what you don't understand. Helping young people better manage their emotions, develop an inner locus of control, higher self-esteem, and sociability can lead to greater well-being.

Developing the courage to work with difficult emotions is fundamental to well-being. Understanding what emotions are and how they affect us is the first step to being able to manage them. Gratitude holds a prominent place throughout human history. The good life is easy to observe and relish when we come to acknowledge and appreciate all that we have.

The goodness in our lives can be found in blessings, not burdens, relishing good experiences, and appreciating how we dealt with adversity. Gratitude becomes a meta-strategy to navigate difficult times. As a positive emotion, gratitude also has the potential to energize, heal, bring hope, cope, and help to become more resilient to stress while opening a doorway of awareness to goodness in our lives.[9]

Embracing optimism and broadening and building our lives allows us to turn the lemons that life throws at us into lemonade. It also provides us the means to build our lives toward goodness and broaden our positivity ratios. Barbara Fredrickson's research reveals that positive emotions allow us to broaden our view of ourselves, others, and the world. These positive feelings that come from experiencing positive emotions often lead to better action tendencies improving our relations with others.

When adversity does strike optimists respond in constructive ways. They cultivate acceptance and move forward. Optimists search for ways to turn the lemons thrown at them into lemonade.

Precept #5: To be human is to be emotional, so befriend your emotions

TEACHING WHAT MATTERS PLAYBOOK: TOOLS FOR EXPLORING THE ART OF LIVING

Playbook Lesson Sequence 1: Understanding emotions.

Lesson objectives: Define an emotion and Paul Ekman's "universal human emotions." Differentiate between emotions and moods. Explain how emotions create action tendencies.

Step 1-Guiding Question: What are emotions? What are the 6 types of basic emotions?

- Read *The 6 Types of Basic Emotions and Their Effect on Human Behavior* by Kendra Cherry (available via VeryWellMind)
- Read and access Paul Ekman's *Atlas of Emotions*, http://atlasofemotions.org/#introduction/
- Watch *Alfred & Shadow-A short story about emotions, education psychology health animation* (available via YouTube)

Step 2-Answer the following questions based on what you read. What are emotions? What are triggers associated with different emotions? What are various action tendencies associated with different emotions? What are ways we can choose to respond to emotions? Is it better to discuss one's emotions or stifle them? Should the expression of emotions be encouraged or discouraged? Why or why not?

What can be taught & learned about *Happiness?*

What are emotions? Emotions are complex responses to our immediate perceptions or appraisals about a situation and/or something that has happened. Humans can experience a multitude of emotions. Especially during adolescence, it is common to experience more than one emotion at the same time.

An emotional reaction is based on our appraisal of almost anything, a trigger of some sort, which is usually important to us. This results in physiological changes in our body and motivates behavior that helps to deal with what we have perceived.

Some theories argue that emotions are a result of physiological responses. We feel the beating heart and sweaty palms, the heat of anger, and that evokes an emotional reaction. Emotions are fundamental in influencing our decision-making and behavior on a daily basis.

Emotions often lead to action tendencies. Various emotions influence how we act in response. There are components fundamental to an emotion. We feel an emotion, then an action tendency is activated. We try to make meaning from what we are feeling, then determine how we express or show what we are feeling along with the physiological changes that accompany the emotion we are experiencing. Emotions can intensify if we are unable to identify what we are feeling.

All emotions are necessary. Emotions evolved to ensure survival. Feelings proved advantageous to our early ancestors. Negative emotions activated behaviors that avoided potential dangers. It made our early human ancestors sensitive and alert. Whereas positive emotions encouraged behaviors that led to creativity, communication, and connection that promoted healthy living.

What are differences between moods and emotions? Psychologists sometimes use the term "affect" to describe moods, feelings, and emotions we experience during the course of our daily lives. An emotion tends to be brief. Emotions are triggered by events that occur in the present. Emotions can be set off by memories or thoughts of past or future situations.

In contrast, moods tend to last longer, hours, days, or weeks. Moods tend to be in the background of our minds. Moods are less prone to specific stimuli. Whereas emotions tend to be front and center in our awareness.

How many emotions can we experience? Psychologist Paul Ekman identified six basic or "universal" human emotions: fear, anger, sadness, disgust, surprise, joy, and happiness. He proposed that these are expressed in similar ways around the world and are recognized in different countries and cultures. Psychologist Robert Plutchik put forth a wheel of emotions that looks like a color wheel. Emotions can be combined to form different feelings, much like colors can be mixed to create other shades.

Plutchik's research led to eight primary emotions that serve as building blocks. These foundational emotions blend with other colors (emotions) to create secondary or more complex emotions. Plutchik's wheel of emotions visually illustrates this. The wheel provides insight into understanding the intensity, duration, and connectedness of other emotions. Our emotional responses are largely shaped by who we are and what we may have experienced in the past.

Playbook Lesson Sequence 2: Developing emotional intelligence

Lesson Objective: Gain emotional awareness by identifying and recording daily emotions.

Step 1-Watch *How Do You Feel? Teaching Emotional IQ in School with Soledad O'Brien* (available via YouTube, WebMD).

Step 2-Activity: Make a list of all emotions you can think of that you experienced today. How many emotions have been positive or negative? Are the positive emotions always good? Or do they result in something bad? Are negative emotions ever useful? Why or why not?

Step 3-Create a monthly emotional tracker

- Note what emotions you feel when you wake up and when you go to bed. It is possible you feel more than one emotion. Use a blank calendar. Keeping track of your emotions will allow you to assess your mood over a period of time. It will also allow you to evaluate any changes that you might want to make regarding your mood and what may affect it during the day. You can color code your emotions.
- Notice and name any emotions you are feeling. Rate the intensity of each emotion on a 1–10 scale. Reflect in your journal. What bodily sensations are associated with these emotions? What seems to give rise to these emotions? Determine whether the emotions energize you or sap energy from you; whether they are pleasant or unpleasant.

Step 4-(Optional) Watch the animated film *Inside Out (2015)*

What can be taught & learned about *Happiness?*

What might students emotional experience be in school? Yale University researcher Marc Brackett and colleagues investigated students' feelings in a nation-wide survey of 21,678 US students in two samples.[10] They asked students to respond to open ended questions and fill out ratings scales. In their responses to open ended questions, 75 percent of feelings students reported were negative.

The three most frequently mentioned negative feelings about school were fatigue, stress, and boredom. Negative feelings about school were similar across demographic groups. High school students did experience positive emotions but in smaller percentages. Plus, the positive emotions they experienced were not linked to learning or achievement.

What is emotional intelligence? Research on emotions suggests that the more specific we can be in naming them the easier it becomes taming or managing them. To become better acclimated with our emotions, it is helpful to have language to name the emotion. Actively becoming aware of emotions can free us from feeling overwhelmed by them. Naming emotions helps us to learn how to better manage emotions regardless of their intensity.

Emotional intelligence was popularized by Daniel Goleman. This is our ability to accurately detect, express, and manage emotions in ourselves. Being aware of what we are feeling, accurately identifying what we are feeling, expressing what we are feeling, and directing and managing our emotions are all essential elements of emotional intelligence.

Understanding emotions leads to creating space and choosing how to react or respond as opposed to relying on habitual reactions. The more specific we can be in differentiating, naming, and describing our feelings, the less likely we are to be overwhelmed by them. This provides the means to better manage our emotions. Our awareness, understanding, the ability to communicate, and finally manage our emotions are all important for psychological well-being.

Playbook Lesson Sequence 3: Negative emotions.
How much negativity is necessary in our lives?

Lesson objective: Identify and explain the negativity bias and its impact.

Step 1-Activity: Write down as many emotion words as possible in five minutes. After the five minutes, determine how many of the emotion words written were positive, negative, or neutral.

Step 2-Whole class discussion. How much negativity is necessary in our lives? How do we prepare ourselves for the worst without becoming a pessimist? Are there benefits in negative emotions?

Step 3-Guiding Question: How can we confront the negativity bias?

- Read *How to Remain Calm When the Rest of the World is Freaking Out* (from the Daily Stoic.com)
- Read Dr. Rick Hanson's *Confronting the Negativity Bias* (available via RickHanson.net)
- Read *How to Stop Negative Thoughts from Getting You Down* by Happify Daily infographic
- Read *How Sia Saved Herself: Before she could have a career unlike any other pop star, she had to learn how to live* by Hillel Aron (Rolling Stone magazine, online).

Step 4-NB-Journal: On average, how much of a typical day is filled with negativity, criticism, gossip, and/or complaints? Why? How much of it is necessary? How does it help you to enjoy the present?

What can be taught & learned about *Happiness?*

What is a negativity bias? We are really good at thinking and behaving in ways that are counterproductive to our own well-being. Our brains lead us astray when we gauge what will bring us happiness. We tend to overestimate the negative effects of our lives. We are loss aversive. As a result, our brains tend to be aware of what is going wrong or could go wrong more than what is going well. We have a built-in negativity bias or a selective attention to the negative. As a result, negativity makes a greater impression on our brains.

Dr. Rick Hanson explains that our brains are "Velcro for negativity and Teflon for positivity. Our negative experiences stick to us like Velcro, while our positive experiences slide right off our consciousness like Teflon. No life is without stress, adversity, or crisis. It is estimated that close to 50% of adults in the United States will experience a traumatic event during their lifetimes.[11]

Happiness is largely determined by the state of our minds. We must accept negative emotions along with positive emotions. To really enjoy the good in our lives we have to be able to contrast that with the tough times.

Why do negative emotions command greater attention than positive emotions? Social psychologist Roy Baumeister and colleagues found that the response to negative emotions is stronger than to positive emotions. In a meta-analysis research study,[12] Baumeister and colleagues noted that we pay closer/longer attention to negative information than positive. Having a bad day tends to impact the next day.

Major traumatic events have a longer-lasting negative effect on people's lives than major positive events, such as a lottery win. We have evolved brain mechanisms and tendencies that lead us to pay more attention and give more weight to what is wrong and less to what is right. This usually impacts how we feel.

What is the purpose of negative emotions? Evolutionary psychologists point out that worrying kept our ancestors alive by being alert, hyper-vigilant, and hardwired to potential threats. This ensured human survival. This was helpful 200,000 years ago. Not so much in our daily lives.

Research indicates that affective forecasting, our predictions on how good or bad things will affect us in the future, is often wrong. When adversity of any kind strikes, like missing a game-winning free throw in a basketball game, we are devastated but not as long or as emotionally intense as we believed. We can learn how to regulate our negative emotions and work to cultivate position emotions. However, our beliefs about adversity can alter our thinking, feelings, and behavior. Not everything happens for a reason. Hardships will always happen. No one is immune to adversity.

What is the relationship between negativity and stress? Our brains are differentiated engines constantly scanning for changes in our environment that may affect our survival. We focus our attention more easily on negative differences externally and internally. Long-term negative effects of chronic negative stress are well documented.

Chronic stress often leads to other health problems. In the modern world, we all experience various stressors that affect our well-being. A recent survey from the American Psychological Association found the following most common sources of stress:[13]

- Health care costs
- Mass shootings
- Pressure to succeed in life because of social comparison
- Economic pressures
- National concerns and concern about the future
- Body and health concerns
- Information overload via social media

Playbook Lesson Sequence 4: Befriending difficult emotions and stress

Lesson objective: Assess the validity of the different strategies to cope with adversity.

Step 1-Reflection in NB-Journal: How do you typically react to life difficulties? To what extent do you engage in each of the following strategies (see below)? How effective have they been in the past in coping with adversity or stressful situations?

- Do nothing (a kind of learned helplessness)-Learned helplessness occurs when an individual continuously faces a negative situation and believes that nothing they do can help. The result is the individual does nothing or stops trying in response to the harmful situation. This inaction is learned.
- Engage in John Henryism-you can overcome almost anything or even control certain outcomes if only you stay determined and you work hard enough to do so.
- Problem Based coping-Do something about it. People try to take the situation into their own hands. People act to resolve the situation somehow, and make a bad thing go away, thereby reducing the stress.
- Emotion-focused coping-If the event or situation seems uncontrollable or a person feels unequipped to resolve it, then people focus their attention on reducing the negative emotions associated with the event. This is done by employing a variety of techniques from distraction to journaling to mentally reappraising a situation to acceptance to suppression of negative emotions. When we can't change a situation, we can change how we feel about it.
- Try and get advice from someone on what to do.

Step 2: Guiding Question: How do cognitive interpretations or mental traps undermine one's ability to cope with adversity and stress?

- Determine whether you fall into the following cognitive distortions[14] or mental traps when feeling stressed, triggered, and/or fatigued.
- All or nothing thinking-you look at things in absolute, black and white categories.
- Overgeneralizing-you view a negative event as a never-ending pattern where you apply it to all aspects of the categories of your life (e.g., relationships).
- Mental filter-you dwell on the negatives and ignore the positives.
- Discounting the positives-you insist that any accomplishment or positive qualities don't count.
- Jump to conclusions-you either mind read assuming that people are reacting negatively to you when there's no definite evidence for this or engage in fortune telling where you arbitrarily predict things will turn out badly.

- Magnification or minimization-you blow things way out of proportion or you shrink their importance inappropriately.
- Emotional reasoning-you reason how you feel, concluding that your emotional reaction proves something true.
- Labeling-you identify with your shortcomings by becoming them.
- Personalization-you blame yourself for something you weren't entirely responsible for, or blame other people and overlook ways that your own attitudes and behavior might contribute to a problem. You take things personally.

Step 3-Guiding Question: How can we support ourselves and others during difficult times?

- Watch *A Heavy Load: Teens and Homework Stress* with Soledad O'Brien (available via YouTube)
- Read *How to Beat Stress Infographic* (available via *Happify.com*)

Step 4-Guiding Question: How to cope better with adversity? Coping and dealing with stress takes a variety of different skills, strategies, and styles for different circumstances and personality types. There is no one right way to deal with stress or adversity. Resilience is the ability to withstand or recover from difficult situations. It includes our capacity to make the best of things, cope, and rise to the occasion.

Research Tip #1: Practice self-compassion

- Read Dr. Kristin Neff's *Changing Your Critical Self-Talk* (available via self-compassion.org)
- Watch *Dove Real Beauty Sketches, You're more beautiful than you think.* (available via YouTube)

Research Tip #2: Find outlets for your stress, like exercise. Work it out.

- Read *How Inuit Parents Teach Kids To Control Their Anger* by Michaeleen Doucleff and Jane Greenhalgh (available via NPR.org)

Research Tip #3: Find meaning and possibly a silver lining. Transform the adversity.

- Watch Andrew Solomon's TedTalk *How the Worst Moments in Our Lives Make Us Who We Are*

Research Tip #4: Lean on others. Get and receive the right kinds of support from the right kind of people at the time when you are ready.

Research Tip #5: Don't take your adversity so seriously. Try to laugh or be lighthearted.

Research Tip #6: Use other strategies. Rely on signature strengths, problem-based coping, emotional-based coping, journaling, or mindfulness.

What can be taught & learned about *Happiness?*

What is learned optimism? People are generally pretty good when bad things happen. We generally bounce back and recover. Some people are wired to be more resistant to stress.

About 80 years ago, 180 nuns entered into a study about life longevity where they were asked to write autobiographical statements describing their lives and their feelings. The nuns lived very similar lifestyles having the same socioeconomic condition, same environmental conditions, same access to medical care, etc. Their brief autobiographical statements were analyzed.

Researchers Deborah Danner and David Snowden compared which nuns frequently used more positive words, described positive experiences, and expressed more positive emotions like gratitude than nuns who did not. The nuns who expressed greater levels of happiness in their writing, evidenced by positive feelings, lived longer. Danner and Snowden concluded there was a strong association between happiness and life longevity.[15] The nuns appeared to have engaged in learned optimism.

Learned optimism as defined by Martin Seligman involves explaining events to ourselves in ways that help rather than distort our thinking. This explanatory style develops into positive internal dialogue where people believe that the causes of setbacks are temporary and changeable.[16] This internal dialogue is constructive rather than destructive.

What is John Henryism? John Henryism is described by Sherman James of Duke University after the American folk hero who beat a steam-drill machine by outpacing and outworking the machine through a tunnel only to die from his efforts. Research from James is primarily focused on the impact of racism, discrimination, micro-aggressions, and stereotype threats on African-Americans and POC. His research notes that African-Americans are at a higher risk for hypertension, cardiovascular disease, and strokes.[17]

Why do meanings we give to adversity both help and undermine our ability to cope? Cognitive interpretations are very common as most people fall into these mental traps. This often happens when people are feeling stressed or fatigued. Our brains are wired to focus attention and energy on counteracting the stressor or trigger.

Cognitive traps lead people to look for evidence to support the cognitive bias while unconsciously ignoring evidence that disputes the bias. This leads to the perpetuation of people's feelings in response to the stressor, creating an unintended self-fulfilling prophecy. Cognitive distortions are not helpful. These mental traps make it difficult to cognitively reconstruct hardship and change our life perspective. When adversity strikes, being flexible and realistic is more helpful. Interpreting adversity practically helps to cope more effectively and constructively.

What is self-compassion? Coping with stress often requires the flexibility and ability to switch strategies. Every situation is different and may require a different response. We all experience loss, failure, disappointment, and pain. Adversity is universal and inevitable, but it doesn't have to be feared. Adversity provides opportunities to know ourselves better. Strength, perspective, and the cultivation of self-compassion can be galvanized.

When adversity strikes, why not offer ourselves a bit of kindness and self-care? According to researcher and author Kristen Neff, self-compassion consists of many different components that combine and intersect. Self-compassion entails treating ourselves with the same level of kindness, compassion, patience, and comfort that we afford others.

Seems easy, but generally we are harsher to ourselves in our times of need than we would ever be to another person. To practice self-compassion Neff explains that one must be kind and caring to oneself, understand that all people fail and make mistakes, and be mindful of one's suffering to be able to be compassionate to oneself.[18] Self-compassion often leads to making instructive changes to one's life.

How to control what we can control? The Stoics, a school of philosophical thinkers in ancient Greece and Rome, taught people to focus on things that are in their power. That is to control what we can control. Stoicism urges avoiding worry about things that we can't control. And what we can control is how we think and choose to respond to life experiences.

Most of us engage in unrealistic optimism. It is a way to protect ourselves from the unpredictability and unpleasantness of possible future realities. Psychologists define unrealistic optimism as believing that good things more than bad things are more likely to happen to us in the future but bad things are more likely to happen to other people.[19] Stoic thinkers recommended that we should think about hardship proactively. This is called negative visualization. The Stoics taught that if hardship should strike, people would be better able to cope and respond more favorably.

Playbook Lesson Sequence 5: Reframing Adversity and Post-Traumatic Growth

Lesson objective: Investigate personal growth that can develop from adversity and/or trauma.

Step 1-Guiding Question: How might people grow or even thrive because **of adversity?**
Almost all people can expect to be impacted by a significant form of adversity. In the list below are individuals who have experienced childhood adversity.

- Select 1 individual from the list below and research A) the adversity they experienced, B) what they did to overcome the adversity, and C) determine whether they survived but with impairment (e.g. PTSD), recovered (returned to the person they were prior to the adverse event(s), or did they thrive and flourish, that is did they experience post-traumatic growth. Post-traumatic growth is a positive change that is experienced as a result of the struggle with a major life crisis.

  - Andre Agassi, tennis champion
  - Maya Angelou, author
  - Alison Bechdel, cartoonist
  - Johnny Cash, country singer
  - Stephen Colbert, comedian
  - Howard Schultz, former CEO Starbucks
  - Paul Ryan, 54th Speaker of the House
  - Misty Copeland, ballet dancer
  - Sonia Sotomayor, U.S. Supreme Court Justice
  - Barack Obama, former president
  - Monica Seles, tennis champion
  - Or you pick someone not on the list
  - Alan Cumming, actor
  - Viktor Frankl, psychiatrist/author
  - Oliver Sacks, neurologist
  - LeBron James, NBA champion
  - Akhil Sharma, author
  - Elizabeth Warren, U.S. Senator
  - Oprah Winfrey, media mogul
  - Jay Z, rapper and entrepreneur
  - Elizabeth Smart, child advocate
  - Mary J. Blige, singer
  - Charlize Theron, actor

Step 2-Guiding Question: Is all adversity bad?

- Read *Post-Traumatic Growth: Finding Meaning and Creativity in Adversity* by Scott Barry Kaufman (available via Scientific American).
- Research Emily Werner's Kauai Longitudinal study of at-risk infants across time. Identify and explain what you learned.
- Engage in NB-Journal reflection. Is all adversity bad? What explains why some people might experience growth after a major adverse life event?

What can be taught & learned about *Happiness?*

How can adversity make us stronger? As Friedrich Nietzsche and Kelly Clarkson noted, that which does not kill us makes us stronger. Researchers have labeled our ability to overcome trauma and grow from tragedy as post-traumatic growth. Psychologists believe that finding meaning or benefit in trauma can lead to a personal transformation. When faced with a life challenge or trauma, people can not only recover but thrive developing a renewed sense of meaning. Adversity often can make us stronger. It might even simplify our lives.

Psychologists Richard Tedeschi and Lawrence Calhoun who pioneered this discovery of post-traumatic growth note, *"People develop new understandings of themselves, the world they live in, how to relate to other people, the kind of future they might have and a better understanding of how to live life."*[20] This is not to say that all life traumas are good. Nor is post-traumatic growth universal.

There are multiple possible outcomes that an individual may incur. One involves succumbing to the detrimental effect of the trauma where survival involves a permanent impairment of function, losing much happiness and motivation to enjoy love, work, or leisure. Another outcome from trauma might result in a return to pre-adversity levels of functioning. That is people recover. Another outcome involves a person not only returning to their previous level of functioning but surpassing it. This is post-traumatic growth.

Here are some factors that might explain recovery and/or post-traumatic growth: An earnest and steadfast optimism, one's perceived control over events; coping style; and a strong sense of self and your strengths. Generally post-traumatic growth manifests in the following ways. People report having a greater appreciation for life, are more open to newer possibilities and opportunities, reprioritize one's time and what's valuable, a strengthening and development of closer relationships, a strengthening or revitalized religious or spiritual belief, or a newfound sense of one's strength via resiliency.[21] Post-traumatic growth doesn't mean however, there isn't suffering endured or adverse life events are good.

Playbook Lesson Sequence 6: Assess Understanding and Learning

Reflection journal-students explain what they have learned about the various lesson steps. Explain what they agree with or disagree with. Also, they could explain how to incorporate information into their lives and discard other types of thinking and behaving from their lives, if applicable. In the journal students should document (1) the extent to which they have changed as a result of the lessons (this includes habits of thinking, behavior, actions, experiences, epiphanies, insights, philosophies, accomplishments, goals, etc.) and (2) their plans for themselves in the future. This includes all that they want to accomplish in terms of goals; aspects of themselves that they want to discard; and practices, ideas, actions, and experiences that they want to add to their lives that they hypothesize will bring them closer to a good life.

Draw what you've learned-Explain the applicability of the information to your life. Also explain what you have drawn, how it represents what you've learned. Summarize why you chose to express your understanding in this way.

Analogy concept paper-explain how what has been learned is like a _____ (e.g., an acorn). Make specific connections between assessed concepts and whatever the object may be.

Life Maps-A summation of what students learned in a unit, mapped with images, quotes, and multi-page reflection that explains the map and how if followed, helps one to attain a good life. This should also critically analyze rather than merely summarize what students learned or found applicable to understanding well-being.

Precept #6: Let positivity reign. Cultivate positivity, positive emotions and optimism.

TEACHING WHAT MATTERS PLAYBOOK: TOOLS FOR EXPLORING THE ART OF LIVING

Playbook Lesson Sequence 1: A Thought Experiment on Positivity

Lesson Objective: Appraise the meaning of the Myth of Sisyphus

Step 1-Guiding Question: Is it possible to imagine Sisyphus with a smile? Explain the myth of Sisyphus. He was punished by the Gods for eternity to push a giant boulder up a mountain, only to have it roll back down as he approaches the top. He then repeats this day after day, for eternity. He is never successful in accomplishing the task. That is his punishment, an exercise in futility. Or is it?

Step 2-Watch Marcela Janovics film "Sisyphus" (2 minutes) https://www.youtube.com/watch?v=QujiLG93BKw

- Ask students: What connections can be made between Sisyphus and living? Is it possible to imagine that Sisyphus is pushing that boulder for eternity with a smile on his face? Why or why not?

Step 3-Watch: Disney Pixar short: *Boundin.* What difference is there between Sisyphus and the lamb? Is there one? How are their mindsets similar or different? Can you simply choose to think and act in ways that stir up positivity and optimism? How is it that we can imagine Sisyphus with a smile?

Step 4-Read *A Life Worth Living: Albert Camus on Our Search for Meaning and Why Happiness Is Our Moral Obligation* by Maria Popova (available via Brainpickings.org)

- In journal notebooks, write down any information that helps to explain and understand how we can imagine Sisyphus with a smile.

Step 5-How might you explain how Sisyphus may have a smile? What might he have figured out that the rest of us have not, independent from the explanation given by Camus? What is the lesson? How can you apply this lesson to the future?

What can be taught & learned about *Happiness?*

With regard to Sisyphus, Camus urges us to view Sisyphus as a tragic hero. We are left to wonder, like Camus, what must Sisyphus be thinking as he walks back down the mountain to begin anew.

Camus suggests that Sisyphus must be able to smile because he has accepted the absurdity of this task. This has led to an inner contentment. Every step that Sisyphus takes is an exercise in acceptance. He does not engage in counterfactual thinking like what if things were different. He doesn't compare this moment with some future moment that has yet to come. Sisyphus doesn't seem to live daunted in the past. Camus concludes that "all is well . . . one must imagine Sisyphus happy."[22]

Playbook Lesson Sequence 2: What is optimism? What are the benefits of optimism?

Lesson Objective: Describe optimism, its benefits and an optimistic explanatory style.

Step 1-Guiding Question: What are **the benefits of looking on the bright side?**

- Engage in the following thought experiment: You are out walking alone with gaze fixed on the ground you are about to look more carefully at something, when you are hit in the head with something. You feel it but it doesn't hurt. Now your gaze is distracted. You scan the environment, looking up and all around. No one else is around or visible. How do you react?
- Now ask yourself, what's right about your current situation? Ask yourself, what's wrong about your current situation? Which appraisal of your situation is more valid? Why? Discuss. Were you able to look on the bright side? Why or why not? Why are some people more apt to adopt a positive attitude?

Step 2-NB-Journal: How has the Covid pandemic changed you? Take 15 minutes and write.

- When done, examine what you wrote. To what extent do you think you are an optimist or a pessimist?
- Use the following to evaluate what you wrote. According to researcher Martin Seligman, optimists explain life events differently than pessimists. Optimists explanatory style consists of three basic dimensions that contrasts with pessimists. While on a continuum, individuals with a pessimistic explanatory style generally perceive and explain why something happened by viewing problems as internal, unchangeable, and pervasive (affecting all aspects of my life) whereas optimistic people are the opposite. Keep in mind that optimism can be learned. No one is born an optimist or a pessimist.

Step 3-Guiding Question: What is optimism?

- Define optimism. Optimism is a mood or attitude associated with an expectation about the future, one which the evaluator regards as socially desirable to his or her advantage. Optimism is about perception. Martin Seligman defines optimism as a way of reacting to events in our lives with confidence and the ability to affect change. Optimists generally believe that negative events are temporary, are limited in their impact in the other areas of our lives, and can be managed.

Optimism is often a fluid mindset, existing on a spectrum where levels of optimism change to fit various situations. Optimism is both a personality trait and influenced by our environments (for example parents, friends, peers, and socioeconomic status). Many of us learn our explanatory styles. Optimists are not Pollyannish, or unrealistically optimistic. A Pollyanna is someone who holds a positivity bias focusing irrationally on the positive without taking into account critical, rational thought.

Step 4-Guiding Question: What are the benefits of thinking like an optimist?

- Read *The Benefits of Looking on the Bright Side: 10 Reasons to Think Like an Optimist b*y Jessica Cassity (available via Happify Daily)
- Read *The Benefits of Optimism Are Real: Having a positive outlook is the most important predictor of resilience* by Emily Esfahani Smith (available via The Atlantic)
- NB-Journal: What might be the benefits of optimism?

Step 5-Guiding Question: What does optimistic thinking look like really?

- Watch and evaluate how optimistic thinking is revealed and the benefits of optimistic thinking. Write down 2–3 examples of optimistic thinking. Turn your examples and interpretations into a guide for understanding optimistic thinking or an explanatory style.
- Watch Randy Pautsch's *The Last Lecture* (available via DVD through Carnegie Mellon)
- Watch Michael J. Fox, staying positive through Parkison's disease (available via YouTube)
- Watch Bert Jacobs, co-founder of *Life is Good, The power of optimism* (available via Tedx Talks)
- Watch *Is Your Glass Half Empty or Half Full?* (available via Soul Pancake YouTube channel)
- Watch The Power of Optimism Man on the Street (available via Soul Pancake YouTube channel)
- Watch Tiffany Haddish interviewed on David Letterman's Netflix show *My Next Guest Needs No Introduction*
- Watch *An Astronaut's Guide to Optimism, 2020* by Chris Hadfield (available via YouTube)

What can be taught & learned about *Happiness?*

What is optimism? Optimistic thinking is a helpful tool in the world today. Research shows that optimists are happier, healthier[23] and tend to be more successful in many different domains of one's life.[24] Fortunately, optimism is a learned skill.

Genetics plays only a small role of inherited personality temperament that may or may not incline us to optimism. Optimism is about perception and explaining the world, often to ourselves. According to Martin Seligman, optimists explain life's events differently than pessimists do. Whether we see things as good or bad determines whether we are optimistic or pessimistic. We develop explanatory styles to define the reasons why events happen and whether they are good or bad.

Optimists believe that adverse things happen for a variety of reasons often independent of us. Optimists have confidence and belief in the ability to change the causes of the adverse events. Lastly optimists believe that problems are not likely to bleed into the other aspects of our lives. Optimists generally hold that problems are one and done.

Optimism can protect individuals from stress, anxiety, and depression by fostering better means to cope with life difficulties. Optimism fosters problem-solving and thought-catching, evaluating the validity of our automatic thoughts, helping generate more accurate explanations when life throws lemons.[25] Optimism is a positive mindset which opens us up to opportunities, growth, and overall psychological well-being.

What are the benefits of looking on the bright side? Compared to pessimistic people, optimists are:

- More successful in school, at work, and in athletics
- Healthier and they live longer
- More satisfied with their marriages
- Less likely to suffer from depression
- Less anxious[26]

Playbook Lesson Sequence 3: Positivity and The Broaden and Build Theory

Lesson objective: Explain the benefits of positivity.

Step 1-Guiding Question: What's good **about feeling good?**

- **Life-Lab: Experiments in turning positivity on in our lives.**
- Write about time in your life when you were truly happy.
- Write down 5 quotes that inspire and uplift your spirits. Ultimately the message(s) shift your thinking and allow you to experience positive mindset upon being repeated. (e.g., "Use the force, Luke.")
- Create a positive movie or a positivity portfolio of your life based on each of the positive emotions. More specifics can be found: *What are the top 10 positive emotions?* (Kari Henley, June 2009, huffpost.com).

Barbara Fredrickson, the leading researcher on positive emotions, recommends creating a physical iMovie or scrapbook or art portfolio of photos, objects, momentos, music, or letters which make you feel awe, inspired, love, joy, gratitude, hope, or pride. Be certain to include specific details and keep your portfolio in a place that is readily accessible. Take at least 5 minutes and marinate in your movie.

Step 2-Guiding Question: How do positive emotions creative positivity and can you increase your positivity ratio?

- Explain Barbara Fredrickson's broaden and build theory. Decades of empirical data show that positivity broadens or amplifies positive possibilities for our lives. Positivity opens one up to life. People's thoughts, actions, awareness, and ideas expand. Positive emotions then help to build new ways of living. Positive emotions encourage new habits and new ways of thinking that improve optimal functioning. Positive emotions aren't simply the absence of negative emotions but a means to flourish by encouraging active engagement in the many provinces of our lives.[27]
- NB-Journal: Reflect, how do you apply positive emotions in your life? Can you define each of the following positive emotions? What do they feel like? What kind of action tendencies have they cultivated for you in your life? How have these emotions impacted your life?
  - Joy-what are the sources of joy in your life? When did you act from a place of joy?
  - Gratitude-what are reasons to be grateful? When did you act from a place of gratitude?
  - Serenity-what brings you serenity? When did you act from a place of calmness?
  - Interest-when was the last time your curiosity was stirred? When did you act from a place of interest?
  - Hope-what gives you hope? When did you act from a place of hope?
  - Pride-what makes you proud? When did you act from a place of pride?
  - Amusement-when was the last time you were amused? When did you act from a place of amusement?
  - Inspiration-when was the time you were inspired? When did you act from a place of inspiration?
  - Awe-when was the last time you felt part of something larger than yourself? When did you act from this place?
  - Love-when was the last time you felt love (a combination of all of these)? When did you act from a place of love?

- Reflect: To what extent did these positive emotions and your actions from these emotions enrich your life? To what extent did you increase your positivity ratio?

What can be taught & learned about *Happiness?*

What is the broaden and build theory? Positivity is transformative. A goal can be to plan ways to incorporate positive inducing experiences into our daily lives. Barbara Fredrickson reveals in her broaden and build theory that positive emotions broaden our awareness and then build upon prior held learnings to create emotional and intellectual thought-action skills.

For example, if fear is linked with the urge to flee, positive emotions like gratitude and joy promote different ways of thinking and actions. These culminate in building various personal, physical, intellectual, and psychological resources that encourage new ways of being.

How much positivity do we really need? Is there an optimum amount of positive emotions? Barbara Fredrickson and Marcel Losada suggested cultivating during the course of our day a mean ratio of 3 positive emotions for every 1 negative emotional experience or unpleasant feeling. For example, if you have negative emotional experience (you get into a fight with your friend), the theory holds that to offset the negative effects, deliberately cultivate 3 positive emotional experiences to uplift you.

As an unofficial benchmark, they determined a mathematical ratio of 3 to 1.[28] For every one criticism you endure during the day, offset that by marinating in the 3 compliments you received. After scientific scrutiny, they have retracted the exact mathematical quantification of positivity.

But Fredrickson's research still supports the importance of increasing positivity in our daily lives. Building up positivity in our emotional bank accounts helps to provide the currency and means to navigate the emotional complexities of our days. Regularly experiencing pleasant emotions along with feeling infrequently unhappy is now considered a feature of flourishing.

Why is positivity complimented by negativity? Positivity and optimism are not about eliminating or avoiding the negativity or difficult emotions. Optimists are not immune to the suffering in the world. The positivity ratio is not about zero negativity. Negative life experiences are an important part of our lives and can be motivators to improved behaviors.

However, this emotion will motivate you to take action to improve upon those aspects in your teaching which will lead to a positive outcome. Negative emotions are a normal part of the human experiences. By looking for the silver lining, we can turn the lemons that life throws at us into lemonade.

Playbook Lesson Sequence 4: Generating more positivity and positive emotions in our lives

Lesson objective: Assess the benefits of positivity interventions.

Step 1-Guiding Question: How can we generate more positivity **into our lives?**

- **Positivity Suggestion #1: Journaling about three good things.**

  Before going to bed or at various points during your day, write down at least three things that went well. You can also identify things that you have done well. Provide an explanation for why they went well. As you write, provide as many details as possible, including dialogue, where you were, who was present, etc. Also, write about how each even made you feel. The joy can be found in the details.[29]

- **Positivity Suggestion 2: Create a movie of your life or a positivity portfolio.**

  Barbara Fredrickson, the leading researcher on positive emotions, recommends creating a range of physical portfolios of objects and mementos to evoke particular positive emotions. Go on a positivity scavenger hunt. Gather together photos, gifts, music, and letters which make you feel any of the various positive emotions. You can keep digitalized photos on a computer or phone, in a scrapbook, or in a journal. Remind yourself to take 5–10 minutes out of your day to marinate in your scrapbook or digitized portfolio. Write in a journal how it feels to engage with your portfolio. How do you feel?

- **Positivity Suggestion 3: Fake it to you make it! The power of a smile.**

Step 1-Guiding Question: What are the benefits of lightheartedness?

Smiling is a universal form of human communication. All people smile, and do so frequently. Research on the facial feedback hypothesis suggests that we can literally laugh or smile ourselves into a better state of mind, change negative emotions into positive ones, or simply make us feel better. We can fake it until we make it. That is feel a little bit better, even when you aren't feeling it. Even when experiencing stressful situations, a fake smile can go a long way in undoing the negative emotions.

When we show the physical manifestations of an emotion like a smile, our facial movements can intensify the emotional state. When you smile, you might begin to feel happier, or when you scowl you might feel angrier. This works because your face or voice sends signals or feedback to the brain letting it know that you are experiencing a particular emotion and leading you to feel it.

A 2010 Wayne State University baseball card study[30] found a clear connection between how big a smile someone made on a baseball card photo and life longevity. Players who smiled the most lived seven years longer than those who did not smile. The researchers, Abel and Kruger, analyzed photos of baseball players from the 1952 season. The photo ratings were no-smile (42 percent of players), partial non-Duchenne smile (43 percent), to full Duchenne smile (15 percent). The players who did not smile on average lived for 72 years. Players who smiled a bit lived on average 75 years. Players who smiled fully lived an average of 80 years. The conclusion being a smile is worth an extra 5 years of life.

Step 2-Watch and analyze short film *Validation*.

- Watch the film available on YouTube, *Validation* by Kurt Kuenne
- What are the messages from the film? How does smiling affect individuals but also others?

Step 3-Watch Ron Gutman's TEDTalk: *The hidden power of smiling* (and his review of many studies about the benefits of smiling).

POSITIVITY SUGGESTION 4: LAUGH AND PLAY THROUGH YOUR DAY.

Step 1-Conduct a laugh yoga session.

Laughter and play are essential to humans and create joy. Joy is a positive emotion and contributes to feeling fully alive. Laughter both signals this but also helps to access joy. Laughter can be contagious. It can connect you to others. But you don't need others to laugh. In fact, you don't need a reason to laugh. You can laugh for no reason even if there is nothing funny.

Laugh yoga helps teach people how to do just that. Laugh yoga is just like conventional yoga, you use the same breathing techniques as regular yoga, but the focal point is laughter. The mantra of laughter yoga is *you fake it until you make it.* There is no pressure to laugh. Even a fake laugh will provide the same health benefits as you would gain from real laughter. Your brain can't tell the difference between real or fake laughter. You get the same release of the feel-good chemicals in your brain.

While it is estimated that children laugh hundreds of times a day authentically and adults average well below that, the point is laughter is an outward reveling of amusement. Since you can't consciously worry and laugh at the same time, laughter is a tool that helps create space from stressful thoughts and emotions.

- Watch the following: *Breath, laugh and be happy. The science behind laughter yoga* (CNN https://www.cnn.com/videos/health/2018/08/14/sw-laughter-yoga.cnn)
- Watch *Laughter Yoga, CNN Report* (available via YouTube)
- Watch, *Unexpected benefits of fake laughter* (available via YouTube)

Step 2-Watch https://www.wikihow.com/Do-Laughter-Yoga or you can simply have students place their heads on their desks and continuous laugh for 10 minutes. Fluctuating from tiny, baby laughter, to robust laughter. It can be fake laughter until they make real laughter. Know what isn't funny. Make it a point to NOT laugh at the expense of others—via gossip, ridicule, alleged superiority, etc.

Step 3-Debrief/NB/Reflection: How do you feel? What worked, what did not? Once you've had your chuckle, take stock of how you're feeling. Are your muscles a little less tense? Do you feel more relaxed? How can you increase your laugh quotient?

POSITIVITY SUGGESTION 5: CULTIVATE AN ATTITUDE OF GRATITUDE

Step 1-Self teaching experiment: Write and read a gratitude letter

Write a letter of gratitude to someone you have not properly thanked who has made a difference in your life.[31] In the letter describe what this person did and why you are grateful to them. You can describe the impact this person had on you using anecdotes, feelings, and emotions. It is up to you whether you choose to read this letter in person or over the phone.

You can simply send your letter or even keep it to yourself. Upon completing the experiment reflect on your experience with gratitude. How did it feel for you to express gratitude? How did it make the other person feel? What did you learn about gratitude? What makes gratitude easy or difficult to practice?

- Watch the following *Happiness Challenge Part 2-Being grateful for the good things (Action for Happiness)*

Step 2-What is gratitude? What are the different ways in which people express gratitude? What are the methods? What were the effects on them and on others? List all that you observe.

- Watch Brene Brown on Joy and Gratitude (available via YouTube). What are the various ways she practiced gratitude with her family and why did it make her happier?

- Watch *Nature, Beauty, Gratitude* by Louie Schwartzberg (available via YouTube).
- What are the suggested ways by which we can practice gratitude?
- Watch *The Science of Gratitude* (via SoulPancake YouTube Channel).
- Watch *365 Days of Gratitude,* Brian Doyle TedxYouth.

Step 3-NB/Journal: What are the different ways in which people expressed gratitude? What were the effects on them and on others? List all that you noted. Why is gratitude good? How does gratitude make us happier?

Step 4: What is good about gratitude?

There is a long body of research that supports the benefits of gratefulness. Robert Emmons, a psychologist at the University of California, Davis has shown in his research that ingratitude limits our sense of self. Ingratitude can foster negative emotions like envy, resentment, and bitterness, which undermines our relationships with others and with ourself. Focusing on the achievements of others can make us feel inadequate. Gratitude helps to block this. You can't feel envious and grateful. That is how gratitude can fortify and encourage stronger relationships with others and yourself.

Gratitude is simply the affirmation of goodness in your life. It is a felt sense of appreciation and thankfulness. Gratitude has two mindsets. One is an acknowledgement of the good or abundance present in your life and recognizing that the source of this goodness comes from outside or larger than yourself. As Robert Emmons writes in his book *Thanks! The New Science of Gratitude,* people feel and express gratitude in multiple ways. They can apply it to the past (retrieving positive memories and being thankful for elements of childhood or past blessings), the present (not taking good fortune for granted as it comes), and the future (maintaining a hopeful and optimistic attitude).[32]

There is a difference from short term gratitude like saying *thank you* and being someone who holds gratitude as a way of thinking and behaving. Gratitude helps marinate in the present magnifying the good and the positive emotions associated with the goodness. Instead of adapting or simply being an autopilot, gratitude helps us to slow down and savor the good.

While gratitude focuses attention on the good, it doesn't assume that life is perfect or without hardship. In times of adversity, gratitude can help develop a growth mindset by helping you to find the silver lining in the situation. Gratitude can help to redefine and reframe hardship and find the positive. Simply counting your blessings rather than your burdens can increase optimism about the future and overall life satisfaction.[33]

Step 4-Create a class culture of gratitude

- Create a Gratitude Jar. Each day students fill their own or a class gratitude jar with reasons to be grateful. In the expression of gratitude, briefly explain why it is good and why did it happen? At the end of class or during class, read one expression of gratitude.
- Try a no complaint day. Identify issues that you find yourself currently and frequently complaining about to yourself or to others. Brainstorm at least three creative solutions that might resolve these issues and take action on them daily.
- Keep track of your number of expressions of gratitude for one week. Keep a record of the number times you use the words "thank you" or recognize thankfulness in a day. During the course of this exercise, every day, thank someone for something that you might otherwise take for granted (e.g., thanking the janitor who cleans your hallways)
- Recognize the good in others by giving compliments—practice giving people compliments. Watch Purdue University's *Compliment Guys* (available via YouTube).
- Create a class gratitude wall. Create and display various expressions of gratitude just like Michel de Montaigne. Whenever a positive boost is needed, one can look up and find uplifting affirmations of goodness.

What can be taught & learned about *Happiness?*

Why appreciate the good in your life? It appears that what we do in life matters only in how we feel about it. What have Olympic bronze medalists figured out that silver medalists have not? Why might Olympic bronze medalists be happier than silver medalists? This should not be so.

Silver medalists were in second place among the most elite athletes in their sport, ahead of the third-place finisher. Due to counterfactual thinking, a human tendency to create possible alternatives to life events that have already occurred, we tend to create a narrative that is composed of thinking "what if things turned out differently."

Psychologists Victoria Medvec and Thomas Gilovich analyzed reactions to the achievements of Olympic medalists during the 1992 Olympics and the 1994 Empire State Games. They found that silver medalists, who were objectively better off than bronze medalists, were less happy with their accomplishments than the bronze medalists both during the medal ceremony and for a time after the Olympics.

They concluded that the difference could be explained by counterfactual thinking. The silver medalists compared their accomplishment with a gold medal winner, deeming their own achievement as less significant. The bronze medalist however, compared their achievement with the prospect of not earning a medal at all.

Silver medalists had more counterfactual thoughts overall, more counterfactual thoughts about how things could have gone better, thus deeming their accomplishment as less important than just missing out on a gold medal. Whereas bronze medalists evaluated their accomplishment in terms of finishing in fourth place, almost not winning a medal at all.

This unequal comparison explains the difference in their happiness levels. Bronze medalists appreciated their accomplishment far more than silver medalists who viewed their accomplishment as less because they did not win the gold.[34]

Playbook Lesson Sequence 5: Assess Understanding and Learning

Concept check, quiz-Do you understand the research, the theories, the data, and philosophical considerations behind the various ideas. (Points subject to assessment.) Traditionally designed quizzes along with using scenes from films by which students must demonstrate application of their knowledge based on what is seen in the film. Students can select any film and identify and explain scenes from the film that illustrate each of the assessed concepts.

NB-Journal-students explain what they have learned about the various lesson steps. Explain what they agree with or disagree with. Also they could explain how to incorporate information into their lives and discard other types of thinking and behaving from their lives, if applicable. In the journal students should document (1) the extent to which they have changed as a result of the lessons (this includes habits of thinking, behavior, actions, experiences, epiphanies, insights, philosophies, accomplishments, goals, etc.) and (2) their plans for themselves in the future. This includes all that they want to accomplish in terms of goals; aspects of themselves that they want to discard; and practices, ideas, actions, and experiences that they want to add to their lives that they hypothesize will bring them closer to a good life.

Draw what you've learned-Explain the applicability of the information to your life. Also explain what you have drawn, how it represents what you've learned. Summarize why you chose to express your understanding in this way.

Analogy concept paper-explain how what has been learned is like a _____ (e.g., an acorn). Make specific connections between assessed concepts and whatever the object may be.

Life maps-A summation of what students learned in a unit, mapped with images, quotes, and multi-page reflection that explains the map and how if followed, helps one to attain a good life. This should also critically analyze rather than merely summarize what students learned or found applicable to understanding well-being.

Chapter 4

It's About Time

Giving Some Intention to Our Attention

This chapter is about time. During any given day, how present are we for any of it? Attitudes about time as well as the pace of life often impact happiness.

American culture marinates in messages that promote the notion that faster is better. This can make anyone feel like they are busy. People are surrounded by stimulus. This stimulation can create a climate of distraction often leaving people feeling rushed.

It can feel as though giving our full attention to anything or anyone is becoming increasingly difficult. As Pico Iyer has noted, *"Many people feel as though they barely have enough time to see how little time they have."*[1]

Time doesn't have to feel adversarial. There is value in slowing down. The average adult spends as much as 12 hours a day in front of TVs and computers.[2] People often lament how screen time is incongruous to how they want to be spending their time. Charlie Chaplin hinted at this in his satirical film *"The Great Dictator"* when he said:

> *We have developed speed but we have shut ourselves in: machinery that gives abundance has left us in want. Our knowledge has made us cynical, our cleverness hard and unkind. We think too much and feel too little: More than machinery we need humanity. More than cleverness we need kindness and gentleness. Without these qualities, life will be violent and all will be lost.*[3]

Psychologist Tim Kasser has researched the effects of time poverty and time affluence on people's happiness. Time poverty is feeling time starved because we are often overworked, over-scheduled, and lack leisure time. There is a host of physical and mental health issues associated with the stress that accompanies time poverty.

Often time poverty is a matter of perception. People today enjoy more leisure than in the 1950s.[4] To many people, however, it doesn't feel that way. The most important aspect of time is how we decide to use it. Busyness, like leisure, is a choice.

How does one take control of their attention? Mindfulness is a particular way of simply paying attention and anchoring us to greater awareness to moments in our lives. Being mindful is simply being more aware of what is around us. It also helps us to be more conscious of our inner lives, more aware of thoughts and feelings. Mindfulness is a foundational skill that grounds us in the present. It also is a tool to help us recognize when we are feeling overwhelmed and respond compassionately and constructively.

People are also engaging in ways to spend time independent of screens. Happy people engage in pursuits that are fulfilling and rewarding for their own sake, like playing an instrument for hours alone. The reward for playing music or reading a book is the enjoyment and engagement with the activity itself.

In this chapter, there is an examination and evaluation of one's relationship with time. Mindfulness practices will also be explored to better understand the anatomy of the present and calmness. Lastly, experimenting with time in novel ways using strategies like savoring, rediscovering playfulness, and flow, will attempt to foster an appreciation for time.

*Precept #7: Maximize aliveness **by** examining your relationship **with** time.*

TEACHING WHAT MATTERS PLAYBOOK: TOOLS FOR LIVING MORE FULLY

Playbook Lesson Sequence 1: Nozick's Experience Machine Thought Experiment

Lesson objective: Examine Epicurean philosophical views of the attainment of pleasure and evaluate them within the context of Robert Nozick's thought experiment.

Step 1-Guiding Question: If we only have one life **to live, do we have duty to pursue as many pleasurable experiences as possible?** Watch an explanation of Epicurus (available via *The School of Life*, YouTube channel).

Step 2-Discuss as a whole class the guiding question. Epicurus would urge all people to figure out those things that bring us pleasure. Our attention and awareness should be directed to finding ways to enjoy ourselves rather than feeling miserable. On a scale of 1–8 (highest) How certain are you that the best way to transform your relationship to the present is to engage in more pleasurable experiences? What kind of pursuits would be pleasurable?

Step 3-NB/Journal: Students personally reflect on the following: To what extent is happiness about the attainment of pleasure throughout one's life? (How might the Hedonic Treadmill factor into your decision?)

Step 4-Guiding Question: Do you plug **into Nozick's experience machine?** Introduce Robert Nozick's experience machine thought experiment from his 1974 book *Anarchy, State and Utopia.* Here is the thought experiment. You go into a technologically elaborate lab and sit down with the staff. You talk to them about everything. All you ever wanted to do in life, all that you wanted to experience.

You describe your perfect, most ideal, most pleasurable, most joyous, most satisfying possible life. While in the machine the scientists can ensure any experience. They can also have you never endure the loss of loved ones or other painful experiences. As preparation for the experience machine, they induce you into a coma that you will never emerge.

They put your unconscious body into a tank of fluid in a pitch-black room. Your head is then covered with electrodes as you are connected to the machine. Your body is placed in the tank. Then, the simulation begins. While in the tank, you will experience everything you expressed to the researchers.

They have adapted multitudes of programs to simulate the days of your life. You will feel as if you are living everything you dreamed and wanted for the duration of your life. The machine will keep you alive and healthy as long as you want. Your body will stay the same age that you enter. You will have no memory of going into the experience machine or knowledge that your world is a computer simulation. You will experience your perfect life in its entirety, feeling as if it is really happening.

In reality, none of it is real. You are actually floating in a vat of fluid preserving your body in the room stored in a warehouse. You will never again wake up to experience the actual world or interact with actual people, but you won't know that, and you will feel like you did.[5]

- Small group discussion, consider and discuss the following questions. If given the opportunity, would you enter the experience machine? If not, why not? What makes the experience machine enticing? What might make it terrifying? What if all humans plugged into experience machines? Would this make for a better planet?

Step 4-NB/Journal: Did you choose to plug into the machine? Why or why not?

- What does the experience machine teach us about experiencing life as it is?
- Is life really all about obtaining pleasurable experiences? Does your response to the experience machine refute or support your thinking about Epicurean philosophy?
- Can we consistently create for ourselves a steady influx of engaging, satisfying, pleasurable, and positive experiences throughout our lives? How much is needed in order to feel satisfied?

Playbook Lesson Sequence 2: Our attitudes about time and well being

Lesson objective: Identify your perspective about time and its usage.

Step 1-Read *The Importance of Our Time Perspective* by Rosemary Sword and Philip Zimbardo (available via Psychology Today).

What can be taught & learned about Happiness?

What is time perspective theory? According to TP (time perspective) theory, our biases about time create cognitive processes, like attention and perception, that shape how we live. TP influences many of our decisions and behaviors. Time perspectives shape our moods, sleep habits, health, relationships with others, work choices, and leisure activities.

Time perspectives also largely determine how the past, present, and future are viewed. While influenced by other factors, like culture for example, perspectives on time often become a personality characteristic.

Researchers Philip Zimbardo and John Boyd developed a Time Perspective Inventory (TPI). They determined five main types of time perspectives consisting of the past-negative TP, past-positive TP, present-hedonistic TP, present-fatalistic TP, and future TP.[6]

Future oriented people work for the future often sacrificing enjoyment of the present. A present-hedonistic person lives in the moment and is a pleasure seeker. A past-positive person holds a nostalgic view of the past relishing the days gone by. Past-negative person feels the past unpleasantly and has an aversion to recalling experiences that were difficult. A present fatalist person feels helpless and hopeless and regards outside forces as controlling one's life.

Research from Ilona Boniwell and colleagues reveal that the time perspective that fosters well-being is the past-positive. Past-positive individuals tend be satisfied with who they are and with their past and present lives.[7] Like all things, having a balanced time perspective as opposed to a rigidly defined perspective has been shown to be correlated with greater well-being.

Flexibility and fluidity are the key. Being able to shift our goals, plans, and attention to the dictates of a given situation proves to pay dividends. With a balanced time perspective, we can gain higher self-esteem, agency, optimism, greater sense of meaning and purpose, higher life satisfaction, and generally feel happier.[8] Most people can change their time orientation if they are motivated and are shown how.

Playbook Lesson Sequence 3: Examining one's relationship to time.

Lesson objective: Investigate and apply the meaning of time.

Step1-Guiding Questions: Do you understand time? Do we need constant stimulation or do we enjoy creating idleness?

- Introduce and engage students in the following experiment about time. Explain that as a class you will be exploring whether busyness is a choice. The purpose of the activity is to create some space within time, to simply do nothing. Students sit for 15 minutes.
- They are not allowed to talk, leave their seat, fall asleep, put their head down on their desk, check cellphones in backpacks, draw, or read. They must simply sit there for 15 minutes.
- After 15 minutes, have students reflect on what they did with that time. Debrief and discuss. What did you experience? Specifically. Did you enjoy it? What was easy? What was difficult? Is doing nothing difficult for you to do?

Step 2-Guiding Question: Why might being alone with thoughts difficult? Introduce the following ubiquitous study conducted by Timothy Wilson and colleagues that made news headlines. *Just think: The challenges of the disengaged mind.*[9]

The researchers found that participants sitting passively in a room for 6–15 minutes in some cases, preferred giving themselves an electric shock rather than sitting passively. Being alone with one's own thoughts (or simply just thinking) was less enjoyable than giving oneself pain. At least 67 percent of men (with one male shocking himself 190 times) in comparison to 25 percent of women chose to give themselves a shock. And this was after reporting that they would pay to not get shocked again.[10]

Step 3-Guiding Question: What is **the significance of John Cage's silent musical piece?** Read *The Story Of '4'33'"* (available https://www.npr.org/2000/05/08/1073885/4-33) or watch William Marx perform John Cage's 4'33" filmed at the McCallum Theatre (via YouTube). What is the point of the performance?

Discuss as a class conversation. Is silence and stillness welcome in our lives? Or do we prefer distraction or busyness?

Step 4-**Guiding Question: Has the pace of life increased?**

- Examine the following from the Pew Research Center: *How Americans feel about the satisfactions and stresses of modern life*. https://www.pewresearch.org/fact-tank/2020/02/05/how-americans-feel-about-the-satisfactions-and-stresses-of-modern-life/
- According to the Pew Research Center, in a 2016 survey, about half of Americans (52 percent) said they're usually trying to do two or more things at once. But just 11 percent of Americans said the fast pace of their lives was harming their health. In a 2018 survey, 60 percent of U.S. adults said they at least sometimes felt too busy to enjoy life, but just 12 percent said they felt this way all or most of the time. In a 2006 Pew Research Survey, 26 percent of women and 21 percent of men felt that they were "always rushed."[11] In 2012, 50 percent of working Americans reported they were "always rushed," and 70 percent "never" had enough time, while in 2015, over 80 percent said they didn't have enough time.[12]
- What does it mean to be idle? Is there a difference between idleness and unproductive?
- Share Pilvi Takala's performance in "The Trainee" (available at https://pilvitakala.com/the-trainee). Discuss how idleness is regarded by others and the culture of work. What social norms does Takala seem to be breaking? In order to generate ideas or thoughts, time and the space free from distraction are needed. How much time is permitted to think? To ponder? To create?
- Ask students to research and investigate Karoshi in Japan and Gwarosa in Korea. What explains why people are literally working themselves to death?
- Discuss and define slowness. Slow means movements or actions at a relaxed or leisured pace, unhurried. Discuss in small groups. What does slowness mean to you? Is it appealing or unappealing? Why or why not? Is faster better? What kind of life can you have if you are overworked, stressed, and don't sleep enough?
- Watch the sloth scene at the DMV from the movie *Zootopia*. What lessons do they provide us with regard to time? What does slowness mean

to you? Is it appealing or unappealing? Why or why not? Whose pace is errant: The character Flash the Sloth or Officer Judy Hops? Why?

Step 5-Guiding Question: What is time?

- How can time be defined?
- Research time. How is time used and understood in other cultures and throughout history? What is the difference between linear and circular time? What is the international Slow Movement?

Step 6-NB/Journal: How would you characterize your relationship to time? How do you value the time in your life? How do we use our time to really live? Is there anything about linear time, cyclical time, and multi-linear time that is appealing to you? Why or why not? What impact has culture had on our view of time? Have students share their responses with the class. When given leisure time, do you know what to do with it to make your life a little bit better? To what extent is busyness a choice?

What can be taught & learned about Happiness?

What is time? The mechanical clock was invented in thirteenth century Europe. When Galileo invented the pendulum in the seventeenth century, it allowed people to count minutes in a day for the first time. Long before the use of the Gregorian calendar, farmers in China and Japan reduced each year into 24 *sekki* or small seasons. Sekki was a collective term to describe the seasonal days. No dates were used, but the seasons were identified by natural phenomena or changes in weather that occurred during the year.[13]

Ancient Babylonians and Egyptians, because of the necessity of living in agricultural-based societies, began to measure and place a value on time. They also measured their time based on the seasons. They did not have a need to fill the minutes of a day. In ancient Greece, they had two different words for time: *chronos* and *kairos*. Chronos is clock time, or water time (the Greeks used water clocks) and sequential time. Kairos is qualitative time. It is concerned with *the kind* of time it is.

In Roman times, time was differentiated by *negotium* and *otium*. Negotium was business time, one's duties or obligations that had to be fulfilled, like work or military service. In contrast to this was *otium*. Otium was leisure time, a time for idleness, reflection, thinking, conversing, and existential considerations. People's relationship with and to time is different around the world.[14]

The ancient Greek Stoics urged people to seek ataraxia or the tranquility of the soul. In the United States, time is linear. Time is viewed as use it or lose it. In other countries the idea of linear time has cultural differences. Some European countries set meeting times which are not to be recognized as an exact time to meet, but rather a basis by which people could meet. Punctuality is seen as unusual. The meeting, the relationship forged, the conversation, and the enjoyment of all of these, is valued. Not being on time.

In some eastern cultures time is viewed cyclically. The value of time is not how much time one possesses but rather what *kind* of time it can be. In cyclical time, days are structured to do certain activities. In cyclical time cultures people think deeply about time. This allows one to live not only a long life, as Roman philosopher Seneca had suggested, but also a life that is wide.

What is leisure? According to a 2018 study happiness peaks around 2.5 hours of leisure per day for people who work and 4–5 hours for those who don't.[15] Like most things, balance is the key. Time to be scheduled but not over-scheduled. Not having enough free time makes us feel stressed. Too much free time leaves us feeling aimless and that time lacks purpose. Leisure historically has been a luxury. People did not have leisure. They worked to survive.

Have we today changed, emphasizing living to work rather than working to live? How do Americans on average spend their leisure time? Data seems to show that people feel, either actual or perceived, that they don't have enough time.[16]

Psychologist Tim Kasser has researched the effects of time poverty and time affluence on people. Time poverty is feeling time starved because often we are overworked, over-scheduled, and lack leisure time. There is a host of physical and mental health issues associated with the stress that accompanies time poverty. Often time poverty is a matter of perception. Most people today paradoxically enjoy more leisure than in the 1950s.[17] Having time affluence promotes greater life satisfaction.[18]

Eric Carle's classic children's book *"Slowly, Slowly, Slowly," said the Sloth* reminds us of about the nature of slowness. At the end of the book, the sloth replies, *"I am relaxed and tranquil and I like to live in peace. But I am not lazy. That's just how I am. I like to do things slowly, slowly, slowly."*19

Robert Levine in his book *Geography of Time* attempted to measure the pace of life around the world and investigate differing cultural attitudes toward time. His research attempted to examine the relationship between people who live in slower pace cultures and happiness. Are people happier living a slower pace? Are they healthier? What is the quality of their lives?

He used three different measures to determine the pace of life of people around the world: Average walking speed of a randomly selected pedestrians, time taken for a postal clerk to fulfill a request for stamps and make change, and gauging the accuracy of the time on the clocks of fifteen randomly selected bank clocks in a center of a city.

The fastest people were found in North America, Northern Europe, and Asian nations. The slowest were in countries found in South and Central America and the Middle East.[20] As Levine noted in his book, *"the truth of the matter is that there are no overriding rights and wrongs to a particular pace of life. There are simply different ways of life, each with their pluses and minuses. All cultures, then, have something to learn from others' conceptions of time."*[21]

Why does it feel like we always have to be busy? Leisure is not necessarily idleness. Leisure can be anything that challenges, adds value to our lives, or relaxes us. Leisure is choosing to do or do nothing. Today we experience boredom differently in the eighteenth and nineteenth centuries. The word "boredom" did not come into use until the nineteenth century.[22] Unlike the past, people today react to boredom with distaste and revulsion.[23]

Playbook Lesson Sequence 4: Digital Technology, Social Media, and Time

Lesson objective: Create a set of principles for using as opposed to being used by digital devices.

Step 1-Guiding Questions: Are digital technology and social media liberating or tyrannical in their effects of being present? How does your smartphone affect your relationship with time, both in beneficial and detrimental ways?

- Read *Weapons of Mass Distraction: Why we have lost the ability to focus* by Larry Rosen (available via *Psychology Today*).
- Watch Tristan Harris (available via Big Think). *Social Media's Dark Side: How Facebook and Snapchat Try to Steal Our Self-Worth.*
- Read *The Joy of Quiet* by Pico Iyer (available via *New York Times*).

- Discuss. What rings true and what doesn't? What are some of the ideas/ points you agree and disagree? Why? Should you reassess your relationship to technology and smart devices? What could you do with all the leisure time instead of using your smart device? Use the following parental guidelines from Alicia Blum-Ross and Sonia Livingstone's parental recommendations to assess your relationship with your smart device.[24] Are you sleeping enough? Are you healthy? Are you connecting socially with family and friends? Are you engaged in and achieving in school? Are you pursuing hobbies and interests in any form? Are you having fun and learning in your use of social media? Also consider the following questions from DigitalDetox. Does your smart device

interfere with your sleep, self-esteem, relationships, memory, attention-span, creativity, productivity, and decision-making skills?
- NB-Journal: Address the guiding question.

What can be taught & learned about Happiness?

How do American spend their time in leisure? According to the U.S. Bureau of Labor Statistics, on an average day in 2019, nearly everyone aged 15 and older engaged in some sort of leisure activity. Watching television accounted for about half of all leisure time while socializing with friends was the next most common leisure activity.[25]

Americans between the ages of 18–24, send and receive over 128 texts every day. Data from 2021 indicate that 44 percent of 18 to 49-year-olds say they go online almost constantly.[26] The average American watches over 30 hours of television a week, about 4 hours a day.[27]

How do smartphones affect the quality of leisure time? A Harvard Business Review survey found that 60 percent of those who carry smartphones are connected to their jobs 13.5 hours or more each day on weekdays and 5 hours on weekends. We are not wired to multitask. The quality of what we are working on diminishes as our focus becomes diluted. This also includes leisure time. Distraction makes it difficult to pay attention to anything fully.

According to Mary Meeker's *Annual Internet Trends Report* Americans are spending more time with digital media than ever: 6.3 hours a day in 2018, up 7 percent from the year before.[28] Two or more hours are spent using a digital device by 95 percent of Americans.[29]

The average smart phone user takes approximately 1 minute to open and close their phone about 58 times a day. That translates to about 1 hour out of every day of your life just opening and closing your phone. College students at Kent University found that consistent use of their smartphone negatively affected their happiness, finding they felt more uptight, stressed, and anxious in their free time.[30] Researcher Ashley Whillans calls this time confetti, little bits of seconds and minutes lost to unproductive multitasking. This distraction negatively impacts our enjoyment of leisure time.

Research from Amy Blankson who has interviewed some of the world's most successful individuals reveal that happiness, balance, and greater life satisfaction in this digital era is dependent on many different strategies. Blankson writes about these individuals, *"They generally stay grounded in the face of distraction. They use technology to know themselves on a deeper level. They know when and how to use technology to train their brains to reach their full potential. They structure their surroundings to create a* *habitat for happiness. Lastly they innovate consciously to enrich the world around them."*31

Much of the emerging research on social media reveals that the impact on children or adults are neither inherently positive or negative. It really boils down to how smart devices are used as well as the users themselves.

Devices like smartphones often amplify positive and negative effects. There is hyperbolic concern about screen usage and young people.[32] Research suggests a rule of thumb, the Goldilocks analogy when using a smart device. The right amount of screen time, about 2 hours a day, seems just about right for teenagers.[33]

Precept #8: Exploring mindfulness helps to better understand the anatomy of the present and calmness in those moments.

TEACHING WHAT MATTERS PLAYBOOK: TOOLS FOR LIVING MORE FULLY

Playbook Lesson Sequence 1: Examining the play *Waiting for Godot*.
Lesson objective: Hypothesize the meaning of the play *Waiting for Godot* and the meaning of unused time.

Step1-Guiding Question: What can one interpret **from Samuel Beckett's play about how idle time affects our thinking and behavior?**

- Watch *Why should you read "Waiting For Godot"?* by Iseult Gillespie (available via TedEd)
- Read *Themes and Related Quotes from 'Waiting for Godot'* [34] by Esther Lombardi (available via ThoughtCo.)
- Discuss in small groups and whole class. What do Estragon and Vladimir do with the time while they wait? What should they do? What can they do? What do people generally do with idle time? Does anyone actually wait? Where and how do we direct our attention? Is waiting a waste of time? Do people have an uncertainty about idle time?

Step 2-Guiding Question: What do our brains do when we are waiting, doing nothing? What is the default mode network of the brain?

- Watch Neuroscientist Marcus Raichle's *What Your Brain Does When You're Doing Nothing*. Raichle explains the default mode network of the brain. (Available via YouTube)

What can be taught & learned about Happiness?

What does the play *Waiting for Godot* illustrate? The play *Waiting for Godot*, written by Samuel Beckett, consists of two men, Estragon and Vladimir, who wait by a tree at dusk to wait for someone named Godot. Godot never comes. As the two characters wait, they meet others and discuss many different things including their lives.

As they continue to wait Vladimir and Estragon engage in circular discussions about whether Godot will come and what they will do if he doesn't show up. The play entices the audience to wait with Vladimir and Estragon for Godot.

While there have been many attempts to interpret the meaning of Beckett's play using a variety of academic disciplines, no one knows for sure its meaning. Beckett himself never intimated what his play suggests. Like most art, *Waiting for Godot* is best left for the individual to interpret and extract personalized meaning.

What is attention? How do we take control of our attention? We might think we are simply waiting, mindlessly doing nothing. However, as soon as we stop doing or focusing our attention, our brains immediately start thinking about other things. Research tells us that one of the great sources of unhappiness is when our minds wander. Our brains wander a lot, 47 percent of the time our brains are thinking about something other than what we are doing.[35]

Researchers Matt Killingsworth and Dan Gilbert have shown that the more the mind wanders, the less happy we are. Typically, mind-wandering leads to thinking about things from the past and predicting future events negatively. Many of these thoughts are disconcerting.

When you think you are zoning out, you engage a brain circuit called the default mode network (DMN). The DMN activates when you stop intentionally focusing on something. When our brain is supposed to be at rest, the DMN becomes active. This activity is usually under our conscious awareness.

It is estimated that we have thousands of thoughts daily. The majority of thoughts are the ones we had yesterday. The majority of those thoughts are negative. That means on an average day most people think thousands of negative thoughts. What people think often impacts people's happiness more than what they are doing. Practicing various mindfulness meditation practices by experienced meditators has been shown to alter the activity of the DMN and keep present-focused attention.[36]

Playbook Lesson Sequence 2: Introduction to Mindfulness.

Lesson Objective: Explain what mindfulness is and what mindfulness is not.

Step 1-Engage in the following thought experiment. At the end of any day, what percentage of the time are you present for any it? What percentage of your day is spent on autopilot, distracted, or unaware of what you were doing?

Step 2-Guiding Question: **What is mindfulness and why practice it?** One way to create a better relationship with time is to give more *intention* to your attention. Watch the following videos introducing students to a generalized understanding of mindfulness meditation.

- Watch Dan Harris, author of *10% Happier* explain what brought him to mindfulness and why he practices it. *Dan Harris' Panic Attack (and Discovery of Meditation) Big Think* (available via Big Think YouTube channel).
- Watch Dan Harris: *Hack Your Brain's Default Mode with Meditation* (available via Big Think YouTube channel).
- Watch *Mindfulness and how the brain works* (available via Mind the Bump, Smiling Mind YouTube Channel.)
- Watch Jon Kabat-Zinn's talk, *Mindfulness Dissolves Thoughts—Attention Is What's Left Over* (available via Big Think YouTube channel).
- Examine what might mindfulness look like in school: Watch two videos from mindfulschools.org *"What Is Mindfulness?" Awakening Kindness and Curiosity at School* and *"Just Breathe" How Can Children Process Difficult Emotions?*
- Discuss as a whole class or students can turn and talk. What are your initial impressions of mindfulness? What is mindfulness and what isn't it?

Step 3-NB-Journal: *Address the guiding question.*

What can be taught & learned about Happiness?

What is mindfulness? The opposite of mindfulness is mindlessness. Mindlessness means going through the motions, usually on autopilot. Selective attention is difficult. Mindfulness is being aware of what you are doing or thinking. It cultivates habits of being that allow us to pay attention to the things that matter. That is how mindfulness is useful and beneficial.

Mindfulness is the secularized companion to Buddhist meditation. Mindfulness is about incorporating meditation practices that have been in use for thousands of years without the religious and spiritual teachings.

Mindfulness is simply bringing attention to the present by using breath as the focus of attention. Mindfulness is defined by Jon Kabat-Zinn (the founder of Mindfullness-based Stress Reduction [MBSR] program and mindfulness expert) as "paying attention in a particular way, on purpose, in the present moment, and non-judgmentally."[37]

Mindfulness is a practice that allows us to ground ourselves in the present moment. By focusing our attention on something specific, like our breath, sensations in our bodies, emotions, or any of our senses, we begin to control our attention. When the mind begins to wander, mindfulness allows us to anchor our attention intentionally.

Mindfulness encourages conscious breathing, becoming aware of each breath. From this place mindfulness becomes an integral tool in interacting with the world. It helps to see and accept things as they are. Mindfulness is a means of living more fully.

There has been incredibly promising research over the last two decades regarding the benefits of mindfulness practice. Mindfulness has been shown to help feel less affected by stress, mentally and physically healthier, more creative, foster resiliency, sleep better, increased awareness and attentiveness, self-regulation and emotional control, and feel happier and more satisfied.[38]

The point of engaging in mindfulness practices is not to leave the benefits in the classroom. Despite being a solitary endeavor, mindfulness can foster deeper connections with others. This can be done by taking the benefits of mindfulness practices like calmness, clarity, greater attentiveness, and compassion out into the world and applying them to our daily interactions.

How not to use mindfulness in the classroom. Within school settings it is important to note that mindfulness isn't a classroom management tool. Mindfulness should never be used as a disciplinary tool. Like all the activities presented, student participation should be voluntary. It is not easy sitting in stillness for extended periods of time. Note that during any mindful practice, students can simply put their heads down on their desks.

The best way to teach mindfulness is to practice it yourself. Practice what you teach. It becomes easier to foster discussion and identify with student experiences. There are many organizations that provide mindfulness courses. Consider developing your own practice out of school if you don't already do so.

Playbook Lesson Sequence 3: The science of mindfulness

Lesson objective: Explain how mindfulness meditation affects the brain.

Step 1-Guiding Question: How does Rumi's poem *The Guest House* **relate to mindfulness practices?**

- Read the poem by Sufi poet Rumi "*The Guest House*."

- Students reflect in their journals. Then discuss responses to the following questions with their peers. What is the meaning of the poem? How does it relate to mindfulness? What does Rumi mean by "guests?" What "guests" visit you on a daily basis? How many are welcome? How long is their stay? To what extent do these guests affect you?
- Provide a sample of various guests, and have students raise their hand if they are visited by these guests. Sample guests might be emotions, like fear, anger, joy, sadness, and stress.

Step 2-*How does mindfulness help to cultivate amor fati, to accept life as it is, the good, the bad and the ugly and to love it?*

- Make a Glitter Jar (instructions available at http://www.mindful.org/how-to-create-a-glitter-jar-for-kids/). Use it as analogy for our minds responding to emotions, environmental stimuli, stress, anxiety, and unwanted thoughts. Each color of glitter can represent emotions, thoughts, sensations, or stimuli.

The jar of water represents your mind. When the jar is still, the water or our minds are at peace. There is a sense of tranquility. When glitter is added, the jar gets cloudy. The mind is not clear. The purpose then is to focus on breath and relax the mind. This allows the glitter to settle at the bottom. Then the water (mind) is clear again. With time the mind can be calm and settled.

- Show a picture of the brain with the amygdala, prefrontal cortex, and hippocampus labeled within the brain. Explain the various functions of these parts of the brain. The amygdala is the emotional center of the brain. Activation can occur when detecting threats, differences, and reacting to emotions such as fear. The amygdala activates the flight, fight, or freeze responses. Cortisol is released in response to stress along with epinephrine to get the body ready to deal with the perceived or actual threat. The hippocampus is where new information that is learned is stored or it aids in the ability to recall prior information. The prefrontal cortex is the rational center of the brain. It controls executive functions like self-regulation and problem-solving. When the amygdala becomes activated all cognitive and physical energy goes to alleviating the threat inducing the flight, fight, or freeze response.

Anyone in this flight, fight, or freeze response finds it inhibits learning new information or recalling prior information. By controlling breathing, slowing it down, choice moments are created which gives time for the prefrontal cortex to critically evaluate the nature of the threat. Engaging in reasoned thinking allows us not to give in to habitual, automatic responses. We can choose a different response to stress, fear, etc.

In doing so, we develop and strengthen new neural pathways. As Rick Hanson notes, neurons that "fire together, wire together" and are more likely to do so in the future.

Step 3: Assess student understanding of mindfulness. In a paragraph explain to someone, using 2–3 empirically-based reasons, why mindfulness practice is worth the time. Or pretend that a person is skeptical of mindfulness, what reasoning can you provide that could illustrate the benefits of mindfulness practice?

What can be taught & learned about Happiness?

What does it mean to create choice moments? Many of the great thinkers throughout history have urged us to embrace the concept of *amor fati,* to accept life as it is, the good, the bad, and the ugly and to love it. In every part of our lives, we should learn to value, appreciate, and celebrate them.

Viktor Frankl in his memoir *Man's Search for Meaning* wrote, "*Between stimulus and response, there is a space. In that space lies our freedom and our power to choose our response. In our response lies our growth and our happiness.*" What this means is we are able to train ourselves to respond to emotional stimulation and create the ability to choose how we want to react. This is typically known as response flexibility. Breath creates space for the examination of what is going on inside our brains, the thoughts, emotions, and what we are feeling in our bodies.

Mindfulness helps to not get swept up in an emotion, or to feel as though we are the emotion, but to notice what we are feeling, where we are feeling it and how to simply let go of it and its hold on us at that moment. We come to realize that we are not sadness ("I am sad") but that we feel sadness ("I feel sad"). We identify where we feel sadness and notice it, compassionately and without judgement.

We come to learn that thoughts are not facts, no matter how powerful the emotions associated with them. When negative thoughts develop mindfulness helps us to notice them and view them non-judgmentally. Mindfulness also lets us be attentive to good things that happen. We learn how to lean into these positive experiences and marinate in them as opposed to rushing through them.

What is the science behind mindfulness? At the heart of mindfulness is present-time awareness and equanimity working together. When experiencing something that triggers our amygdala (the older part of the brain that deals with fear), the flight, fight, or freeze response is activated.

This served a purpose through our evolutionary history. We need to be on the look-out for danger, especially with a T-Rex roaming around, and be ready to run (flight), fight with the T-Rex to avoid being eaten, or freeze with fear because the danger is paralyzing to us. This helped our ancestors and allowed for the continuation of our species.

Unfortunately, this evolutionary biological mechanism does not help when we experience the fight, flight or freeze response in a supermarket or stuck in traffic. The amygdala is constantly scanning and searching for potential threats. As a result, we often develop habitual ways of responding.

When the amygdala gets activated, the other regions of our brains get deactivated. For example, our prefrontal cortexes help to regulate fear and other emotional responses. It is also the part of the brain that allows us to reason, rationalize our experiences, make decisions, and engage in executive planning.

The other important part of the brain affected by the flight, fight, or freeze response is the hippocampus. The hippocampus is important in storing new memories and retrieving memories. For teenagers, the prefrontal cortex takes the longest to fully mature as it continues to develop well into their twenties. When a stress response is triggered, the amygdala becomes active and the body and brain go into automatic mode.

For teenagers, this means that executive functioning and reasoning are diminished. The hippocampus is deactivated making learning new information and/or recalling prior information from memory more difficult.

What is the importance of labeling any emotion? In brain scans done by Matthew Lieberman, he found that affective labeling or labeling an emotion as you are feeling it helps to control that emotion and the response to it. His research suggests that labeling an emotion creates a mental brake pedal, which then allows for an increased activation of the prefrontal cortex allowing for executive functioning.[39] This diminishes the physiological and emotional affects, allowing you to cognitively reappraise it to achieve neutrality and/or relaxation.

That is why mindfulness has at its core two fundamental aspects, present-awareness and equanimity. Mindfulness however isn't about clearing the mind or preventing any thoughts. Mindfulness meditation helps create space between the thought and your reaction to it.

Mindfulness meditation practices examine thoughts as they arise and simply notices them to determine the causes behind them. Response flexibility is cultivated. This allows us to think about different ways to respond to emotions, feelings, or thoughts. Then we can be the driver and not the passenger to our responses.

Psychologist and author Elisha Goldstein illustrated this wonderfully when he wrote, *"You can become naturally flexible in your decision making, become able to regulate your body in moments of distress, calm your anxious mind when it's snowballing with thoughts, have greater focus at home and work, feel empathy and compassion toward yourself and others, communicate more effectively, and be more aware of what is most important to you."*[40]

How does mindful breathing promote equanimity? When experiencing an amygdala trigger, our breath becomes shorter, shallow, and increases in speed. Our breathing is controlled by our autonomic nervous system. When we are stressed or anxious our sympathetic nervous system gets stimulated which is connected to the flight, fight, or freeze response. It is the gas pedal to the flight, fight, or freeze response.

However, when we focus our attention on breath and regulate our breathing by slowing down our inhalations and exhalations, we stimulate the parasympathetic nervous system (PSNS). The PSNS basically undoes the work of the sympathetic nervous system. The PSNS actually slows down our heart rate and fosters the rest and digest response. The PSNS is the brake pedal. Stress or anxious stimulation leads to activation of sympathetic nervous system, the gas pedal to the fight, flight, or freeze response. This results in rapid breathing and the impetus to alleviate the trigger.

Becoming aware of this response, pausing, and regulating breathing by slowing down inhalations and exhalations stimulates the PSNS as a brake pedal. This allows for executive functioning, reappraisal, and choosing a response for a different desired outcome.

Can mindfulness rewire our brains to respond to stress more favorably? Mindfulness has been shown to increase the growth of more gray matter in parts of the brain believed to be involved in learning, memory processing, emotional regulation, perspective, and overall executive functioning.[41] Mindfulness done by experienced meditators has also been shown to decrease the activation of the default mode network as well as the influence of the amygdala.[42] Mindfulness also strengthens brain networks that improve emotional regulation and emotional well being.[43]

Researchers at the Massachusetts Institute of Technology suggested in a recent study that for the first-time mindfulness training can alter brain activity in adolescents. Middle-school-aged youth in Boston charter schools were divided into two groups, a control group that took a coding class and another group of students who received an eight-week training in mindfulness awareness of breath.

Students who received mindfulness training reported feeling less stressed and fewer negative feelings, such as anger or sadness. Brain scans of students both before and after the mindfulness training revealed reduced activation of the amygdala, when they viewed images of fearful faces.[44]

Mindfulness meditation is easier to do when we are relaxed. It can be difficult to sit in stillness and welcome unpleasant sensations, feelings, and thoughts. Mindfulness allows for training in responding differently to the triggers, stressors, and the associated physiological sensations. This repeated exposure can be beneficial.

Robert Sapolsky noted in his book, *Why Zebras Don't Get Ulcers* the repeated experience of doing something can change activation of your stress response. He cites a study involving Norwegian soldiers learning to parachute. These soldiers were studied over months of training. When they jumped for the first time, they were extremely nervous. They would stress about jumping days before they had to jump and days after they jumped. Physiologically, they experienced stress responses both before and after the jump.

By the end of their training as they continued jumping, they experienced a reduced activation of their stress response.[45] They didn't stress out about the jump days before or after the jump. Nor did they experience the same physiological effects of stress. They still got nervous, just not to the same degree. After significant hours of habitually practicing jumping out of a plane, they were able to diminish their stress response simply by repeatedly experiencing the very thing that was causing them the stress.

Playbook Lesson Sequence 4: How to practice/teach each mindfulness

Lesson objective: State the ways to practice mindfulness.

Step 1-Guiding Questions: How does one practice mindfulness? **Like anything, how do you teach the fundamentals?** Incorporating your own experiences from your own practice will be extremely helpful. If you don't practice mindfulness yourself, no worries, you can experience it with students with the help of guided meditations and/or other credentialed instructors.

- Read *What is Mindfulness?* Here is an introduction to the fundamentals: mindful.org.
- Or students can follow the steps via the *New York Times* infographic *The Calm Place*.

Step 2-Guiding Question: What are the fundamentals of a mindfulness meditation class practice?
Create a routine. Consider integrating mindful minutes of practice at the beginning or end of a class period. Begin every class with different mindfulness practices to cultivate greater experiential knowledge. Intention begins with a purpose. Giving intention to our attention is habit-forming. What habits do we want to strengthen? What is the purpose of the mindful practice? Is it for cultivating emotional intelligence, well-being, compassion, or to reduce stress?

An intentional daily practice will provide opportunities to experience various practices and ways to incorporate mindfulness into one's life. For any mindfulness practice, the purpose is for students to develop and find their own mindfulness style.

Various practices can be incorporated. Building an anchor breath, breathing and sound meditations, body-scan meditations, mindful eating, mindful conversations, mindful listening, loving kindness or compassion meditations, and noticing unwanted thoughts can be introduced.

- In the beginning of practicing mindfulness do so in short amounts of time. One minute or less early on in the practice is recommended. Then you can build up to five minutes or longer.

It is extremely important that you give students the time to discuss their experiences with practices with others and to reflect. Give students opportunities to write in their reflection journals. Here are sample discussion/reflection prompts. How would you describe your experience? What did you notice while you were practicing? Do you have any questions? How do you feel during and after practice? Do you enjoy mindfulness practice, why or why not? What do you enjoy the least? Have you experienced any changes as a result of your practice?

- Read *Integrating Mindfulness in Your Classroom Curriculum* by Giselle Shardlow (available via Edutopia).
- Watch short films about mindfulness in education (available via Mindful Schools).
- Remind students that mindfulness is about gaining self-awareness, from a place of non-judgement. It isn't easy. It isn't a quick fix. Taking mindful minutes is a choice to learn about ourselves. It is like choosing to go to the gym. Instead of lifting weights to build strength or tone muscles, mindfulness commits us to befriending emotions, sensations, and feelings, positive or negative. We get stronger in our emotional regulation and awareness. Mindfulness meditation is really about practicing being human.[46]
- **How does one sit during a mindful meditation practice?** In traditional Buddhist meditation, there are 4 main meditation postures: sitting, standing, walking, and lying down. Have students pick one that allows them to be alert and relaxed, not sleep inducing.

If sitting, make sure one's back is straight like an arrow. Legs crossed if sitting on the floor or if sitting in a chair, feet are comfortably placed on the floor uncrossed. Shoulders relaxed and back. Chin tucked in slightly, head slightly bowed to chest. Eyes closed or soft gaze with eyes open (some students might be uncomfortable with their eyes closed so always allow them the opportunity to keep their eyes open). Lips can be slightly

apart, teeth unclenched. Hands placed on legs or comfortably in lap. The goal is to be comfortable, not in pain or holding any tension in the body.
- **How do I focus my attention on breath?** Build a practice to anchor breath. Try sitting just in stillness noticing the inhale and exhale. Don't try to control the breath, simply notice each breath. You don't do anything. Try focusing on an anchor spot on their face, the place by which you notice your breathing. This can be the nickel-sized spot at the end of your nose, your chest, or stomach. Students can place their hands in front of their nose or on their stomach to feel each breath. If you mind drifts or gets distracted welcome to the club. Don't get frustrated or feel like you are doing something wrong. Gently notice that you are distracted but softly remind yourself to return to awareness and sensation of breath.
Sometimes counting breaths can help. Expert meditation teacher Sharon Salzberg recommends inhaling then as you exhale count as one. Take another inhale, then as you exhale count two. Try to count to ten. Then begin again. Other practitioners recommend visualizing inhalations as white, soft, gentle light, and exhalations as grey smoke, releasing any negative sensations.
- What are some recommended guided meditations?
- UCLA Mindful Awareness Research Center: http://marc.ucla.edu/mindful-meditations
- Tara Brach https://www.tarabrach.com/guided-meditations/
- Mindful: https://www.mindful.org/mindfulness-meditation-guided-practices/
- Mindful: Best Practices for Bringing Mindfulness into Schools: https://www.mindful.org/mindfulness-in-education/
- Kristen Neff, Self-Compassion exercises: http://self-compassion.org/category/exercises/
- Contemplative Mind and Life: https://contemplativemind.wordpress.com/how-to-meditate-links-for-guided-meditation-practice/
- Body Scan, Elisha Goldstein
- Popular apps that can be used for guided meditations: *10% Happier, Buddify, Headspace, Calm*

Precept #9: Savor more and improve your relationship with time.

TEACHING WHAT MATTERS PLAYBOOK: TOOLS FOR LIVING MORE FULLY

Playbook Lesson Sequence 1: What does it mean to savor?

Lesson objective: Synthesize what it means to savor and why might it work to make people more satisfied with their lives.

Step 1-Guiding Question: What is savoring?

- Discuss. When was the last time you took the time to marinate in something that brought you joy, contentment, happiness, etc.?
- Define savoring. Everyone experiences stress, hardship, and difficulty. Savoring is simply stopping and smelling the roses and giving ourselves the time to enjoy the good things that happen to us. It entails slowing down to enjoy marinating in memories and feelings from past experiences, anticipating and thinking about future experiences, and being mindful of the present moment and what is happening around us.

Savoring helps to amplify positive feelings when thinking about the past, future, or present. Savoring involves ruminating on the good. This affords time for relishing positive experiences afforded to us. Other researchers define savoring as any thoughts or behaviors capable of generating, intensifying, and prolonging enjoyment.

- Read *What Is Savoring—and Why Is It the Key to Happiness?* by Tchiki Davis, available via *Psychology Today*. Write down at least 3–5 insights you gained about savoring and its relationship to well-being.
- Show an example of savoring. Watch Julie Andrews sing *"My Favorite Things"* from the movie *The Sound of Music*.
- Read the poem *If The Moon Came Out Only Once a Month* by Cathy Ross.
- One of the fundamental aspects of savoring is being present in the moment to connect with the experience, whether external (warm sun on your shoulders) or internal (feeling joy). Awareness is one of the keys. Watch Carl Honore's TedTalk *"In Praise of Slowness"* (the talk begins with his recalling reading bed-time stories to his son and what a fast-paced culture had done to him. A moment that he felt he should have savored, bed-time reading with his son, turned into an internal struggle to get back to his work-related tasks. Something he later laments). Discuss reactions to his talk.

Step 2-Guiding Question: How do you savor?

- Read *The Science of Savoring* by Jan Stanley (available via Livehappy.com) Write down at least 3–5 insights you gained about savoring and its relationship to well-being.
- **How to savor practice #1.** Transport yourself into a mental-time machine. In your notebook make a list of happy memories. Pick 1 positive memory from your list and take 10 minutes to reflect upon it.

Take a deep breath and relax. Close your eyes if that is comfortable and begin to recall the memory. Think of the details of the event. Allow images to come into your mind. Let your mind freely wander through the details of the memory, while you are imagining it. If you can remember, what were you feeling? What were you thinking?

Replay the details of the events. Was anyone with you? NB-Journal: Reflect on what you learned about savoring. In this activity, what seemed to work and not work for you? Is this a practice that you would incorporate into your life? Why or why not? How might this be a tool to enhance greater well-being for you or someone else?

- **How to savor practice #2.** Invest in your future self by embracing your inner James Van Der Zee, Ansel Adams, and Annie Leibovitz and savor with a camera. Either during school or after school, take photographs that capture or reflect an experience that uplifted you or that you savored. Prepare a slide show presentation of at least five of your photographs. Provide a caption for each photograph that helps the viewer understand the importance of the image. Be prepared to discuss what you attempted to savor in each of the photographs.

Devote a class period to a savoring gallery of student photographs. Have students share their photographs and discuss the sensory experiences involved with the photographs. NB-Journal: Reflect on what you learned about savoring. In this activity, what seemed to work and not work for you? Is this a practice that you would incorporate into your life? Why or why not? How might this be a tool to enhance greater well-being for you or someone else?

- **How to savor practice #3**. Take the class around the school and outside for a savoring walk. Students could also do this again at home. Students should bring a notebook.

Here is how it works. Look for good things. When you notice something good, something positive that happens, that you see, hear, touch, taste, smell, experience, or observe, take about 1 minute to stop and smell the roses (so to speak).

Marinate in the good. Try to identify what makes it pleasurable to you. Write it down in your journal. Identify what it is, specifically, that captured your attention. In the next class, have students discuss what prompted them to savor.

Have students share their experiences with each other. Rotate through partners. NB-Journal: Reflect on what you learned about savoring. In this activity, what seemed to work and not work for you? Is this a practice that you would incorporate into your life? Why or why not? How might this be a tool to enhance greater well-being for you or someone else?

- Some other optional ideas on how to practice savoring. Savor some good music. If you could select one song to change people's perceptions of something, or if you could move someone's consciousness, awareness, or emotions, to think differently about life, a cause, a belief, behavior, something, what would the song be?

Or make us fall in love with music by playing one song. Select a song that best exemplifies our ability to marinate in the emotions conveyed or experienced, messages or associations of the song? Elaborate why, specifically and generally why you selected the song you did. Another practice is to take the time to share our good experiences or emotions with others. This is called capitalization. Another practice is when you feel yourself about to complain, gossip, or criticize stop yourself. Stop being a wet-blanket and instead share something good.

What can be taught & learned about *Happiness*?

What is savoring? Savoring is one of those ways in which we can transform our relationship to the present. Bonnie Raitt illustrated the importance of savoring in the song *Nick of Time*, when she sang *time gets mighty precious when there is less of it to waste.* Reminding ourselves once in a while that time is scarce (to live each day as fully as we can as it is our last) can prompt us to seize moments that matter and extract more life satisfaction.[47] It is literally an empirically-based reminder to stop and smell the roses.

Savoring also has a past and future component to it as well. Reminding ourselves of the good and beautiful in the world, both from our past, and what we can anticipate in the future makes us feel good. By recalling the good in our lives, we also can stimulate positive emotions and garner greater well-being.[48] Experiencing regularly positive emotions is essential to well-being and generally feeling happy.

What is the relationship between savoring and well-being? Fred Bryant and Joseph Veroff were the pioneer researchers who characterized the process of savoring and measured its benefits on well-being. They identified four processes involved in savoring.[49]

Basking means receiving praise and congratulations. Marveling is getting lost in the wonder of a moment. Luxuriating entails indulging in a sensation.

Thanksgiving involves expressing gratitude. We have all savored various experiences throughout our lives. Be it sunsets, laughter, the birth of children, graduation, the day we got married, these are events that we consciously savor without really realizing it.

Habitual savoring has been found to be correlated with life satisfaction, feeling grateful, and feeling that life overall is good. Savoring helps generate positive emotions and make these feelings last longer. When we anticipate future experiences, we realize that anticipation provides free happiness.[50]

In addition, savoring increases when we share our good news or experiences with others especially if people respond actively and positively to our good news.[51] This is called capitalization.

It is important to incorporate different ways to savor to thwart hedonic adaptation but also to fully generate positive feelings. Researchers call these various strategies regulatory diversity. People who were able to use various strategies rather than a few specific ones proved more beneficial to overall happiness.[52]

The ability to regulate our emotions has been shown by sharing positive events (usually face-to-face) called capitalization and up-regulation, when we try to make the best of a situation when it did not meet our expectations (think rain on your wedding day).

There also numerous other strategies that help to celebrate the good. Express your joy out loud. Hear yourself say it. Sing it out loud. Avoid killjoy thinking. Focus your attention on what is good as opposed to what it bad. Count your blessings and write down people and experiences for whom you are grateful. Remind yourself that life moves pretty fast so take the time to enjoy it.[53]

How might savoring work? What makes recalling positive memories or imagery actually work is that our brains don't know the difference between what we think and what we experience. Imagine a spider slowly descending from its web about to land on someone's neck without them knowing? What if someone put on a metal claw glove and proceed to walk up to a chalkboard and make a scratching back and forth motion on the board? Would you react? Would you cower? Would your shoulders rise up to your ears? Most of us would react as if the spider was on our necks.

Simply imagining the sound that transmits from the chalkboard causes us to raise our hands to our ears, even though there is no actual sound. We think it did happen and experience all physiological, mental, and emotional reactions that come with it. There is no spider or blackboard, but we can imagine it and recall the reactions to it.

This is an evolutionary mechanism. It is known as our imagination or kinesthetic imagery or kinesthetic visualization. This means experiencing things in our body through the mind and thus mentally rehearsing something. Often times if we imagine or think about something related to the past or future, we will experience that event, including all the emotions it entails.[54]

Precept #10: Redefine your relationship with time by rediscovering playfulness and flow.

TEACHING WHAT MATTERS PLAYBOOK: TOOLS FOR LIVING MORE FULLY

Playbook Lesson Sequence 1: Introduce flow, the theory of optimal experience

Lesson objective: Understand what is flow, the theory of optimal experience.

Step 1-Guiding Question: What is flow and why should you strive **to get into it?**

- Engage in the following activity to induce a flow state. Bring in balloons and have each student blow up a balloon. Bring students either outside or rearrange the classroom to allow students to lie down comfortably on the floor or ground. Introduce the game.

  The purpose of the game is to keep as many balloons in the air without hitting the ground. They can use any parts of their body, hands and feet. The idea is for the teacher to keep track of time, not the students. Don't tell the students, but let the game run for about 15 minutes. After that time, tell them to stop and close their eyes and have them guess how much time had elapsed. Announce the time to them.

  Debrief. How did they feel while playing the game? Did they have fun? Were they bored? Did they lose track of time? Were they disappointed when the game was stopped?

- Next, draw the flow channel chart on the board (available via any web-search). The chart illustrates the flow channel. The y-axis represents how challenging an activity is. The x-axis represents one's abilities to complete the activity or task. If an activity is too challenging and you lack the ability to do it, then it produces anxiety. If your abilities far exceed the challenge of the activity, it leaves you feeling bored. The key is to find the right balance between skills and challenges in an activity. The concept of flow was developed by psychologist Mihalyi Csikszentmihalyi (pronounced cheeks-sent-me-high). Ask students to determine while they were playing the game to plot where they were on the flow chart.

Step 2-Define flow or the theory of optimal experience.
- One way to increase greater life satisfaction is to engage in more activities that puts you in a flow state and/or transform boring, mundane activities into challenging activities. Do you ever find yourself so completely immersed in what you're doing that you lose track of time? This loss of self-consciousness that happens when you are completely absorbed in an activity, either mental (e.g., reading or writing), social (e.g., in a deep conversation with another person), or physical (e.g., mountain climbing) is described as flow or being in the zone.

Flow has been defined as being in a mental state in which the person is fully immersed in what he, she, or they is doing, coupled with a feeling of energized focus, full involvement, and success in the process of the activity.

Csikszentmihalyi describes this optimal experience in his book *Flow, The Psychology of Optimal Experience*, *"Contrary to what we usually believe, moments like these, the best moments in our lives, are not the passive, receptive, relaxing times-although such experiences can be enjoyable if we worked hard to attain them. The best moments usually occur when a person's body or mind is stretched to its limits in a voluntary effort to accomplish something difficult and worthwhile. Optimal experience is thus something we make happen."*55
- Watch animated summation of the theory of flow available via FightMediocrity on YouTube.

Step 3-Guiding Question: What does it look like to be in a state of flow?

- Watch the following scenes or the whole films. Have students turn and talk to exchange ideas and report out as a whole class. How did these characters generate flow? What did they do?
- Watch the film *Free Solo*.
- Watch various music playing scenes in the movie *Soul*.
- Watch various scenes in *The Legend of Baggar Vance* (the scene begins with Randolph Junah finishing the first day of the tournament).
- Watch various scenes from the animated film *Surf's Up* (the three scenes are "Let's Surf," "Being Inside the Tube," and "Building Cody's Board."
- Watch the tightrope walking scene from the documentary *Man on Wire*. In 1974 Philippe Petit tightrope walked across the Twin Towers successfully. Use the footage from when he actually walks on the wire.

Step 4-Guiding Question: Do you experience flow during leisure time? Conduct a flow diagnostic of the ways in which you spend your leisure time. List all the activities that you engage in during a typical weekday and weekend. Determine where each activity fits in Csikszentmihalyi's updated flow channel diagram.

- Create a class micro-flow bank. Now make a list of possible micro-flow activities that can transform boring, mundane experiences into positive ones. Brainstorm micro-flow strategies. Some examples are counting ceiling tiles, categorizing classmates into teams based on the color of their outfits, drawing mazes, coloring, etc. From this list, create a class bank. Use some of these tools to help transform any tedious, mundane, boring, or stressful experiences into more positive ones.

What can be taught & learned about *Happiness*?

What is flow? Flow is a feeling of great pleasure and well-being that comes when one is engaged in mental and/or physical activity, hobby, etc. with great concentration and effectiveness leading to peak performance or outcome that is intrinsic in nature. During states of flow our minds are clear, free of mind wandering and negative thoughts.

One of the significant names in Positive Psychology is the researcher Mihalyi Csikszentmihalyi. His original research focused on numerous interviews with various people as to why they engaged in tasks, activities, hobbies, etc. for hours on end without any external benefits. No one receives a trophy after playing a piano for hours alone. There is no applause from a small audience. He wondered why would anyone utilize their leisure time this way. Csikszentmihalyi found that people found an internal satisfaction in this state he called flow.

That is why Csikszentmihalyi refers to flow as being autotelic, or an intrinsically rewarding experience. The reward is the activity. For athletes, this state of flow is often referred to as "being in the zone" as depicted in this iconic image of Michael Jordan making yet another three-point shot in a 1992 playoff game.

For athletes the game seems to slow down, crowd noise dissipates, and there is a feeling of enjoyment more than pressure. The game becomes easier to anticipate and play. Often individuals lose track of time, mental and physical discomfort, and are emotionless. One's brain quiets down, maintaining a semblance of control as you strike the right balance between being challenged, yet having the capacity/skills to perform favorably during this experience.

How does flow occur? Flow can occur playing sports, or music, interacting with friends and family, while in conversation, writing curriculum, or playing with toys. Flow is different than savoring because flow involves the present only. Savoring has a past, present, and future component to it.

Also, Flow does not have to be solitary. Other people can help you to experience flow and greater joy.[56] It was easy for all of us to find flow when we were younger. In fact, we were probably in flow quite a bit. Research from Howard Gardner stresses that schools should strive to create flow-like learning opportunities for students. Not only would this enhance learning, but it would also strengthen one of Gardner's intelligences, namely intra-intelligence, a good sense of one's emotions, intellect, and intrinsic motivators.

Is there such a thing as junk flow? There are different kinds of flow. There are general flow experiences like rock climbing, painting, playing an instrument, and conversing with friends. There are also micro-flow activities. These are leisurely activities involving a simple task that transform a boring, stressful, or tedious task into a more enjoyable one. For example, when stuck in traffic, you can tap your fingers along with a song. At a faculty meeting you count the number of vocal filers used in an hour-long meeting. You can create a list of favorite music albums of all time.

Noted psychologist Chris Peterson distinguished flow from junk flow, a way of being where we are seduced into a state of leisure but in actuality are simply vegetating. The activity we are engaged in, like binge watching television, lacks the challenging element of flow. Emerging from junk flow engages our attention but does not energize or satisfy. Flow is about engagement rather than withdrawal.

Chapter 5

The Heart of Altruism
Compassion, Human Goodness, and Helping Others

The Josephson Institute of Ethics released its findings about the relationship between high school attitudes, behavior, and later adult conduct. Their survey found that for adolescents aged 17 and under and ages 18–24, *"64% cheated on an exam, 42% lied to save money, and 30% stole something from a store."*[1]

The findings also revealed that *"teens 17 or under were five times more likely than those over 50 to hold the cynical belief that lying and cheating are necessary to succeed, nearly four times as likely to deceive their boss, more than three times as likely to keep change mistakenly given to them, and more than three times as likely to believe it's okay to lie to get a child into a better school."*[2]

Character education isn't a novel idea. Schools have taught what it means to be a good person for a long time. This can be done by learning how principled men and women have responded to ethical issues. This knowledge isn't to create a moral agenda but to celebrate integrity.

This ethos can be an ingrained part of education, not independent of it. Helping students cultivate their own moral, ethical reasoning and decision making is the ultimate application of education. A high school principal illustrated this when he placed letters in the mailboxes of teachers and staff at the beginning of the school year. The letter read:

> *My eyes saw what no man should witness: Gas chambers built by learned engineers. Children poisoned by educated physicians. Infants killed by trained nurses. Women and babies shot and burned by high school and college graduates. So I am suspicious of education. My request is: Help your students become more human. Your efforts must never produce learned monsters, skilled psychopaths, educated Eichmannns. Reading, writing, arithmetic are important only if they serve to make our children more human.*

—School Principal Letter to teachers, and Holocaust survivor[3]

Humans are social creatures. Our happiness is interwoven with those around us. You can derive happiness from looking outward. Doing acts of kindness for others can be more meaningful and fulfilling than acting selfishly.

Are people inherently good? This chapter encourages investigation into the biological propensities for kindness, compassion, and altruism. Research has shown that helping others benefits our well-being. If human nature is primarily selfish, why does anyone help others? Why is heroism commonplace?

An exploration into these questions and on how to cultivate being kinder, more compassionate, and altruistic is emphasized. These lessons are intend for students to develop their own capacities and limits for other-centered behavior.

Wesley Autrey was a construction worker who was dubbed "The Subway Superhero" and the "Hero of Harlem" by the press for his heroism in 2007. Autrey was on a subway platform with his two younger daughters, when Cameron Hollopeter had a seizure and fell off the subway platform. Hollopeter landed on the tracks just as the subway train was beginning to arrive at the platform.

Within seconds, Mr. Autrey made the decision to leave a point of safety and tried to pull Hollopeter off the tracks to save him from the incoming speeding subway. He couldn't get a good grip on Hollopeter. With seconds to spare, Mr. Autrey threw himself on top of Hollopeter, wrapping his arms around him so an appendage would not be lost. Autrey pinned both of them in between the tracks. Suddenly five subway cars flew into the platform swiftly rolling over them.

Autrey had adeptly calculated that the space between the tracks and the bottom of the subway cars was enough for them to fit safely. The only damage either of them suffered was a speck of grease on Mr. Autrey's hat. No one was injured.

Mr. Autrey became known as the "Subway Superman." What motivated Mr. Autrey to risk his own life to save another? Research on heroism has shown that the motivations that lead to someone performing a heroic act are rather ordinary. What makes someone a hero? Are they born or are they made by environmental circumstances?

Researchers have found that one-time acts of bravery are rather conventional. Whereas people who demonstrate valor in their daily jobs, like firefighters or nurses, appear to demonstrate deep-rooted personality traits like empathy and strong moral codes.[4]

What are those mechanisms within human nature that are evolutionarily wired to allow humans to be other-centered? What have various scientific disciplines revealed about human nature and its ability to love (in the agapic tradition that Dr. King espoused) your fellow man as your own brother or sister. Are we equipped with the ability to put other people's needs above our own, even at a cost to ourselves? To what extent are kindness, compassion, and altruism awaiting to be cultivated?

Altruism exists and is demonstrated daily. Altruism occurs when one acts for the sake of another or others. The well-being and welfare of another become the ultimate object of one's concern. When someone acts altruistically, it usually, but not always, entails a cost by the altruist and results in a benefit to the recipient.

There is no singular academic discipline alone that explains why humans act altruistically. However, human nature is not some uniform mechanism. It is complex and multifaceted. There are a multitude of theories from a variety of academic disciplines that attempt to help understand altruism.

The chapter precepts explore case studies, exemplars, and research into why people *do* help others, both in mundane and extraordinary ways. Altruism illustrates what Columbia University professor Jeffrey Sachs has written, "Compassion is the glue that holds society together."[5] In addition, further exploration into extraordinary acts of courage reveal what Ervin Staub has identified in his research that *"Heroes aren't born; They evolve."*[6]

By studying evolutionary biology, the research of Frans de Waal on chimpanzees and bonobos along with Darwin's conclusions he wrote in *Descent of Man,* one begins to form a different understanding of human nature. The theories that solely paint human nature as "red in tooth and claw" or selfish appear limited in comparison. Compassion, cooperation, and altruism are evolutionary mechanisms that are evident in our primate relatives (the chimpanzee and bonobo). These traits are an ingrained part of human biology and evident in brain mechanisms. These traits are waiting to be developed and bolstered.

Research on the neuroscience of empathy and Daniel Batson's empathy-altruism theory, along with the promising discovery of mirror neurons, results in behavior economics, game theory, and compassion research from the Max Planck Institute, all have advanced understanding of altruistic behavior in humans. In many ways all of this research has put the human back into human nature.

This research also affirms the hopefulness of what Robert Kennedy exhorted, *"Few will have the greatness to bend history itself, but each of us can work to change a small portion of events, and in the total of all those acts will be written the history of this generation. . .Each time a man stands up for an ideal, or acts to improve the lot of others, or strikes out against injustice, he sends forth a tiny ripple of hope."*[7]

Precept #11: The world is not broken. There is another side to human nature, one that is constructive, benevolent, and good.

TEACHING WHAT MATTERS PLAYBOOK: TOOLS FOR EXPLORING THE ART OF LIVING

Playbook Lesson Sequence 1: Perceptions of human nature and moral responsibilities to others

Lesson objective: Defend your assessment of doing the right thing to do, along with defending whether we have a moral responsibility to help others.

Step 1-Guiding Question: When thinking **about the state of the world, is there more kindness or unkindness in the world? Why? Prove it.** Begin with gathering perceptions of the state of the world. Encourage students to make a ledger with 2 columns where they listed events or examples of acts of human kindness vs. unkindness. How many and what kinds of examples are cited for each column?

Step 2-Guiding Question: **As a spectrum with good at one end and evil at the other, is human nature good or evil? Put individual responses on the spectrum to determine the extremes.** Have students provide evidence and/or examples that supports your answer.

Step 3-Debate. Select students for small groups [5–10 minutes] to discuss the following two questions.
Question 1: **Do we have a moral responsibility (duty) to help others?**
Question 2: **Should there be a *legal* responsibility to help others?** (A legal responsibility might entail a civil punishment similar to traffic infractions. The greater the negative effect of an inaction, the greater the punishment. A person could appeal, like a speeding violation. (The reason a person didn't jump into the river to help someone was because they couldn't swim.) Thanks to the television series *Seinfeld*, there was an episode based on this dilemma. The Seinfeld four were arrested for not helping another person in need. They violated a so-called "Good Samaritan Law" in fictitious Latham, Massachusetts.

Massachusetts does have a Good Samaritan law and various clauses to it. The law protects anyone acting in good faith in their attempt to help another person from any liability or lawsuit. The law protects your actions in an attempt to help another.

What can be taught & learned about **Human Goodness?**

Is the Golden Rule relevant in any discussion of a moral responsibility to others? The Golden Rule appears in almost every spiritual and religious tradition. Treat others as you yourself would want to be treated. It has been argued that the Platinum Rule is a better moral imperative for helping another. It states, treat others as *they* would want to be treated. Take the time and effort to get to know another person and their needs, preferences, etc. It is the difference between buying a gift for someone that *you think* they will like as opposed to buying a gift that you know *they would want*.

Who or what determines a moral responsibility to help others? Philosopher Immanuel Kant argued that helping others is an unconditional moral obligation, always actionable in every situation. Kant instructed that the way to obey this obligation was to use rational thinking as a third person observer to determine the ways to help others.

When it comes to determining what is morally right, this is for every individual to determine for themselves. Young people should determine, nurture, and cultivate the highest form of ethics, morals, and ideals for themselves.

Playbook Lesson Sequence 2: Plato's Allegory of the Cave and Mean World Syndrome

Lesson Objective: Explain Plato's Allegory of the Cave. Apply Plato's metaphor of the cave to the positive progress around the world.

Step 1-Guiding Questions: How might your worldview be fallible? Does love win in the world?

How well do you know the world? Are you optimistic or pessimistic about the state of the world? Are you optimistic or pessimistic about human nature? How about the future? How broken is the world in your view? Discuss as a whole class.

- Watch the beginning of the film *Love Actually* (the arrivals gate at Heathrow Airport scene).

Step 2-Watch Plato's "Allegory of the Cave" (via Ted-Ed).

- Discuss, what is the message of Plato's allegory of the Cave? What does the cave symbolize? How are our inner lives influenced by the time and place in which we live? What contributes and/or influences people's perceptions or knowledge of the world?

Step 3-Does America's individualistic culture promote selfishness?

- Watch via YouTube, Abigail Marsh: "Human nature is not fundamentally selfish"[8] April 17, 2016 UCal-Berkeley events.

Step 4-Guiding Question: Overall do you feel as though the world is getting better, worse, or staying the same? Why is progress met with denial or cynicism? If some things are getting better in the world, why do some people feel worse or worry more about the future?

- Examine the following data: https://ourworldindata.org/a-history-of-global-living-conditions-in-5-charts and also use Gapminder https://www.gapminder.org/ and use *23 charts and maps that show the world is getting much, much better these are bleak times—but a lot of things are improving.* https://www.vox.com/2014/11/24/7272929/global-poverty-health-crime-literacy-good-news
- To what extent might people be influenced by mean world syndrome?

*What can be taught & learned about **Human Goodness**?*

What is mean world syndrome? Mean world syndrome, first coined in the 1970s by Dr. George Gerbner, is a cognitive bias where the world begins appearing and feeling to be more dangerous than it actually is, due to repeated exposure to violence-related content on mass media. Thus, increased feelings of pessimism, fear, and even a hyper-vigilance of perceived threats may develop. This bias impacts people's beliefs and attitudes about the world.

What might Plato's cave represent? Why is it challenging seeing the positive possibilities of the future? The allegory of the cave appears in Book VII of Plato's *Republic*. The cave can be interpreted to symbolize many different things. The cave can represent a schema or perceptual set. Much of what we know is shaped by prior experiences, ideas, knowledge, biases, etc. Much of what we don't know remains hidden from us. Plato encourages us to see things as they actually are, habitually uncovering truth, beauty, and goodness. What we come to understand about the world comes from critical thinking and shared knowledge.

Thanks to social media, information can be done quite easily. People are bombarded with massive amounts of information. Raw and unedited footage from all parts of the world can be seen at any time. Humans have a built-in negativity bias prone to having negative information grab our attention and stick in our memories more than positive news. Humans are aversive to loss and threats to our survival. That is one of many reasons why negative information affects us more than the positive.

Another reason may be because of declinism, or the idea that humans are predisposed to view the past positively, and worry that the future is going to be bad. News generally doesn't highlight the slow, gradual positive improvements in global living standards and progress that have been witnessed over the last 200 years. Systematic misconceptions about the world continue to persist. Seeing positive progress requires reexamination and hindsight.

Repeated surveys and polls in the United States and around the world reveal that people hold a pessimistic outlook about the world and about the future of the world. The late author and researcher Hans Rosling in his book *Factfulness* noted that if he went to the zoo and hypothetically quizzed chimpanzees by throwing three different bananas with three different answers to questions about the positive progress happening in human society around the world, the chimps would outperform well-educated humans.

The chimps through the pure luck of selecting and eating a banana would score better on evaluating positive trends in human societies than humans. Rosling's experiences working with international organizations around the world has led him to lament that, "every group of people thinks the world is more frightening, more violent, and more hopeless than it really is."[9]

Does America's individualistic culture lead to a denial of social responsibility? Across many different studies and measures of individualism the United States has ranked consistently as one of the most individualistic countries. A culture that is individualistic values autonomy, self-expression, the pursuit of personal goals, and achievements rather than prioritizing the interests of the community, country, or group. In contrast, people living in collectivist countries find meaning in life through building social relationships, identifying with the group, participating in its shared way of life, and striving toward its shared goals.

Conventional wisdom suggests that individualism promotes selfishness or self-centered behavior. How can an individualistic culture lead to beliefs about responsibilities to others? Georgetown University researcher Abigail Marsh has found that greater levels of individualism were linked to *more* generosity, not less.

Research from Marsh and colleagues suggest that individualistic countries like the United States and Netherlands were more altruistic than collectivist countries like Ukraine or China. The research data from 152 countries evaluated seven different forms of altruism and generosity like donating blood, organs, or bone marrow; giving money to charities; volunteering and helping strangers; and humane treatment of animals.[10] On average, Marsh found that people in individualist countries help others in need more often as well as treat animals more humanely.

Playbook Lesson Sequence 3: Beliefs about people's personal responsibilities to others

Lesson objective: Identify and differentiate your interests from the interests of others.

Step 1-Guiding Question: **To whom or for whom is part of your universe of responsibility?**[11] Create a series of concentric circles like a solar system. At the center should be the strongest and most commitment you have to others or to nature or animals. Then add with the farthest circle from the center being a feeling of responsibility, just not as strong as those in the center.

NB-Journal reflection. What explains who or what appears in your universe of obligation? Why are some valued more than others? If you believe we have a responsibility to help others, why are some more important than others? How might your values, beliefs, and experiences explain this? What prevents everyone from being equally as important and part of a universal brotherhood/sisterhood of humanity? Do you hold all human life to be sacred and important? What about non-humans? Or the environment? Do you consider those as part of your universe of obligation?

Playbook Lesson Sequence 4: Explore the tragedy of the commons thought experiment

Lesson objective: Evaluate whether the tragedy of the commons is actually a tragedy and whether humans are equally as constructive as they are destructive.

Step 1-**Guiding question: Where is the line between individual needs and the needs of community?**

- Explain Garrett Hardin's tragedy of the commons thought experiment.
- Watch the following, a different variation of the tragedy of the commons thought experiment: https://wi-phi.com/videos/tragedy-of-the-commons/.
- Turn and talk conversation. Where does our own individual interests begin and end in relation to any commons? In a society that is deemed a dog-eat-dog world or in an economic system that encourages pursuing one's economic interests which results in an *invisible hand*, to what extent should someone sacrifice their own interests for the common good?

The Heart of Altruism

Step 2-Guiding Question: If the future is a kind of commons, what might it mean to be a good ancestor?

- Watch: "Why Humanity Destroyed Itself" (available via *The School of Life*) To what extent do you agree with the causes of the destruction and the proposed solution to avoid this destruction?
- Watch Roman Krznaric's *How to be a good ancestor?* (available via TedTalk). In the future an estimated 6.75 trillion unborn generations will inherit a world we relinquish. As their ancestors, what political, environmental, cultural, or technological responsibilities[12] do we have to them, if any?
- Research the *Alaska Permanent Fund*. What insights does it provide on how to navigate the "problem of the commons?"
- NB-Journal: What might it mean to be a good ancestor? What responsibility, if any, do we have to the estimated 6.75 trillion unborn generations?

Step 3-Guiding question: Is selfishness in your self-interest?

- Engage in a discussion of the following thought experiment: When was the last time you made a decision with the *Seventh Generation Principle* in mind? When was the last time someone you know made a decision with the *Seventh Generation Principle* in mind? Can this principle be applied to almost all our decisions? Is it practical to do so? Why or why not? The *Seventh Generation Principle* is based on the ancient Haudenosaunee (Iroquois) philosophy that the decisions we make today should result in a sustainable world seven generations into the future. It is the idea that we are connected as a community to a community.[13]
- Watch Amy Alkon's *The surprising self-interest in being kind to strangers* (available via TedTalk).
- What is the difference between selfishness and self-interest?

Step 4-NB-Journal: In the case of the commons, where do you believe your individual interests begin and end in relation to the commons (community interests and/or interests of others)? Do we have a moral responsibility to help others? To be good ancestors?

What can be taught & learned about **Human Goodness?**

What is tragic about the tragedy of the commons? In 1968, ecologist Garrett Hardin published an essay in the journal science called *The Tragedy of the Commons*. It remains one of the most cited scientific papers of all time.

It provides an oversimplified explanation for the failure of human cooperation and destructive capabilities. Hardin's views and solutions to global problems during his lifetime revealed explicit racism (non-profit Southern Poverty Law Center continues to classify him as a white nationalist and extremist).[14] Hardin advocated population control of only certain groups/ethnicities of people and discouraged aid and assistance to poorer countries for fear of overpopulation from them.

In his version of the tragedy of the commons, he asks the reader to picture a pasture that is shared by an entire village. Each day, the farmers that live near the common bring their own cattle to the common area so their own cows can graze. If each farmer is careful and limits the amounts of cows and how much the cows are able to graze on the common grass, the commons could last a lifetime.

However, if every farmer brings all their cows and allows them to graze without limit, then there won't be enough grass to sustain all herds. Thus lies the tragedy. The more selfish the farmers act, thinking only about themselves and their own herd, the less likely the commons are able to sustain everyone. By thinking about oneself without considering the needs of the many, the commons become exploited as a result.[15] Thus, Hardin wrote, *"the logic of the commons remorselessly generates tragedy . . . freedom in the commons brings ruin to all."*[16]

Interestingly, history proves that people often work together and when they do, it leads to positive outcomes. The Disaster Research Center at the University of Delaware has proven in over 700 field studies since 1963 of major catastrophes, like natural disasters, there is never anarchy, chaos, or even a mentality of every person for themselves.

Rather a cooperative mentality develops, where a sharing of resources and helping behaviors emerge to ensure collective survival.[17] Catastrophes often bring out the best in people, which often includes ensuring the welfare of others as much as oneself.[18]

Elinor Ostrom, a Nobel Prize researcher in economics, studied examples of commons (collaborative management systems of resources) around the world from cattle herders and shared pastures in Switzerland, farmland sharing in Japan, to communal irrigation in the Philippines.[19] Ostrom and her team of researchers set up a database to record examples of commons from all over the world.

Ostrom concluded that for centuries people had been sharing resources like water, forests, and fisheries successfully, not tragically. When it comes to pooling resources, human behavior can be wonderfully constructive, not tragically destructive.

What is the difference between selfishness and self-interest? Selfishness is taking care of your own needs usually *at the expense of another.* Selfishness is zero-sum. For you to win, someone has to lose. Whereas self-interest is pursuing one's personal interests, but not always at the expense of others. Your self-interest might also align with another's needs where both of you win.

Playbook Lesson Sequence 5: Introduction to the Bystander Effect

Lesson objective: Describe the bystander effect and why people may not help others who ordinarily do assist others.

Step 1-**Guiding Question: If people have a moral responsibility to help others, why don't people always help others?**

- Watch *Seinfeld* "The Good Samaritan Episode" (it was the second to last episode of the show) *Eventually someone will require assistance and the Seinfeld four will do nothing to help. They will be bystanders to a car-jacking.*
- Discuss, should Jerry, Elaine, George or Kramer have helped? What could they have done? Was it better not to? What might explain why they didn't help?
- At one point, Jerry's lawyer Jackie Chiles (famed fictitious lawyer) says, "Good Samaritan Law? I never heard of it. You don't have to help anybody. That's what this country is all about." Are the Seinfeld four, Jerry, Kramer, Elaine, and George, bad people? Did they have a moral responsibility to help? Why or why not? Or is not helping others what life is all about in the short and long run?

Step 2-Relate the fictious good samaritan law in Latham, Massachusetts to the question of whether or not people should have a legal responsibility to help others.

Step 3: Share the Good Samaritan parable from the *Bible*.
Jesus tells a story to a lawyer, who, in all other ways, is blameless and upright in God's eyes. He obeys the Ten Commandments, and loves his neighbor as himself. But he asks Jesus, "Who is my neighbor?" Jesus then explains, with the following parable, that everyone is everyone's neighbor, and that help should be offered to anyone in need of it, regardless of who or what that person is. A Jew is going along the road, and is beset by bandits, who beat him severely, strip his clothes, and rob him. They leave him for dead. Later, a priest walks by. He sees the Jew, moves to the other side of the road, and walks by without helping. Later, a Levite goes by, sees him, and gives him a wide berth, going on without helping. Later, a Samaritan (considered by Jews

to be outcasts) comes by, sees him, and immediately helps him, taking him to a nearby inn, caring for him, and paying the innkeeper.

"Which of these is the neighbor of the Jew who is beaten by robbers?" Jesus asked.

"The merciful one," replied the lawyer.

"Go and do likewise."

Step 5-NB-Journal: Students reassess their journal responses in Lesson step 1.

Step 6-Share examples from your own life or from a book or movie in which you or someone else were bystanders and another example where you chose to give help. Have students assess inaction and action collectively.

What can be taught & learned about **Human Goodness?**

What is the bystander effect? The bystander effect is a social-psychological concept, individuals are less likely to offer help in an emergency situation when other people are present. There are many intangible forces and/or variables that affect human action and inaction when it comes specifically to helping another person.

Oddly, the bystander effect is more likely to occur when there are more people present. The probability of help is inversely proportional to the number of bystanders. In other words, the greater the number of bystanders, the less likely it is that any one of them will help.

When other people act as if there isn't an emergency, it signals to other people who take cues on how to act in a given situation from others, that maybe there isn't an emergency. If everyone remains calm, and no one helps, this can influence others to do the same.

When help is needed, why do people decide not to help? The world has seen some of the greatest crimes against humanity perpetrated as millions were bystanders to these atrocities. Many people didn't partake in these atrocities. But many also didn't do anything to stop them, prevent them, or try to make things better. The bystander effect phenomenon isn't something that we automatically succumb to in every situation that requires assistance.

Like most human behavior there are environmental and social factors that play a role that influences whether we choose to help. Consciously we all make the decision to help or not. Much of this is determined by personality, past experiences, as well as the values that guide behavior. As Shakespeare famously wrote in Hamlet, "For there is nothing either good or bad, but thinking makes it so."

Playbook Lesson Sequence 6: Understanding the Bystander Effect, The Catherine "Kitty" Genovese Case

Lesson objective: Summarize and hypothesize what caused the people to be "bystanders" during the attack and murder of Kitty Genovese.

Step 1-Guiding Questions: How did **the "bystanders" explain their inaction? If people have a moral responsibility to help others, why didn't someone help Kitty Genovese?** Introduce the Kitty Genovese story. It is one of the more popular case studies of the bystander effect. The story, as documented in the New York Times in 1964,[20] appears below.

There were 38 "witnesses"—people who heard Genovese yell out *"he stabbed me, oh my god he stabbed me. Please help me. Please help me! I'm dying! I'm dying! I'm dying! I'm dying!"* Winston Moseley stabbed her one time, and after a neighbor opened his window and yelled *"let that girl alone"* he ran off.

He returned after seeing no one helping her and stabbed her again until she died. She was attacked at 3:20 am. Police received the first call at 3:50 am. It would have taken the police 2 minutes to arrive on scene. Many of the neighbors thought it was a lover's quarrel as reported in their interviews. Two people actually did call the police.

The question researchers asked was, why did Kitty Genovese die if there were 38 people available to help her? As the New York Times reported in 1964, why didn't any do anything to stop the attack and eventual murder?

- Perhaps there was ambiguity about the situation. Analyze the reasons for inaction by the 38 "witnesses." These were some of the reasons given by the "witnesses" that were reported in newspapers:
  - *"We thought it was a lover's quarrel!"*
  - *"Frankly, we were afraid."*
  - *"I tried to call, I really tried, but I was gasping for air and was unable to talk into the telephone."*
  - *"We went to the window to see what was happening, but the light from our bedroom made it difficult to see the street."*
  - *"I didn't want to get involved."*
  - *"I told [my husband] there must have been 30 calls already."*
  - *"So many, many other times in the night, I heard screaming."*
  - *"I was tired, I went back to bed."*
- Discuss and list options of what people could have done to help Kitty Genovese.

Step 2-Guiding Question: Based on the witness responses, what variables or other psychological decision-making conditions are present that prevented people from helping?

Analyze the witness responses to determine if some, none, or all of the following are present. Bibb Latane and John Darley first conducted research on the bystander effect in 1968. Much of their research has shed light on factors that influence people to inaction in cases of emergency.

Imagine a small child falling into the deep end of a public Olympic sized swimming pool with multiple lifeguards and over hundreds of people inside and outside of the pool. In this situation you notice a child around 3 years of age walking on the edge of the pool near the deep end. They accidentally slip and fall into the water. You observe this and see that the child is treading water but ultimately keeps dropping below the surface. Each of the following thought processes or steps in thinking happens pretty quickly.

This quick decision making determines whether someone often helps or not. There isn't a slow cost-benefit analysis taking place. Below is a list of decision-making processes and factors.

Notice the emergency. You have to be attentive first to the need in order to determine whether to act. Research has shown that feeling rushed can influence both your willingness to help and whether you actually notice the need of others.

Ambiguity: "Is this really an emergency"—this is the first question people ask. Can people clearly interpret this to be an emergency. If not, what do people do?

Pluralistic Ignorance: "No one else is doing anything; I guess there's no problem." Typically, people will take their cues from others. People might begin to look around at other people. Do they look concerned? Are they calm? Perhaps people glance at the lifeguards. People scan for the child's parents to see if anyone is running to the pool nervously. People conclude that if no one is acting like the child is in danger, maybe the child isn't in danger.

Fear of Looking Foolish: "I don't want to look stupid." No one wants to be that person that goes diving into the pool only for the child to scream with fear that you are grabbing them and bringing them out of the pool. The parents run over as do others. You now have to explain with considerable embarrassment why you went rushing into the pool when in fact there was no need to do so. Tied to this is a fear of retaliation. Bystanders may feel less inclined to help if they assume that others will react negatively, lose the respect of others, or endure physical harm. We wrongly assume the beliefs and actions of others. This discourages us from helping.

Diffusion of Responsibility: "Someone else will handle it." Typically, if a person still has not helped, they will rectify any guilt or concern by telling themselves that this is someone else's responsibility. They might say to themselves "that is what lifeguards are for or the parents should be watching out for their child." If it is no one's responsibility then it is not my responsibility either.

High Intervention Costs: "It's dangerous; rather be safe." If a person's intervention into a situation requires a certain degree of cost, for example, they may not be the best swimmer, this will deter people from helping. One can't help because they are not equipped with the skills to help.

Conformity and Obedience: "I just do what I'm told to do; If no one tells me to do anything then I won't do it." When you train for CPR, and if you have ever performed CPR, you need help. You don't just yell out "please, someone help me." People will be reticent about getting involved and many will back out of the circle that enjoins you. That is why you must point to people, ask them for their name (personalize your connection) and direct them as how best to help. For example, "Karen, please hold this person's head. Andrew, call 911." Unfortunately, because people take their cues from others, people need to be told what to do when it comes to helping and/or told how they can help.

Step 3-Watch: "*Remembering Kitty*" The New York Times https://www.nytimes.com/2016/04/11/us/remembering-kitty-genovese.html

What can be taught & learned about **Human Goodness**?

Were there really 38 bystanders to Kitty Genovese's murder and were *all* of Ms. Genovese's neighbors indifferent? Recent research has revisited the facts of the Kitty Genovese case. The *New York Times* revisited the reporting of the facts of the case and has shed new light on the tragic death of Genovese. Not all 38 people directly witnessed the attack. Not all 38 people stood by and watched the attacks unfold. It is not accurate to state that no one called the police.

Someone did in fact call the police. Did others hear an attack? Yes. Did what they actually heard reveal what was taking place? This isn't so clear cut. They hear something. It was winter in New York City and people did have their windows closed. In fact, many people didn't wake up. Ms. Genovese's neighbors weren't evil, apathetic, or indifferent. They acted as many people do who are confused, afraid, and coerced by ambiguity.

As former assistant district attorney Charles Skoller noted, "I don't think 38 people witnessed it," "I don't know where that came from, the 38. I didn't count 38. We only found half a dozen that saw what was going on, that we could use."[21]

One of the people who called the police was Ms. Genovese's friend Karl Ross. He first called Ms. Genovese's neighbor Sophia Farrar. Mr. Ross was reticent about calling the police at first (he was the witness who said he "didn't want to get involved." He had been drunk that night and was fearful of any publicity. As a gay man living in a time period where homosexuality was illegal in 1963, he was fearful of any publicity.

Police documents confirm that Sophia Farrar and her husband both jumped out of bed upon the phone call. Mrs. Farrar found Ms. Genovese lying and bleeding. She lay with Ms. Genovese holding her while attempting to comfort her by telling her that help was on the way and instructing a neighbor to call the police.[22] Ms. Genovese's partner Mary Ann Zielonko identified her body upon her death.[23]

Playbook Lesson Sequence 7: Understanding the Bystander Effect

Lesson objective: Summarize and explain the various social-psychological factors and intangible forces which may contribute to the bystander effect.

Step 1-Guiding Question: **Why does the bystander effect occur?** Introduce the following additional psychological factors/aspects which can also paralyze people into action. With education, the more you understand the variables that induce becoming a bystander, the less likely you are to succumb to these social-psychological forces. At the very least, people can decide for themselves what the right thing to do might be for them. Whether people have the courage to act is difficult to determine.

- Assign the following activity. Read through each of the different social psychology concepts and have students reflect on a time in their life where they became a bystander because of one or all of these forces. Definitions are provided below.
- If they can't think of time for themselves, see if they can remember a time where someone they know actually was a bystander because of the psychological forces. If that isn't applicable, have them refer to a piece of literature they have read or a movie that they have recently watched. Next, ask students to remedy inaction. Now knowing what you know about the bystander effect, if you could go back in time, what would you do differently? Meaning how would you overcome the bystander effect? Explain.

Sympathetic paralysis-the problem faced appears so enormous, a person can suffer paralysis of action from an over-analysis of not knowing where to begin. Our brains become averse to feeling overwhelmed and helplessness. The empathy parts of our brain, our ability to put ourselves in the shoes of another which can motivate us to help others, is deactivated before we become crippled with the suffering of so many. Because the need is so large it becomes depersonalized. This can influence inaction.

Cognitive dissonance-This is the tension or psychological stress that occurs when one's actions don't align with one's morals. When a person behaves inconsistently with the way they believe they ought to be acting, one can experience psychological tension. In order for one's brain to alleviate this tension, a person will justify their inconsistency to themselves in order to alleviate this tension (perhaps guilt).

People will quickly adjust their values to fit their behavior, even when it is immoral. They will change the way they explain a situation to themselves. For example, those stealing from their employer will claim that "everyone does it." Or alternatively that "I'm underpaid so I deserve a little extra on the side." People resolve dissonance through rationalizations. Being aware of this can help avoid one of the most dangerous consequences of cognitive dissonance: believing our own lies and justifying our inaction to those in need of help.

Social Proof Error-this psychological error causes inaction because when faced with ambiguity and uncertainty we need proof of what we should do. We falsely believe that other people's actions or inaction in a situation are probably more correct. Faced with uncertainty, people often mistakenly believe that other people know better.

Thus, people's decision to be inactive is determined to be the correct course of action. Social proof is a kind of conformity. Large groups of people can influence us to conform to mistaken or correct group choices. What the group signals by their inaction or actions ignoring the need, often influences us. If we follow the herd, it is one way for us to avoid being embarrassed.

Characteristics of the victim-research has shown that people are more likely to help those they perceive to be similar and deserving of their help. It is the dark side of empathy. We tend to be more empathetic and helpful to those that are like us or appear not entirely responsible for the emergency situation.

This type of thinking falls into the us vs. them mentality. This includes people who are similar to us racially and ethnically. Stereotyping others leads to bias and inaccurate judgements where we inaccurately categorize another person as part of an out-group. This then can influence us not to help. This relates to the just-world phenomenon (or cognitive bias that people use to rationalize their behavior). It is the idea that the world is just and people get what they deserve. People blame the victim to rationalize their inaction.

Pluralistic Ignorance-Pluralistic ignorance is a systematic error in our estimation of the beliefs of other people. When everyone in a group is uncertain and looking for information on what the right thing to do might be, this can result in a pluralistic ignorance. We guess at the group members' beliefs and norms based upon our observations, and our guess is wrong. The more people that are observed as bystanders confirms to us that inaction is the right course of action. This can inhibit our willingness to act. All people wrongly assume what others believe about a situation.

Obedience and conformity-Humans tend to be herd animals. We follow the group. We defer to authority figures who demonstrate superior knowledge and power in certain situations. This holds true when responsibility is assumed by someone in a position of dominance or authority. This deference to authority has led to disastrous effects. This has been evident in the Holocaust, the Rwandan genocide, and in the genocide in Darfur, Sudan.

Step 2-Guiding Question: **What experiments illustrate the psychological elements of the bystander effect?** Present the following research experiments and ask students why people behave the way they do in each of the experiments.

Research study 1: The Asch Effect. https://www.youtube.com/watch?v=NyDDyT1lDhA&t=34s Solomon Asch in the 1950s conducted experiments assessing the pressure of conformity. In one study, he showed a group of individuals images of three printed line segments of different lengths. They were then shown a fourth line and were asked to determine if that line matched one of the three original lines shown.

In each group of individuals, all but one was confederates (that is they had knowledge of the experiment and who were instructed to think and behave in ways to test the behavior of the one individual who was the subject). There is one line that is obviously the match. There is no ambiguity.

However, the confederates all pointed to the wrong line match and expressed certainty and agreement. The question The Asch effect illustrates is how the group can influence the judgment of the individual. People deny *unambiguous* information from their own senses just to conform with others.

Research study 2: Diffusion of Responsibility. https://www.youtube.com/watch?v=KE5YwN4NW5o "Smoke Filled Room Study." Bibb Latane and John Darley illustrated the bystander effect over many decades of research. In a number of experiments, they tested whether people would succumb to diffusion of responsibility, being misled by the reactions of others. In this case the inaction of others was misleading. In one experiment subjects were asked to fill out a questionnaire in a waiting room. Smoke began to pour into the room under the door.

In one variation of the experiment the subject was alone. In another variation of the experiment there were two other people (confederates) in the room who were instructed to purposely notice but ignore the smoke. As more smoke poured into the room, they continued to fill out the questionnaire without making any movements or indicating that they were concerned about the smoke.

75 percent of subjects in the room by themselves calmly noticed the smoke and left the room. But only 10 percent of the subjects with the confederates left the room. Most subjects who remained in the room later justified their inaction by stating that they believed the smoke was not dangerous. None of them, however, identified the presence of others in the room as a reason for their inaction.

In another similar experiment subjects either waited alone, with a friend, with a passive confederate, or with a stranger in a room. The room was separated from another room by a curtain. While remaining in the waiting room subjects would hear a tape-recorded message (unknown to them that it was a recording) of someone falling and becoming audibly hurt. Would people leave the waiting room and attempt to offer help of any kind to the hurt individual in the next room?

Overall, 61 percent pulled back the curtain to check on the experimenter. 14 percent entered via another door, and 24 percent simply called out.[24] Nobody went to report the accident. 70 percent of alone subjects reacted, but only 7 percent of those with passive confederates reacted.[25]

Latane and Darley concluded that a "confusion of responsibility" took place. In post-experiment interviews, the subjects who attempted to offer some help claimed they acted because the fall seemed serious and it was "the right thing to do."[26] The subjects who did not make any attempt to help claimed they were unsure what happened. Or they determined the accident probably wasn't serious. People felt they weren't highly influenced by others.

Research study 3: Feeling rushed. John Darley joined with psychologist Daniel Batson in a classic experiment to assess the variable of hurriedness on helping versus non-helping behavior. Watch a summation here by Bo Bennett "The Good Samaritan" (available via YouTube). In addition they were also curious about whether the number of people would affect an individual's inclination to help.

Batson and Darley investigated whether personality disposition would ultimately be trumped by other factors like feeling rushed.[27] They recruited seminary school students to participate in their experiment. They asked participants to complete personality questionnaires about their religion and religious beliefs.

One group of subjects were told to prepare a talk about the Good Samaritan parable in the Bible while another group was told to give a talk about seminary occupations. They would be told to begin this process in one building. Then they would be told to continue their preparation in another building.

After participants arrived at the second building, they were told they had to give their talk and then answer a helping behavior questionnaire. While moving from one building to another, they would encounter a "victim" sitting slumped over in an alleyway who would audibly moan and cough a couple of times. The exact condition of the "victim" would be unknown.

Batson and Darley varied the degree of urgency or hurriedness. Before being sent to the other building, one group of subjects would be told they were already late to the other building to complete their task and another group of subjects were told they had some time but they should probably leave for the other building. Darley and Batson set up a scale of helping behavior:[28]

0=failed to notice victim as in need
1=perceived need but did not offer aid
2=did not stop but helped indirectly (told the aide on their arrival)
3=stopped and asked if victim needed help
4=after stopping, insisted on taking victim inside and then left him
5=refused to leave victim, or insisted on taking him somewhere

Feeling rushed did affect helping behavior. We can be subtly influenced by situational factors like time pressure. The results seem to suggest that being cognizant of pro-social norms and ethics does not mean that an individual will act on them.

Batson and Darley also found that there was no correlation between "religious types" and helping behavior. Overall, 40 percent offered some help to the victim. In low hurry situations, 63 percent helped, medium hurry 45 percent and high hurry 10 percent.[29]

In some cases, some participants literally stepped over the victim. This doesn't suggest that these individuals were bad people. Many of them in their post-experiment questionnaire reported feeling stressed, anxious, and in conflict about not helping the slumped man.

Research study 4: The Milgram Experiment. In 1963, Yale University psychologist Stanley Milgram, conducted the famous study of obedience to authority and conformity. At the Nuremberg Trials, one Nazi officer after another who was called to answer for Crimes Against Humanity. They all posited the same defense. All Nazis noted they "were just following orders." They claimed they were doing what they were told to do.

Milgram wondered whether the attitudes and mindset of ordinary Germans who obeyed authority held personality traits that were unique to Germany at the time that "Final Solution to the Jewish Problem" was implemented by Hitler. Milgram wanted to test whether other people in other parts of the world in a different time shared a tendency to obey authority figures even when this obedience contradicted their own better judgments.

All the participants were white males, ages 20–50 in New Haven, Connecticut in 1963. They were paid $4.00 to participate which is the equivalent of $35 today. People responded to a newspaper advertisement and voluntarily agreed to participate. Milgram recruited subjects for his experiments from various walks in life. Respondents were told the experiment would study the effects of punishment on learning ability.

All respondents ended up playing the role of teacher in the experiment. The learner was an actor working as a confederate (he was in on the experiment and told to behave in certain ways as directed by the experimenter.) The "teachers" were asked to administer increasingly severe electric shocks to the "learner" when questions were answered incorrectly. The teacher got to meet the student, Mr. Wallace, before the experiment began. The teachers were given a sample shock of 45 volts to get a sense of the voltage. In reality, no shocks were actually given to the student. However, the teacher did not know this.

In front of teachers was a switch board with shock levels that were labeled from 15 to 450 volts. Besides the numerical scale, verbal cues were added above the shock administering levers. Beginning from the lower end, jolt levels were labeled: "slight shock," "moderate shock," "strong shock," "very strong shock," "intense shock," and "extreme intensity shock."

The next two levers were "Danger: Severe Shock," and, past that, a simple "XXX." (It was like having a skull and cross-bones picture over the switch with an informal message of under no circumstances should you hit this switch.) In response to the supposed shocks, the "learner" (actor) would begin to grunt at 75 volts; complain at 120 volts; ask to be released at 150 volts; plead with increasing vigor, next; and let out agonized screams at 285 volts.

Eventually, in desperation, the learner was to yell loudly (things like "get me out of here, you can't keep me here" as well as "I absolutely refuse to answer, I can't stand the pain.") and audibly complain that their chest was bothering them. Finally, at 330 volts Mr. Wallace would be totally silent as if he went unconscious or worse. Teachers were instructed to treat silence as an incorrect answer and continue with the experiment applying the next shock level to the student as a sign of a wrong answer.

If at any point the innocent teacher hesitated to inflict the shocks, the experimenter would assert authoritatively "ordering" the teacher to proceed. Such verbal commands would take the form of statements like, "The experiment requires that you continue."

Many questions arise from this experiment. At what point would teachers disobey the dictates of the experiment and the authority figure in the room with the white lab coat? At what point would these people stop participating in a process that was inflicting pain on another human being? How long would it take for them to interject their own moral misgivings about hurting another human being and refuse to comply? Why couldn't people just get up and walk out of the lab?

Milgram asked his fellow Yale University psychology colleagues to hypothesize the percentage of people they thought would disobey their own judgment, obey authority and potentially continue to deliver lethal shocks up to the 450 volts. They answered less than 1 percent.

What percentage of teachers, if any, do you think went up to the maximum voltage of 450?[30] In fact, in this version of the experiment, 66 percent of people went to the end. Good news, 34 percent of people stopped at some point. What do you think increased and decreased compliance with the perception of authority?

Step 3-Guiding Question: What about those forces for good that lead to positive outcomes?

- One variation of the experiment that reduced compliance down to only 10 percent—that is 90 percent of people stopped when Milgram instructed one person to refuse to comply while saying something like, "No, I'm not doing this anymore. It's wrong" and walked out. This influenced people who were also in the room doing the same experiment to stop 90 percent of the time. Perhaps the lesson is that one voice can make a difference. The fact is that in all variations, a majority of the subjects actually refused to obey.
- Watch Derek Sivers *How to Start a Movement* (available via TedTalk). What are those factors that influence an individual to offer help to another person? Does seeing someone help another motivate another to do the same? Derek Sivers has an interesting take on leadership. He believes leadership is often over-glorified. Why might it be equally important to being the first follower?

Step 4-NB/Journal: Identify and explain ways to overcome the bystander effect. Reassess your thinking: Do humans have a moral responsibility to help others? Should we have a legal responsibility to help?

What can be taught & learned about **Human Goodness**?

What is the point of learning about the bystander effect? The point of this information is two-fold: The more you know about the causes of the bystander effect the LESS likely you are to succumb to it yourself. Reconsider thinking "I don't know what I would do in that situation" but rather "I know what I SHOULD do in that situation, but I don't know if I will have the courage to do it." This is not about instructing or telling others about what the right thing to do is.

What is an inverse bystander effect? Recent research on the bystander effect reveals some positive news. More often than not, people intervene to offer help to others. In fact, in cases of dangerous situations, with more people present, the more likely individuals will intervene.[31] People are more inclined to help than previously thought. The more unusual and less mundane a helping situation appears, the more likely it appears that an individual will offer help.[32]

What can one person do? As the Milgram Experiment instructs, compliance was reduced down to only 10 percent—that is 90 percent of people stopped—when 1 person stood up and said something like "No, I'm not doing this anymore. It's wrong" and walked out. This influenced other people to stop 90 percent of the time.

Psychologist and Holocaust survivor Ervin Staub has researched helping behavior most of his life. After years of research about rescuers during a genocide, Staub has concluded that: "Heroes evolve; they aren't born."[33]

He conducted a study where a participant and a confederate were placed in a room to complete a joint task. Upon working, they would hear a noise and sounds of anguish. The confederate was instructed to dismiss the sounds with some verbal justification for inaction. When this occurred, only 25 percent of the participants went into the next room to try to help.[34]

However, when the confederate said, "That sounds bad. Maybe we should do something," 66 percent of the participants took action.[35] And even more interesting, 100 percent of participants followed the confederate when the confederate suggested that they should go into the next room to check out the "accident" that had occurred.

In another study, Staub found that young children ages 5 through 7 when placed together instead of being alone, worked together to respond to sounds of distress. They actually voiced their concerns with each other and worked together to offer help. This differs from adult subjects in Latane and Darley who internalized their confusion and conflict. As researchers Keltner and Marsh noted, "These findings suggest the positive influence we can exert as bystanders. Just as passive bystanders reinforce a sense that nothing is wrong in a situation, the active bystander can, in fact, get people to focus on a problem and motivate them to take action."[36]

Why might conclusions from the Milgram experiment be misleading? Holocaust survivor and Nobel Peace Prize winner Elie Wiesel reminds us, *"We must take sides. Neutrality helps the oppressor, never the victim. Silence encourages the tormentor, never the tormented. Sometimes we must interfere. When human lives are endangered, when human dignity is in jeopardy, national borders and sensitivities become irrelevant. Wherever men and women are persecuted because of their race, religion, or political views, that place must - at that moment - become the center of the universe."*[37]

Here are some caveats about the Milgram study and the conclusions about human behavior. What Milgram counted as "obedience" was misleading. Recordings of the experiments reveal subjects who repeatedly refused to comply, but reluctantly continued when the researcher insisted. Some protested as many as 24 times before continuing. To Milgram however, as long as they continued with the experiment and gave shocks, they were "blindly obedient."

Recent criticisms of the Milgram Experiment and its findings reveal that not everyone was obedient as Milgram portrayed. According to recently published books and articles that analyzed Milligram's transcripts and audio recordings people did overwhelming disobey authority figures. In his unpublished notes, Milgram recruited pairs of people that knew each other. He had them assume the roles of the teacher and student. In this version of the experiment, disobedience increased to 85 percent.[38]

In addition, many participants were skeptical about the validity of the experiment itself. To what extent did the participants really believe that they were hurting another person? Author Gina Perry who investigated Milgram's conclusions found that only 50 percent of people believed the experiment was real and of those, 66 percent disobeyed the experimenter.[39] When Milgram debriefed the other participants in the study, many of them were ashamed of what they had done. Many felt bad.

Others, however, attempted to justify their actions by devaluing the victims. Some claimed that they would not have shocked them if the students had been smarter or if they had answered more questions correctly.[40] This is often referred to The Just World Phenomenon: the idea that the world is just and people get what they deserve. People rationalize and justify injustice by blaming the victim.

For some, during the Milgram experiment, the reason why people went to the end of the board was somehow caused by the perceived deficient characteristics of the victim. Many participants, just like the Nazi officer's defense at Nuremberg, claimed that they were just following orders—that someone else was responsible for what they have done. There is a tendency to create out-group/in-group biases which manifest as what psychologists call the fundamental-attribution error. A tendency to assume that others are an out-group who behave a certain way based on inherent characteristics, personalities, or flaws.[41]

Playbook Lesson Sequence 8: Assess understandings of the bystander effect

Step 1: Watch the ESPN Film: "*Catching Hell*," the Steve Bartman story (Chicago Cubs Fans).

- Explain the bystander effect in this case. List and explain 2 reasons why no one came to the assistance of Steve Bartman either before, during, or after stadium security came to his assistance. List and explain 2 aspects of the bystander effect, information from the events as they unfolded as portrayed in the documentary, and your own knowledge of the bystander effect. What if anything could people have done to help Steve Bartman?
- Follow up discussion: What is justice for Steve Bartman? Read the following article and discuss. *For Cubs and Steve Bartman, Anger Still Appears to Be in Play* by Filip Bondy, August 2017, *New York Times*

Precept #12: Heroism is always accessible and able to be chosen. We are all heroes in waiting.

TEACHING WHAT MATTERS PLAYBOOK: TOOLS FOR EXPLORING THE ART OF LIVING

Playbook Lesson Sequence 1: Introduction to heroism.

Lesson objectives: Develop a fluid hypothesis which explains the motivation and inclination for people to help another. Identify the roots of moral courage.

Step 1-Introduce heroism.

- Ask students to develop a fluid hypothesis to the following: *What motivates people to help another? What are the roots of moral courage? What makes someone heroic?* (As students discover other pertinent information throughout the duration of the unit, they will add or change elements of their hypothesis. It should be supported with evidence and reasoned conclusions.)

Step 2-Ask students: Who are your role models or heroes? Why? What are the characteristics or qualities that make them effective leaders or role models? List qualities on the board collectively.

Step 3-Students investigate heroes using the following sources below or they can research their own. (They should select no less than 3 individuals). See the following as possible resources.

- *Heroes for My Son* by Brad Meltzer
- Robert Shetterly's "Americans Who Tell The Truth" https://www.americanswhotellthetruth.org/portrait-galleries
- Carnegie Heroes: http://www.carnegiehero.org/awardees/profiles/

- CNN Heroes: https://www.cnn.com/2017/11/02/world/top-10-cnn-heroes-2017/index.html
- Everyday heroes: http://www.dailygood.org/cat/everydayheroes/ (Really excellent stories from around the world.)

Step 4-NB-Journal: Identify and explain, using specific information: What motivates people to perform any act of heroism? What goes through their brains? Can it be quantified? Can it be taught and cultivated? Is heroism that simple?

What can be taught & learned about **Human Goodness?**

What is heroism? The Heroic Imagination Project (HIP), a non-profit organization that focuses on teaching people to become heroes in their everyday lives founded by Philip Zimbardo, defines heroism as taking a personal risk for the common good while others remain passive. HIP identifies the following key elements of heroism:

- It's voluntary and intentional
- It's done in the service of people or communities in need
- It involves some type of personal cost or risk, either physical, social, or in terms of quality of life
- It's done without the need for recompense or gain

What constitutes heroism? Psychologist Frank Farley makes a distinction between what he calls big H heroism and small h heroism. Big H heroism involves a potentially big risk such as getting hurt, going to jail, or even death. Small h heroism, on the other hand, involves things many of us do every day; helping someone out, being kind, and standing up for justice. These things don't typically involve personal risk on our part.

Heroism is different than altruism. Heroes save lives but they also fight for an idea or commitment to principles. Research by Barbara Fredrickson and C. Daryl Cameron asked 313 participants in a survey whether the they had helped during the previous week. 85 percent said that they had done things like listening to a friends' problems, babysitting, donating to charity, or volunteering.[42]

What causes heroic action? Heroic action involves a combination of situational factors and personal characteristics like self-assurance, strength of character, and confidence to act in accordance with one's own morals. Psychological courage is paramount. As Zimbardo's research[43] reveals you can cultivate heroic action and hone your internal moral compasses. As author Elizabeth Svoboda noted in her book *What Makes a Hero,* "We have ample opportunity to *choose* altruism or heroism . . . This is true not just in high-stakes, split-second situations, but over the entire course of our lives."[44]

Playbook Lesson Sequence 2: Introduction to recognized altruism

Lesson Objective: Identify the motivations of various individuals who are recognized altruists.

Step 1-Guiding Question: What is indicative **of altruistic actions?** Introduce and define altruism.

- A simplified definition of altruism is an unselfish motivation to provide for the welfare of another, to promote someone else's well-being, even at a risk or cost to the person helping. An altruistic action can be done for a stranger or someone who has a personal connection to the helper. Altruism has many different definitions depending on the academic discipline.
- What constitutes an altruistic act? Brainstorm a list of possible actions. For example, a solider diving on a hand grenade to save the lives of his fellow soldiers; a fireman rushing into a burning building to rescue someone; a bee stinging and dying in order to protect the hive; penguins huddled together moving concentrically to keep warm.

Step 2-Guiding Question: What motivates people to act heroically? Analyze and hypothesize the motivations of three Carnegie Heroes. Add to any working hypothesis what motivates people to act heroically.

- Listen to Radiolab's *I need a hero* (available from The Good Show, December 14, 2010 https://www.wnycstudios.org/podcasts/radiolab/episodes/103951-the-good-show)
- Identify or explain the motivations of the three individuals featured
  ○ Lora Shrake
  ○ William Pennell
  ○ Wesley Autrey

Step 3-NB-Journal: Add to your working hypothesis: What distinguishes bystanders from Shrake, Autrey, and Pennell? What explains why these people acted the way that they did? Describe at least 2 psychological factors which may have contributed to the heroic act of helping behavior. Briefly describe the circumstances of the heroic act. Discuss possible reasons why the hero helped. Why did the hero assume responsibility for helping? What were the costs and benefits of helping for the hero?

What can be taught & learned about **Human Goodness**?

What is the Carnegie hero? Carnegie Commission's definition of a hero is a civilian who knowingly risks one's own life to an extraordinary degree while saving or attempting to save the life of another person.

What motivates heroic action? In research conducted by Samuel Oliner on Carnegie Heroes, he identified the following motivation factors[45] of heroes:

- Normocentrism-those moral values and norms learned from parents and the wider community.
- Social Responsibility, Empathy, Efficacy-helping comes from as ensue that one has the ability to accomplish the mission, to do the thing to affect an improvement in things.
- Impulse-an instinctive reaction to other people's troubles.
- Religious beliefs and Reciprocity-someone helps because one expects someone might help them in the future.
- Principled Motivation-an internalized universal moral belief in justice and fairness.
- Self-esteem-sensation-seeking-people are more likely to be risk takers.
- Having something in common with all humanity.

Playbook Lesson Sequence 3: The life and actions of Malala Yousafzai or Sully Sullenberger

Lesson objective: Appraise the heroism of Malala or Sully Sullenberger. To what extent are they heroes?

Step 1-Watch and analyze *He Named Me Malala*. What characteristics of heroism are evident? To what extent is Malala a hero? Why or why not? What is the lesson or message of Malala's story?

- Read facts about Malala Yousafzai https://www.nobelprize.org/prizes/peace/2014/yousafzai/facts/
- Or read about Sully Sullenberger https://www.forbes.com/sites/jimclash/2019/11/13/exclusive-interview-capt-sully-sullenberger-a-decade-after-his-heroic-hudson-river-landing/#7eaa51235ae8

Step 2-NB-Journal: Add to your working hypothesis: What distinguishes bystanders from Malala's heroism? What did Malala or Mr. Sullenberger do that makes them heroic? What were the circumstances? What explains why they acted the way that they did? What explains why they took responsibility for helping others? Were there costs and benefits of helping? To what extent were Malala's or Mr. Sullenberger's actions altruistic?

Playbook Lesson Sequence 4: Introduction to recognized altruism-rescuers during the Holocaust

Lesson objective: Identify the motivations and actions of various individuals who are recognized altruists.

Step 1-Analyze and hypothesize the motivations and methods of rescuers during the Holocaust. Analyze the statistics of The Righteous Among the Nations provided by Yad Vashem. (available via https://www.yadvashem.org/righteous/statistics.html).

Step 2-Guiding Question: Who was Sir Nicholas Winton and how did he help save Jewish lives during the Holocaust? Analyze story of Sir Nicholas Winton. Watch the following:

- *He saved 669 children from the Holocaust - now watch the audience when his secret is revealed* (available via YouTube).
- The Story of Sir Nicholas Winton and *60 Minutes* story (available via YouTube).
- Discuss as a whole class. Do you consider Winton an altruist? Why or why not?

Step 3-Guiding Question: What might explain the actions of rescuers during the Holocaust? Use the following resources to investigate rescuers during the Holocaust. Use the following questions to help guide your thinking.

- What insights do these stories reveal on the causes of altruism?
- What characteristics, attributes, and beliefs distinguish rescuers from bystanders?[46]
- Why did people risk their lives for strangers?
- What drove their moral courage?
- Featured Stories from Yad Vashem: (https://www.yadvashem.org/righteous/stories.html)
- About the Righteous (Yad Vashem): (https://www.yadvashem.org/righteous/about-the-righteous.html)
- Read short selections in chapter 8, *Facing History and Ourselves (Resource Book)* and/or extension lesson ideas.[47] (https://www.facinghistory.org/)

- Optional Read: chapter 1, "A Still Small Voice" *Conscience and Courage: Rescuers of Jews During the Holocaust* by Eva Fogelman.

Step 4-NB-Journal: Add to your working hypothesis: What distinguishes bystanders from rescuers and helpers of Jews during the Holocaust? What explains why these people acted the way that they did?

*What can be taught & learned about **Human Goodness**?*

What does Yad Vashem reveal about rescuers during the Holocaust? Yad Vashem, The World Holocaust Remembrance Center, was created in part to honor and express the gratitude of the State of Israel and Jewish people to The Righteous Among the Nations, who saved the lives of Jews during the Holocaust. Yad Vashem is the world's preeminent Holocaust museum, research institution, memorial, and archive. Yad Vashem researches and authenticates stories of rescuers and if validated, a tree is planted with a memorial plaque to honor heroic actions.

Yad Vashem in Israel has officially recognized the names and numbers of Righteous Among the Nations as of January 1, 2019 at 27,362. This reflects both those known and unknown. It does not reflect the full extent of help given by non-Jews to Jews. The actions of rescuers not only took many different forms, the rescuers themselves also came from many different nations, religions, and socio-economic backgrounds. Their motivations were varied and nuanced. However, all rescuers worked to save lives during a time of malevolence and indifference to the plight of European Jews.

Sir Nicholas Winton is an example. He worked and supervised the rescue of almost 700 Jewish children out of Europe. He arranged for their passage and homes for these children once arriving in the United Kingdom.

What is an "altruistic personality?" In Kristen Renwick Monroe's *The Heart of Altruism*, she adopted a stringent definition of altruism.[48]

1. Altruism must entail action.
2. The action must be goal-directed.
3. The goal of the act must be to further the welfare of another as a primary outcome not as an intended consequence.
4. Intentions count more than consequences. Try to do something good for someone else.
5. The act must carry some possibility of diminishment in one's own welfare. They can't also benefit for their action.
6. The purpose is to further the welfare of another purpose or group, without anticipation of reward for the altruist.

Renwick Monroe's research focuses on the motivations of heroic altruism. She found that these heroes maintain an "altruistic perspective" that is central to their identity. This worldview involves a belief in a common humanity, that all people are linked together. There are no strangers, only fellow human beings.[49]

What do the actions of the villagers of Le Chambon reveal about heroism and altruism? The villagers of Le Chambon, a village in southern France, collectively saved about 5,000 people, 3,500 of which were Jewish. When interviewed rescuers all have some things in common. They all had a sense that they did what was required and the villagers had a belief in the brotherhood of humanity, that all humanity is interconnected. The villagers had a concern that extended universally to include everyone, not just family or friends.[50]

Researchers Samuel and Pearl Oliner revealed that for rescuers of Jews during the Holocaust, 59 percent of rescuers had Jewish friends before the war, whereas only 25 percent of bystanders did. Their research also revealed that the personality dispositions of people who were most likely to risk their lives to save Jews were morally principled, strong willed, had been raised to be compassionate, and readily think for themselves.[51]

What were the characteristics of rescuers during the Holocaust? Psychologist Eva Fogelman researched rescuers based on her work as a therapist with Holocaust survivors and rescuers. In her book *Conscious and Courage: Rescuers of Jews During the Holocaust,* she examined the motivations of rescuers. Some of the factors that she focused on was the childhood of the rescuers. What forces from their past and their upbringing may have influenced them?

Fogelman discovered that the seeds of altruism were planted during the youth of rescuers. Most rescuers came from loving and compassionate families.[52] Their parents modeled pro-social behavior and raised them with a firm conviction in morality. They parented them with explanatory style as opposed to authoritatively. Meaning the parents explained the reasons for their decisions with them as children rather than imposing decisions on them. Instead of being punished, they were given explanations as to how their behavior impacted others.

The parents of rescuers also taught them to morally reason. It was apparent that many were being trained in cultivating cognitive empathy. This may have developed in rescuers a strong commitment to moral principles and how to be cognizant of others. Rescuers didn't become seduced by the immense anti-Semitic propaganda. When rescuers witnessed the murder, brutality, and suffering of Jews either firsthand or through other experiences, it awoke their empathy. As a result of their empathic concern, they recognized a shared humanity with Jews and identified with their suffering.

The pattern of rescuing was the same. Some rescuers actively sought out ways to help Jews. Others however, were presented with different opportunities, like a knock on their door deciding in that moment whether to help or not. Rescuers' quick decision making, the cost-benefit analysis didn't entail "how is this going to benefit me?" Instantly they chose to help thinking only of the welfare of another. Fogelman also identified a spectrum of characteristics shared by rescuers.[53]

While not all rescuers fit into all of these characterizations, many shared the following characteristics.

- Moralists or moralist rescuers had an innate sense of right and wrong and a strong humanitarian conscience which manifested in their day-to-day actions. Some gained this morality from religion, while others had an innate empathic intelligence which led to compassionate action.
- Judeophiles were rescuers according to Fogelman who had a personal relationship with Jews that motivated them because of their strong attachment to individual Jews in their lives or felt a closeness to the Jewish people as a whole.
- Concerned professionals were people were already doing assistance jobs, like doctors, teachers, or nurses. They simply expanded the requirements of their jobs to extend help to Jews, usually in defiance of government.
- Networks were people bound together in the same ideal fueled by anti-Nazism working and supporting others in trying to defy the Nazi regime. Lastly, child rescuers were those people as children who helped rescue Jews because their parents involved them in rescue work.

Playbook Lesson Sequence 8: Introduction to altruism: Collective action in response to tragedy

Lesson objective: Identify the motivations and actions of various collaborative actions.

Step 1-Watch and analyze the film *The Martian*.

- The following can be a discussion guide. At the end of the film, students can type a response to the film using the following questions.
- Who helps? Why? Is the motivation selfish or altruistic (meaning did people want Watney to survive for selfish or altruistic reasons)? Who or what felt a personal or collective responsibility to help?
- How did people help? Cite 3–5 examples of help provided? Did knowing how to help foster helping?

- How much of Watney's survival was dependent on his actions versus the actions of others? Explain.
- Watch *The Overview Effect* (on vimeo).

Step 2-Guiding Question: Does disaster and tragedy demonstrate that everything and everyone is connected?

- Read Rebecca Solnit's article about the coronavirus: *The impossible has already happened-what the coronavirus can teach us about hope.* (Available via The Guardian).
- Read Rebecca Solnit's *Paradise Built in Hell* (chapter titled: Mutual Aid in the Marketplace). A short excerpt can be found at *Facing History and Ourselves* website (*Who We Are, Or Could Be, in Times of Crisis).*

Step 3-Debate the following: Does disaster demonstrate that everything and everyone is connected?

Step 4-Guiding Question: How do people work together **at all?**

- Read *Do you believe in sharing?* by Tim Harford (August 30, 2013) *The Financial Times*
- Read "The real Lord of the Flies: what happened when six boys were shipwrecked for 15 months" (Rutger Bregman, May 2020 *The Guardian*) and watch The Real Life Lord of the Flies, ABC News Australia.

Step 5: Watch the documentary (available on YouTube) *What You Do Matters-The Documentary* from the Chicago Community Trust.

Step 6: NB-Journal/Summative Assessment: Add to working hypothesis. A more detailed reflection paper can be collected at this point which asks students to synthesize their thinking and reflections.

What can be taught & learned about **Human Goodness?**

Does collaboration or ruthless competition hold society together? In everyday life, we witness cooperative behavior. We also witness selfless behavior. When we experience the fight, fright, or freeze response activated in extreme situations we feel danger and a desire to survive.

However, our desire to survive and fight for our lives also includes fighting for others. It appears that some people put themselves in harm's way so others can live. Some argue that in order to be successful a person needs to look out only for themselves. Chris Kuuk paints a different picture in his book *The Compassionate Achiever: How Helping Others Fuels Success,* that society works because people simply find ways to cooperate, coordinate, and collaborate.

Can communities arise in disaster? In her book, *A Paradise Built in Hell* Rebecca Solnit examines many disasters throughout history. For example, the 1906 earthquake and fires in San Francisco, the Mexico City earthquake of 1985, the events of 9/11 and Hurricane Katrina. The disasters are different in their causes but her research and writing reveal the altruistic responses to them are consistently the same. She contends that communities (the true sense of the word) arise in disaster, and the best of human nature emerges in tragedy, not the worst.

Playbook Lesson Sequence 9: Assess Understanding and Learning

NB-Journal: students explain what they have learned about the various lesson steps. *What motivates people to help another? What are the roots of moral courage? What makes someone heroic?* (Students should communicate their theories that answer the above questions. Their written response should be supported with evidence and reasoned conclusions.)

> *Precept #13: In search of the antecedents of human goodness altruism turns up not only in nature but also in the evolutionary history of animals and humans.*

TEACHING WHAT MATTERS PLAYBOOK: TOOLS FOR EXPLORING THE ART OF LIVING

Playbook Lesson Sequence 1: Human Nature, Charles Darwin and Survival of the Kindest

Lesson objectives: Explain Darwin's theory of natural selection. Describe how Darwin came to believe that cooperation and compassion were essential to the evolutionary process.

Step 1-Guiding Question: What explains why **a single-celled amoeba acts altruistically, sacrificing itself for the sake of amoeba?**

- Show students a photo of dictyostelium discoideum.
- Present Darwin's problem. According to Oren Harman, in his book *The Price of Altruism,* Darwin recognized the paradox of altruism within the

competitive struggle to survive and reproduce. As Harman noted Darwin proclaimed that his entire theory was suspect if he couldn't explain evidence of altruism.[54] One of the more complex altruistic behaviors that puzzled Darwin was the evolved behavior of dictyostelium discoideum, or a cellular slime mode. These slime mode cells live as individual amoebae until starved, then ultimately transform themselves into a multicellular fruiting body.[55]

In other words, it lives alone in the forest, but when resources are low and survival is threatened, it sends out a chemical signal. Other amoebas (single celled) respond. They start crawling toward each other and meet and become one slug (1 organism). This slug moves along until it finds a windy and sunny place that is more habitable and conducive to life.

About 20 percent of this slug in the head begin to create out of their own body a stalk which hardens. In the process of doing so, the amoebas die. They sacrifice themselves to ensure the other 80 percent of amoebas can live. The rest of the 80 percent of amoebas climb up the stalk into a catapult like catcher and then wait for the wind to disperse them within this new environment. The problem is this: what explains why unicellular slime molds would sacrifice themselves for the sake of others, and is apparently altruistic? Ask students if they might be able to explain it.

- **Here is the problem.** In the traditional Darwinian view, the struggle for existence is based on competition for resources to live and reproduce. Darwin wrote about this in 1859 in his groundbreaking *On the Origin of Species*. In this view it would make no sense to help another, especially if there was cost to the helper. This threatens the helper's ability to thrive and reproduce.

If the story of survival is that nature would never select behavior and traits that would diminish an organism's fitness, how does one explain the continuation or evolution of traits and/or behaviors that produce altruism? And the fact that there is evidence that altruistic behavior occurs consistently amongst all creatures from mammals to bacteria? Charles Darwin had called the problem his "*one special difficulty*." Altruism found in nature made him have doubts about his own theory of evolution.

Step 2-Guiding Question: Could survival be **as much about survival of the kindest as it is the fittest?** Darwin came to believe and wrote later in his life, that everyday existence was not simply competition but also goodness and cooperation. He became convinced of an "ingrained social instinct" particularly in human nature. These beliefs were reflected in later works like

Descent of Man which he published in 1871. Cooperation and mutual aid were as essential as competition.

- Watch Dacher Keltner, *We Are Built To Be Kind* (available via YouTube by University of California).

Step 3-Guiding Question: What are other examples **within nature of altruistic behavior?**

- Students research the following examples to determine whether any animal behavior is altruistic. Students should develop a presentation of their findings. Do these examples support the idea of survival of the fittest or survival of the kindest or both? Why?
  - Antarctic penguins moving in concentrically to keep warm
  - Vampire bats sharing blood
  - Honey Bees sting an intruder, not out of aggression but out of altruistic motivations.
  - Chimpanzees
  - Bonobos
  - Belding's Ground Squirrels give alarms that warn others of danger
  - Leafcutter ants
  - Honeypot ants
  - Meerkats

What can be taught & learned about **Human Goodness**?

What does survival by natural selection mean? By the 1830s Darwin had cemented his thinking about his theory of evolution by natural selection. Darwin's Theory of Natural Selection or survival of the fittest (a term never actually used by Darwin but added later by Herbert Spencer) is that evolution selects certain behaviors that allow for genetic fitness or reproduction of one's genes in their offspring to survive.

Darwin believed that we inherit certain qualities that incline us to survive and reproduce. The struggle to survive wasn't simply direct competition, but a competition to survive against a hostile environment. This led to interpretations that described a competitive world. A world in which everyone is only out for themselves.

However, Darwin wrote both in his early work along with his later writing in *Descent of Man and Selection in Relation to Sex* (1871) that evolution also selected various traits that serve as foundational blocks for human goodness. In the fourth chapter of *Descent of Man* Darwin explained the origins for what he called sympathy or what is commonly referred to today as altruism, empathy, or compassion.

It was his attempt to explain goodness and community in humans and other animals. According to biologists from Darwin to E. O. Wilson, cooperation has been more important than competition for evolutionary success.

What did Darwin reveal about human nature? Darwin also expanded our notion of human nature. Darwin made a series of multi-year voyages. The time spent in the Galápagos islands influenced his theories on natural selection.[56] It was the time in the South American archipelago Tierra del Fuego and his interactions with the Fuegians in Chile which directly influenced his theories about human compassion and sympathy.

Darwin believed humans are a social and caring species with a compassionate instinct. Young Darwin believed that the Fuegians chief means for survival was cooperation and fairness. Darwin theorized that within human communities like the Fuegians, there were altruistic people.

Communities with many altruistic individuals would thrive better than others, and produce more offspring. Populations that have more compassionate members survive more successfully than groups with selfish individuals. Cooperation leads to reciprocity, shared defense, food sharing, and working together. Scientific research is beginning to reveal that evolution is explained not only by survival of the fittest but also by survival of the *kindest*.

How do animals behave altruistically? Darwin also believed that animals behaved altruistically. Honeypot ants extract nourishment from these sacks that grow on some ants. Their sole job is to help others and feed them to help them survive. Ants are one of the most successful forms of life, with at least 14,000 species. Ants have been in existence since dinosaurs roamed the Earth.[57] In these eusocial societies, some group members surrender part of their genetic fitness to benefit fellow members other than their own direct descendants. Social insects are the most abundant of the land-dwelling arthropods.

For Antarctic penguins, they huddle together and move concentrically to keep warm. The warmest spot is in the center while the coldest is the outside. Penguins slowly move so those in the middle gradually make their way to the outside while those outside the circle make their way to the middle.

Vampire bats donate blood to relatives and non-relatives by regurgitating blood and sharing. Two nights without feeding of ample blood and a vampire bat with starve. By sharing resources that are reciprocated in the future, Vampire bats ensure individual and cooperative survival.

Belding's ground squirrels give warning calls of an approaching predator. This draws attention to the squirrel and decreases their chance of survival while it ensures the survival of other squirrels including its offspring.

Meerkats are both predator and prey. They must keep their heads down as they dig in sand for food, while exposing themselves to predators like the jackal. As a result, Meerkats developed a community-based system where cooperative care is given to offspring and community guarding where other Meerkats take turns keeping watch while others feed.

Playbook Lesson Sequence 2: In search of altruistic origins in primate relatives

Lesson objective: Identify from research-based conclusions and theories how compassion, goodness, and altruism are evolutionary mechanisms evident in our primate relatives, the chimpanzee and bonobo.

Step 1-Guiding Question: What can you conclude **about similarities and differences in altruistic behavior between Bonobos and Chimpanzees?**

- Create an anthropological and primatology study. How are both Bonobos and Chimpanzees similar and different? What did you conclude about altruistic behavior? Is there evidence that these primates engage in compassionate and altruistic behavior? Write a brief biography for both Chimpanzees and Bonobos.
- Hominoid Psychology Research Group, Chimps and Bonobos: https://www.eva.mpg.de/3chimps/files/apes.htm
- Photogallery, Hominoid Psychology Research Group: https://www.eva.mpg.de/3chimps/files/research.htm#
- PBS Evolution, Chimps And Bonobos: http://www.pbs.org/wgbh/evolution/library/07/3/l_073_03.html
- New England Primate Conservancy, Bonobos: https://www.neprimateconservancy.org/bonobo.html
- New England Primate Conservancy, Primates at a glance (Old World Monkeys): https://www.neprimateconservancy.org/african-monkeys-at-a-glance.html
- New England Primate Conservancy, Chimpanzees: https://www.neprimateconservancy.org/common-chimpanzee.html

Step 2-Guiding Question: Why are Bonobos considered the happiest and most peaceful of all primates? Investigate a bit more the behavior the Bonobo.

- Watch and meet as *Kanzi Talks to Reporters* (available via YouTube)
- Watch Sue Savage Rumbaugh's TedTalk *The Gentle Genius of the Bonobo*

- Watch *Bonobos in experiments developed by Duke University anthropologists Brian Hare and Vanessa Woods*. National Science Foundation (available via YouTube)
- Watch *Things You Didn't Know about the Bonobo/ National Geographic* (available via YouTube)
- Watch Brain Hare's talk at PopTech *Peaceful as a Bonobo*? (available via YouTube)
- Assess understanding of Bonobo behavior. Have students write a response to the guiding question.

Step 3-Guiding Question: What can be concluded about altruistic behavior? Is this behavior evident of moral behavior? Observe animal behavior in the following videos.

- Watch *Chimp Empathy and Morality, sans Religion* by Frans de Waal (available via YouTube)
- Watch *Monkey cooperation and fairness* (available via YouTube)
- Watch *Chimpanzee Problem-Solving by Cooperation* (available via YouTube)
- Watch Frans de Waal's TedTalk *Moral Behavior in Animals* (2012)
- Read *Scientist Finds the Beginnings of Morality in Primate Behavior* by Nicholas Wade, 2007 (*New York Times*)

What can be taught & learned about **Human Goodness**?

How are bonobos and chimpanzees similar and different? Our immediate primate family consists of the four great apes (chimps, bonobos, gorillas, and orangutans and lesser apes: gibbons and siamangs.) Chimpanzees and bonobos are humans' closest living relatives, sharing about 98.7 percent of our DNA. They make their home along the Congo River in the Democratic Republic of the Congo. They look similar, but fundamental differences in their evolved behaviors, social structures, and biology exist.

Chimps and bonobos shared the same common ancestor until about a million years ago. They lived along the Congo River. Bonobos however, developed on one side of the river and chimps on the other side of the river. Then, they evolved to become different species.

A subtle difference in environment had profound implications for their evolution. Bonobos show less severe forms of aggression than chimpanzees. Researchers suspect that this difference evolved because of relaxed feeding competition.[58] Chimpanzees in this environment south of the river had the forest to themselves, and had access to plentiful food. This allowed them to travel together in bigger groups and form strong social bonds. Chimps had to share their environment with gorillas. Since they both eat the same food, there was competition for food resources.

These changes in environment explain in part, the changes in chimp behavior as they became more apt to violence. Chimpanzees, like most apes, live in male-dominated societies. Chimps use violence to secure mates and status. Chimps will attack and kill other rival chimpanzees.

Bonobos, live in societies dominated by females. There are no confirmed cases of bonobos engaging in deadly aggression with other bonobos in the wild or captivity.[59] Bonobos use sex in a multitude of ways. Sex is primarily used to reduce possible conflict. Bonobos have conflict but it is quickly quelled. Bonobos enjoy being with other bonobos, even strangers. These strangers are often greeted with play and sex.[60]

Does mutual aid emerge among animals in harsh environmental conditions? Peter Kropotkin argued in his 1902 treatise *Mutual Aid,* that many animals display mutual assistance especially facing harsh environmental conditions. Based on his observations of various animal species in Siberia, he witnessed animals working together in order to survive.

He noted that cooperation was commonly seen as musk oxen formed rings around their young to protect them against wolves. He saw individual cattle and horses who had frozen to death. This made him believe that in freezing temperatures you either cooperate to survive like huddling together to keep warm or die alone. Like Darwin he believed that cooperative groups of animals would thrive over less cooperative.

The classic 1964 experiment using Rhesus monkeys illustrated that a majority of monkeys consistently chose to starve themselves by sacrificing food over shocking another monkey. They refused to pull a lever that would give them food, but would also harm another monkey in a different cage. In one instance, a monkey refused to pull chain to get food for 12 days, literally starving itself to death.[61]

Playbook Lesson Sequence 3: Our Hominid Ancestors— In Search of What It Means to Be Human.

Lesson objectives: Identify where humans came from and what it means to be human.

Step 1-Guiding Question: What does it mean to be human? What is part of the history of human nature? Paleoanthropology is the study of human origins and evolution. Students research the history of humans to determine in part, what it means to be human and what is human nature?

- Watch *What does it mean to be human? One species, living worldwide* (available at Smithsonian National Museum of Natural History website)

- Examine and take notes on each of the following
- Examine *Interactive timeline of human evolution* (available at Smithsonian National Museum of Natural History website)
- Examine *Human Characteristics: What does it mean to be human* (available at Smithsonian National Museum of Natural History website)
- Read *The traits that make human beings unique* by Melissa Hogenboom, July 2015 (available through BBC future)

What can be taught & learned about **Human Goodness?**

Who are human beings? Human beings and chimpanzees evolved from a common ancestor around six million years ago. The first human species emerged in Africa around 300,000 years ago. Australopithecines, the name for a group of African fossil apes who started to walk upright about 4–6 million years ago, are the connection between fossil apes and Homo sapiens.[62] Despite differences among individuals, human beings are more alike than we are different. Human beings are considered Homo sapiens, or one species.

Is morality an evolved mechanism? Around 40,000 years ago early human numbers were reduced to dangerously low numbers and almost died off. Christopher Boehm, the Director of Jane Goodall Research Center at the University of Southern California, researches the evolutionary roots of morality and altruism. He theorizes that morality is an evolved mechanism that allowed groups to survive and grow.

Moral behavior like altruism developed when conscience and reason evolved for early humans. Various brain mechanisms, like shame, other-caring, perspective taking, and pleasure evolved which allowed our ancestors to get along and support one another. Social reactions emerged which were regulated by approval and disapproval from other clan members. The only communities that were able to survive were those in which the members supported one another.[63]

This collaboration was rewarded. Family clans grew in size and reproduced more successfully. As trust was built between clans, there was less violent conflict and more sharing of resources to ensure survival. Around 2.5 million years ago as body size increased so did brain size. As cranial capacity increased so did intelligence and brain mechanisms for cooperation.[64]

Playbook Lesson Sequence 4: Young children and the development of morality and kindness

Lesson objectives: Identify how moral understanding and behavior began early in life. Evaluate whether young children have a biological predisposition to morality and altruism.

Step 1-Guiding Question: What is morality?

- NB-Journal: Where are the sources of your morals? What influences your ethical decision making?

Step 2-Guiding Question: **To what extent is morality learned or innate?**

- Discuss the guiding question. What is your hypothesis, where does morality derive?

Step 3-Guiding Question: What does research **on toddlers and young children suggest about the origins of morality?**

- Watch video of research of toddlers and babies. How do toddlers know how to help? Why might toddlers *want* to help?
- Watch Felix Warneken's *Precursor to Altruism in Young Children* (available Dalai Lama Center on Peace and Ethics via YouTube)
- Watch Felix Warneken's *Adorable Altruistic Experiment* (available Dalai Lama Center on Peace and Ethics via YouTube)
- Small group discussion: How do they A) know that someone needs help, B) offer the right help that is needed, and C) do so without being prompted or modeled or rewarded for their behavior? What is their motivation? What explains this behavior?

Step 4-NB-Journal: What theories attempt to answer these questions? How do toddlers know how to help? Why do toddlers *want* to help? Reevaluate your own hypothesis.

Step 5-Guiding Question: **How do toddlers and infants understand fairness and recognize pro-social behavior and rewards and punishments?**

- Watch *Paul Bloom, Yale University, speaks on the topic of Just Babies* (available Oxford Academic, via YouTube)
- Watch *Can Babies Tell Right From Wrong* (*New York Times* video, via YouTube)
- Watch *60 Minutes* story *Born Good, Babies Unlock the Mysteries of Morality*
- Read *Not-so blank slates: What do infants understand about the social world? More than you think*, Kristen Weir, (2014 American Psychological Association)

What can be taught & learned about **Human Goodness**?

What is morality? Morality is complex and difficult to define. Morality can be simply defined as distinguishing between right and wrong. Various theories posit that morality is based on psychological adaptations and foundational pillars. These pillars of morality foster cooperation and benevolent social interactions between individuals. Some of these pillars consist of fairness, loyalty, authority, sanctity, and liberty.[65]

The pillars of morality are influenced by culture and the time period in which we live. Moral pillars are believed to be at the heart of pro-social behavior in humans. The Veneer Theory, both coined and criticized by Dutch primatologist Frans de Wall, argues that humans are essentially bad to their core and that morality is a thin cover that conceals our true nature. Veneer theorists argue that human nature is asocial, egocentric, selfish, and destructive.

Is morality innate? A desire for justice and fairness is universal to all people. While fairness and reciprocity are present in every culture, morality isn't always expressed in the same way within various cultures.[66] For more than two decades, social scientist James Q. Wilson among other researchers have argued that morality is innate. Morality is an inborn component of human nature, cultivated and developed within family and society. Evolution has produced mechanisms for caring about others, but society influences how and the extent to which we care.[67]

The evolution of social emotions has gotten us to do what is socially right, and reward-punishment brain systems reinforce it.[68] Neuroscientists suggest that human morality is an automated process closely tied to social instincts.

Noted psychologist Jonathan Haidt has argued that moral judgments are made quickly, almost intuitively and automatically from what he called moral intuitions. Haidt believes that we have unconscious intuitive heuristics which activate and accentuate moral behaviors.[69] Moral reasoning occurs after the fact which justifies moral judgements to ourselves and to others.

How might morality develop in children? Practically all developmental psychologists see the development of morality as an intersection of environmental, genetic or dispositional factors, and social forces that occur throughout one's life. Psychologist Lawrence Kohlberg's theory of moral development posited that morality was a continual process that progresses with age. Moral development, Kohlberg believed, was based on one's ability to reason at various stages of personal development. This ability to reason would lead to ethical behavior predicated on the principal of justice.

Kohlberg, however, didn't believe that everyone progressed to the highest stages of moral development. For most of the twentieth century, pediatric and developmental psychology textbooks taught that infants and young children were impulsively self-centered and comprehended right and wrong later in childhood.

Much of what was believed about young children was that children were blank slates upon birth. Without rearing or explicit teaching of moralistic principles, children could grow up to be morally deficient. Recent research has painted a different picture about the formation of morality.

As both Piaget and Kohlberg had emphasized, young children engage in perspective-taking. It was widely believed for many years that this wasn't the case. One year old babies have demonstrated the ability to determine another person's non-verbal communicative intent. Babies interpret correctly an adult giving a communicative clue, either by pointing or gazing toward a container with a toy. As researchers pointed out, in order for babies to be successful in the experiment, they had to infer that the adult's behavior was relevant to the situation at hand and that the adult *wanted* the toy inside the container toward which the adult gestured.[70]

Long before walking or talking, around six months of age, human infants can make value judgements, reach out to puppets, shapes, or individuals who demonstrate cooperation or show care for others and pass over individuals who do the opposite. By the time they turn 1, babies have the physical skills to start engaging in helpful behaviors.

Many research studies have shown that babies will engage in helping behavior without being asked and without being praised or rewarded for the effort.[71] Infants and young children are naturally empathetic, helpful, generous, and demonstrate innate preferences. These are the altruistic instruments in humans.

What does research on infants, toddlers, and young children reveal about the origins of morality and pro-social behavior? In the 1980s, Renee Baillargeon, PhD, director of the Infant Cognition Laboratory at the University of Illinois at Urbana-Champaign, and colleagues developed a method to test infant mental states or theory of mind. This method revealed that infants can understand the mental states, emotions, wants, and beliefs of others.

Since babies can't communicate verbally exactly what they are thinking, it has been difficult for researchers to understand what babies understood. Baillargeon and colleagues developed a research technique to do this and reveal in their findings that babies look measurably longer at events that defy their expectations.[72]

Psychologist Carolyn Zahn-Waxler completed some of the early research on child perspective taking capabilities in children. She visited various homes in the 1980s to find out how children respond to family members instructed to pretend cry, fake being hurt, or choke. By watching how children responded she discovered that children as early as one year of age attempted to comfort the adults by touching them and stroking their faces.[73]

Consoling behaviors developed significantly as children aged. Increased age led to increases in empathic concern. This led to increases in helping behavior. Toddlers engaged in a wide variety of spontaneous helping behaviors, such as verbal comfort and advice, sharing, and distracting the person in distress.[74]

Developmental psychologists such as Paul Bloom and Karen Wynn at Yale Infant Cognition Center, study the minds of babies. Through many years of research, they have demonstrated that infants are capable of making certain types of moral judgments based on inborn preferences.[75]

They use puppets to illustrate good and bad behaviors. When presented with a choice of the good and bad puppet, more than 80 percent of the time in various puppet scenarios, babies will "select" (by gazing at the puppet of choice for an extended period of time) the good, helpful, cooperative, and kind puppet. They demonstrate a preference for the good puppet.

In another experiment, Wynn, Bloom, and Hamlin presented infants with different shapes with eyes demonstrating various tasks and behaviors.[76] The circle tries to climb the hill and falters, the triangle enters to help the circle, where the square enters later to prevent the circle from successfully climbing the hill. The sequence is repeated until the babies become disinterested. Fourteen out of sixteen ten-month old babies and all twelve six-month old babies reached out for the helpful triangle over the square.[77]

Playbook Lesson Sequence 5: Assess Understanding and Learning

Concept check, quiz-Do you understand the research, the theories, the data, and the philosophical considerations behind the various ideas. (Points subject to assessment.) Traditionally designed quizzes along with using scenes from films by which students must demonstrate application of their knowledge based on what is seen in the film. Students can select any film and identify and explain scenes from the film that illustrate each of the assessed concepts.

Reflection journal-students explain what they have learned about the various lesson steps. Explain what they agree with or disagree with.

Draw what you've learned-Explain the applicability of the information to your life. Also explain what you have drawn, how it represents what you've learned. Summarize why you chose to express your understanding in this way.

Analogy concept paper-explain how what has been learned is like a _____ (e.g., an acorn). Make specific connections between assessed concepts and whatever the object may be.

Life Maps-A summation of what students learned in a unit, mapped with images, quotes, and multi-page reflection that explains the map and how it followed, helps one to attain a good life. This should also critically analyze rather than merely summarize what students learned or found applicable to understanding well-being.

Precept #14: Human nature is full of goodness, altruism, compassion, and kindness.

TEACHING WHAT MATTERS PLAYBOOK: TOOLS FOR EXPLORING THE ART OF LIVING

Playbook Lesson Sequence 1: Kin-Selection Theory and Origins of Altruism

Lesson objective: Identify and explain kin-altruism and Hamilton's rule as an explanation for altruistic behavior.

Step 1-Guiding Question: How could Robert De Niro's character's behavior be explained by kin-selection theory?

- Watch the circle of trust scene from the film *Meet the Fockers* (Ben Stiller's character is trying on tuxedo and Robert De Niro's character confronts him in the dressing room explaining the tenets of the circle of trust).
- Why is Robert De Niro's character so protective of his daughter and so distrustful of Ben Stiller's character? How could Robert De Niro's character's behavior be explained by kin-selection theory?

Step 2-Guiding Question: What is kin-selection theory and how does it explain altruistic behavior?

- Read *Origins of altruism: Why Hamilton still rules 50 years on* by Ben Oldroyd, Madeleine Beekman, and Rob Brooks, 2014 (The Conversation).
- Assess comprehension of the reading. Have students explain the meaning of the alleged quote from biologist J. B. S. Haldane: "I would lay down my life for two brothers or eight cousins." Note that our siblings on average share 50 percent of our genes and cousins 12.5 percent.

Step 3-Students examine different examples of kin-selection, take notes, and explain how each example supports or refutes the theory of kin-selection.

- Watch the story of Dick and Rick Hoyt (The Dick and Rick Hoyt Story available at Ironman Triathlon via YouTube).
- Watch the alarm sound given by Black-Tailed Prairie Dogs (available via YouTube)
- Have students research Belding's Ground Squirrels
- Does kin-selection explain altruistic behavior between people who are unrelated?

What can be taught & learned about Human Goodness?

What is the kin-selection theory? Altruism seems paradoxical from a Darwinian perspective. In the competitive world of survival, Darwin struggled to explain helping behaviors that involved a personal cost to the helper. Originated by famed biologist William Hamilton, kin-selection attempts to explain any apparent altruistic behavior within various species, including humans. Also known as inclusive fitness theory, the theory holds that instinctual mechanisms like cooperation and altruistic behavior evolved to help those genetically related.

Parental care is the costliest in nature. Generally, most mammalian offspring take the longest to become independent and able to procreate. Thus, parents endure significant costs to their own survival by caring for their offspring for an extended period of time. Kin-selection theory illustrates the powerful social instincts that developed to ensure care for offspring. Nature selected traits that foster altruistic impulses to help those more genetically related to ourselves. Blood, it turns out, is thicker than water.

At the heart of the theory is Hamilton's rule. The rule quantifies a gene-centric view of evolution. Popularized by Richard Dawkin's book *The Selfish Gene,* a gene is only interested in reproducing itself. It can do so in two ways. It can select traits that increase survival and the likelihood of reproduction in the organism in which it resides. Or it can increase the reproduction of close relatives or kin who also possess copies of the same genes. This would require altruistic behaviors to safeguard the chances of reproduction and survival in blood relatives.

From a gene-centered perspective there is no statistical difference between my survival and the survival of two of my siblings. Hence, J. B. S. Haldane's quote. Since my siblings and I share 50 percent of the same genes, and if they are both helped, it is like helping me. This can be expressed mathematically for most species.

Sociobiologists use Hamilton's rule to predict within populations of species that the closer the genetic relationship, the more likely they are to sacrifice themselves for another. This can be seen in various species of ants, bees, Belding's ground squirrels, and other animals. However, we are not beholden to our genes. Genes don't control our behavior and the choices we make in the moments of our lives.

In order to create change, natural selection takes a lot time. Also, environmental factors largely determine whether a gene is activated, deactivated, or altered.[78] Many biologically determined behaviors are controlled by environmental stimuli which trigger innate responses. Humans are imbued with free choices and rational decision making. Many of us engage in maladaptive behaviors which threaten our survival and ability to reproduce. For example, people use birth control, drink alcohol and drive, smoke, free-solo mountain climb, and consume food that is bad for our health.

What about altruism that exists between people who are unrelated? Kin-selection doesn't explain all varieties of altruism that occurs. Hamilton's rule attempts to explain how altruism occurs because of our direct relatedness between individuals. What about altruism that exists between unrelated people? Kin-selection provides no answer why a person would help a stranger.

Another theory called *group selection* posits that altruistic behavior occurs within and between entire groups of organisms. Noted sociobiologist E. O. Wilson and colleagues in 2010 published a contentious paper that mathematically assessed the natural world arguing that altruism evolved for the good of the community rather than for the good of individual genes. Groups that cooperate will be more successful than groups that are selfish. For example, cooperative behaviors such as cooperative hunting by lions, cooperative child rearing, and predatory alarm sounds evolved.[79] Black tailed prairie dogs spend about one-third of their time standing watch for predators. When alarmed, they emit loud and repetitive alarm calls to warn of a predator. Like Meerkats, ground squirrels feed in groups, with certain individuals taking turns watching for predators. When a predator sights the individual who gave the alarm call, it puts the alarm giver at greater risk of being pursued by the predator. Group-selection theory attempts to illustrate how altruism emerged to protect and ensure the success of social groups even when they are blood relatives or not.

Playbook Lesson Sequence 2: Reciprocal Altruism Theory and Cooperation

Lesson objective: Examine how cooperation emerges in competitive environments/society governed by ruthless self-interest. Identify reasons why altruistic behavior develops among non-relatives.

Step 1-Guiding Question: How might cooperation emerge **in competitive environments?** Engage students in the following activity. Each person receives and blows up four balloons. With a permanent marker, have students write their name on one of the four balloons. Combine all the balloons in the middle of the room and mix them all up. Have students turn their backs to the balloons. Give the rules "of the game."

Tell students that they will be given one minute to find the balloon that has their name on it. They are not allowed to talk with others. Your task is to find your balloon. Say go and start the clock. After one minute, see how many students were able to find their balloon.

Now, start the game over. Have students turn their backs as you mix up the balloons in the center of the room. Announce a rule change. For one minute find the balloon with your name on it. This time if you find a balloon with someone else's name on it you can give it to them without talking. (Be certain everyone knows everyone's name.) After one minute, see how many students were able to find their balloon.

- Debrief. In the game of finding the balloon with your name on it, was it better to work individually or cooperatively? Why or why not? How advantageous was cooperation? Does this prove the existence of altruism? Why or why not?

Step 2-Guiding Question: How might cooperation emerge in competitive environments? Engage in a class experiment. Get the harmful parasites off yourself and save yourself.

- Everyone begins with 10 pieces of rolled masking tape on their backs
- Divide class into two groups at random. Have students count off 1–2, 1–2 . . . put the #1 group of students toward one part of the room. Put the #2 students in a different part of the room. As a group have students name their groups. Have them announce their names to each other. As always, students can opt out of participation and merely watch.
- Explain the rules. You can't use your hands. You can't talk either. After 90 seconds, the number of parasites you have remaining on your body will determine whether you survive and evolve.

10–5 parasites remaining=no future, survival rate at 1%
4 parasites remaining=uncertain future, survival rate at 25%
3 parasites remaining=cloudy future, survival rate at 50%
2 parasites remaining=almost full recovery, survival rate at 75%
1 parasite remaining=almost certain recovery, survival rate at 99%
0 parasite remaining=full recovery, continuation of group species.

- Ask students: in 90 seconds, what will be the survival rate of your group members? Will your group species surrender or will they overcome the harm from the parasites? Which group will have the most members with the higher rates of survival? Why?
- Have students begin the process of removing the parasites. Keep the timer visible to students.
- The obvious point of the experiment that many students usually figure out is that it is easier and more efficient to work together to remove the parasites. Some students use elbows or feet or even their teeth to remove parasites. However, some students attempt to work alone scraping their backs up against anything they can find the classroom. Rarely will students cross over and attempt to help those students in the "other group." This is the real point of the experiment. Will they cross over some imaginary group distinction to help others? Which people in their own group did they first attempt to help? Friends? People they knew well? Did they attempt to help people they didn't know? What prevented them from helping more people? Did they only think of themselves? Why or why not? Did they think of only this moment, or did they consider the future? Will your future chances of survival increase or decrease with more people in your group? What about the people in the other group?
- Debrief. What was the purpose of this activity/experiment? How well did you do in achieving this purpose? What explains why you behaved the way that you did? Did you survive? What will help you survive in the future? To what extent are we inclined to be kind and to whom?

Step 3-NB-Journal: Note any emerging thoughts that explain how cooperative behavior develops in competitive environments.

Step 4-Guiding Question: What is reciprocal altruism?
Read *Reciprocal Altruism* by Margaret Levi (edge.org).

The principle of reciprocal altruism holds that people are willing to cooperate and engage in altruistic exchanges even if they are not related.[80] It is another answer to the question as to why anyone helps anyone in the competitive world of survival.

The concept of reciprocal altruism was introduced by Robert Trivers. He showed how altruism, that is helping out another while incurring some cost while helping, can evolve between unrelated individuals. Cooperation emerges even when people act rationally in their own self-interest. The key involves a likelihood of repeated exchanges so individuals can reciprocate or return the favor.

Reciprocity leads to cooperation between people which improves the quality of life of others and ensures our survival and well-being. For cooperation and reciprocity to occur, trust and fairness are important factors. People need to be able to discern whether someone is free-loader or cheater. Evolution has ingrained innate emotions like shame, embarrassment, guilt, sympathy, empathy, and pain of being ostracized that motivate and reinforce moralistic action. As Dacher Keltner points out, "Emotions are signs of our commitment to others; emotions are encoded into our brains; emotions are our moral gut, the source of our most important moral intuitions."[81]

What can be taught & learned about Human Goodness?

How do we think to convince ourselves to help another? When a situation arises in which another person is in need of assistance, a person drops their books on the floor in front of you, a car stops you while you are jogging and asks for directions, a person trips and falls to the ground and asks for help to get up, no one calculates the costs and benefits of helping before actually helping. We have a mental shortcut, a heuristic, that helps us decide what to do. These are the emotions of sympathy and empathy.

On a daily basis people engage in acts of kindness, friendship, generosity, and aid. When asked, we freely pass the salt and pepper at the dinner table and stop feeding ourselves. It feels good to do for others, as much as it feels good when people do things for us. This manifests as the Golden Rule. All major religions have some version of the Golden Rule in common: "Do unto others as you would have them do unto you."

Reciprocity is also evident in our political systems. Enlightenment philosopher Jean-Jacques Rousseau's social contract theory is the bedrock of any democratic society. The theory holds that individuals come together within a society by a process of mutual consent. People agree to sacrifice their individual needs to abide by common rules which benefit everyone. These rules of behavior can be explicit, like laws which enforce a speed limit for the safety of others or implicit like waiting in line with others instead of just walking into a store.

Massachusetts Senator Elizabeth Warren attempted to identify this when she said, *"You built a factory out there? Good for you,"* she says. *"But I want to be clear: you moved your goods to market on the roads the rest of us paid for; you hired workers the rest of us paid to educate; you were safe in your factory because of police forces and fire forces that the rest of us paid for. You didn't have to worry that marauding bands would come and seize everything at your factory, and hire someone to protect against this, because of the work the rest of us did."* She continues: *"Now look, you built a factory and it turned into something terrific, or a great idea? God bless. Keep a big hunk of it. But part of the underlying social contract is you take a hunk of that and pay forward for the next kid who comes along."*[82]

There are also mental shortcuts to help you determine whether your kindness will be appreciated and reciprocated. No one likes being cheated or having their compassion taken advantage of by others. As Trivers noted, one heuristic is moralistic aggression or anger. Another heuristic Trivers calls "reparative altruism" or guilt. As psychologists Jonathan Haidt and Daniel Batson have shown, the innate emotions of sympathy and empathy produce moral intuitions and guide us to help others.

Playbook Lesson Sequence 3: Game theory and the Origins of Altruism

Lesson objective: Examine how cooperation emerges in competitive environments and whether being nice is advantageous in the long run.

Step 1-Guiding Question: Human nature is paradoxical—it is both competitive and cooperative. What does game theory reveal about the *nature* (innate characteristics and ways of thinking, feeling, and acting) of competition and cooperation in social interactions?

- Define game theory. Game theory is the study of mathematical models of strategic interaction among rational decision-makers. Most games that game theory studies are "zero-sum" (the total rewards are fixed, and a player does well only at the expense of other players).[83] Game theory attempts to explain the balance between selfish and selfless behavior in social interactions.
- Debate: Is life zero-sum or non-zero sum?

Step 2-Guiding Question: What explains why and how we can win or lose with others in the zero-sum game of life (where one person gains and one person loses), especially since altruism is not zero-sum?

- Play the Prisoner's Dilemma game as a class. Instructions are as follows: Play 3 rounds against a random opponent in class. Each round consists of 10 moves of the Prisoner's Dilemma game. Add up your total number of points that you score in each of the three rounds. Use the grid below for scoring. Tell students that the lowest scores will be eliminated from the next round and no longer able to play.

Each student on equal sized pieces of paper writes the letter P for peace and W for war on the other piece. Students count down 1–2–3 and then they decide which move to play in that round. Add up their score in that round, keep track of scoring and do this for 10 moves.

- Explain the nature of scoring. Tell students that the objective is to get the most points. You are competing not only against your opponent but also all your classmates. If both players play peace, both players get 3 points. If both players play war, then both players get 2 points. If player A plays peace, but player B plays war, then player A would get 0 points and player B would get 5 points. If player A plays war and player B plays peace, then player A would get 5 points and player B would get 0 points.

	PEACE	WAR
PEACE	3 points/ 3 points	0 points/ 5 points
WAR	5 points/ 0 points	2 points/ 2 points

Step 3-Debrief with students their playing strategies.

- Analyze your nature. Why did you play the way that you did? What factors influenced you? Was it the reputation of your opponent, the playing style of your opponent, your beliefs, etc.?
- Did you win? What did you win? How many of you determined that getting the most points didn't necessarily mean *getting more points than your opponent?* Since life isn't zero-sum, over the long term, what are the advantages and drawbacks of simply cooperating (playing peace) versus defecting/selfishness (playing war)?
- Which strategy ultimately earns the most points? Which strategy earns the least points? If you had to play the same person a number of times, what move would you play to ensure that you moved on to the next round? Does this make you reassess your strategy?
- What is the lesson from the Prisoner's Dilemma Game? Does the game advocate a clear justification for human selfishness (rational self-interest) or does it advocate the best mathematical argument for unselfishness? How could this be applied to human society?

Step 3-Guiding Question: Do nice people finish first or last? Does being nice become advantageous over the long run?

- Students play *The Evolution of Trust Game* (available via Nicky Case https://ncase.me/trust/).
- What is the lesson from the Prisoner's Dilemma Game? Does the game advocate a clear justification for human selfishness (rational self-interest) or does it advocate the best mathematical argument for unselfishness? How could this be applied to human society?
- Watch "*Do Nice Guys Finish First?*" (available via YouTube, asapSCIENCE).
- Watch Yale University researcher David Rand on natural cooperation (PopTech available via YouTube).

- Discuss and/or assess the guiding question.

Step 4-Guiding Question: When is cooperation favored over competition in our daily lives?

- Play the Circle Tennis Ball Game.[84] Bring students to an open space. Students form a circle. Students count off to two around the circle while standing. All the ones will stand. All the twos, sit on the floor, head slightly bowed to chest, hands together with arms outstretched.
- The only rules are the following: The tennis ball must be passed around the circle to the next person. You cannot throw across the circle. How the ball is passed is for everyone to decide for themselves. Second, the people sitting on the floor cannot look up. They must hold out their hands with their gaze fixed on the floor. Lastly, if a person does not catch the ball, they are out of the circle and must stand away from the circle. The goal is to stay in the circle and play.
- Begin play. The purpose of this game is to see what kind of behavior emerges during the game. Will competition emerge where students will try to get each other out of the circle? Will cooperation emerge as students work together to keep each other in the circle? Do students take advantage of the students in the seated position, or will they place the ball in their hands to help them catch the ball? You can announce addendums like one handed catch, or catch the ball between your arms.
- Debrief the game in a whole class discussion in a circle. What is the purpose of the game? Did you succeed? Why or why not? How do you win? What do you win, if anything? If everyone is out of the circle, you cannot play anymore. Why is that more desirable than keeping everyone in the circle knowing that you don't really win anything? What happened to those who cooperated and attempted to play fairly? What about those who were playing competitively and made catching the ball difficult. Why did you take advantage of those that were in a disadvantaged position? Why didn't you help them to stay in the game?

Step 5-Guiding Question: What are examples of cooperation and reciprocal altruism in the real world?

- Read about Ubuntu. Read *How to Be Happy: A Surprising Lesson on Happiness From an African Tribe* by James Clear.
- Watch the Liberty Mutual "Pay It Forward" commercials (available via YouTube).
- Students research about vampire bats sharing blood, meerkats, cleaner stations and cleaner fish, The Kula Ring, and the Christmas Truce in

1914 during World War 1. How do these support the idea of reciprocal altruism?
- Read Adam Grant's *Is Giving the Secret to Getting Ahead?* (*New York Times Magazine*, 2013) or watch his TedTalk *Are You A Giver or A Taker?*
- Read *The Science of Helping Out* by Tara Parker-Pope (*The New York Times*, 2020).

Step 6-Guiding Question: Do humans favor alphas or the Mr. Rogers of the world?

- Discuss as a whole class. What is an alpha? To what extent is life about asserting one's dominance and superiority over another? What picture of an animal and human alpha arises in your mind?
- Watch: Frans de Waal's TedTalk *The Surprising Science of Alpha Males*, 2017.
- Watch the documentary *"Won't You Be My Neighbor"* 2018 Documentary about the life and work of Fred Rogers (available via DVD).
- **NB-journal: Have students produce a written summation of their thoughts and reflections. What type of play kept you in the game? Cooperation or competition? Why? Does either strategy work in our everyday lives? Why or why not? Were you better off in the long-term being selfish? What other factors determined whether you cooperated or competed with certain individuals next to you in the circle? Was cooperative, trustworthy behavior rewarded or punished by others? Was it taken advantage of in the game? Was competitive, cut-throat, untrustworthy behavior rewarded or punished by others?**

What can be taught & learned about *Human Goodness*?

What is Ubuntu? Is it better when together we all win? As Archbishop Desmond Tutu explains Ubuntu is a way of thinking that illustrates trust in a shared humanity that believes "I am, because we are!"[85] Ubuntu redefines what constitutes our self-interest. Out-competing rivals and predators to produce offspring appears to be the rule of nature. This can take the appearance of a showdown with species pitted against species.

Conventional wisdom suggests that we compete in a dog-eat-dog world with a mentality of every person for themselves. Life becomes a zero-sum game. I win, because you lose. Or is it? Cooperation and altruism have evolved and persisted in even the lowliest of species to human beings. The idea of Ubuntu is present in our daily interactions with others. Real life isn't really zero-sum.

What can a computer program called Tit for Tat teach about cooperation? In the height of the Cold War, a professor at the University of Michigan named Robert Axelrod held a pair of tournaments in 1980 using the Prisoner's Dilemma to test the idea of zero-sum thinking. Axelrod had some of the smartest people in the world in various fields send computer strategies to compete in the tournament.

Each strategy would be paired with another strategy for 200 iterations of a Prisoner's Dilemma game. Total points would be tallied throughout the tournament. It turns out that the winning strategy wasn't one that was the most diabolical, selfish, or nuanced. The winning strategy was called "Tit for Tat" and it employed the principle of reciprocity

The strategy submitted by Anatol Rapaport comprised just two lines of code. The strategy was simple. Tit for Tat cooperated on the first move and reciprocated what the other program did on the previous move. It solicited cooperation for as long as it could and would reciprocate cooperation.

However, Tit for Tat did not allow itself to be exploited by other programs that defected. Tit for Tat retaliated by defecting on the next move to signal that it would not be taken advantage of by an aggressive defector program.

If Tit for Tat found enough nice programs who cooperated more than programs that defected, both programs would benefit from this mutual cooperation. The more cooperative programs that there were in the general computer program population, the better Tit for Tat did.

In both tournaments Tit for Tat won and the nicer strategies outperformed the predominate defecting or meaner strategies. Axelrod illustrated that nice guys can win. Cooperation can beat competition.[86] Groups with a high number of altruists do better in the long run than groups comprised of zero-sum exploiters.

What are examples of reciprocal altruism in the real world? Examples of reciprocal altruism in the real world consist of the cease-fire truce that emerged during the trench warfare of the western front in World War I.[87] Soldiers came out of the trenches, walked across the barren no man's land, helped bury each other's dead, exchanged Christmas gifts and even played soccer matches in integrated teams.

Meerkats, as both predator and prey, work together by taking turns keeping guard for predators while others dig in the sand for food. Cleaner stations and cleaner fish work cooperatively. Fish visit the "cleaner stations" and eat the harmful parasites off the coral. This symbiotic relationship helps the coral stay clean while helping the fish doing the visiting get nourished. Vampire bats have been found to regurgitate blood to help kin and non-kin who share the same roost. Bats that don't feed themselves with enough blood are at risk of starving to death in as little as two days. They share some of their own nourishment to help others.

The Kula ring is a network exchange system of the Massim people of the islands near New Guinea. The Kula ring was first publicized by anthropologist Bronislaw Malinowski. Different tribes and tribal leaders travel across the expansive Pacific Ocean exchanging handmade goods. However, the Kula ring is more than the trading of goods. One risks their life and the lives of others while sailing to the different islands. The Kula ring symbolizes the value in strengthening social bonds between communities.[88] There is honor and value in giving more to others than receiving. Not only are objects traded, but also the gift of shared stories, sharing hardships, while exchanging the willingness to help.

The importance of this kind of giving has been written about by University of Pennsylvania psychologist Adam Grant. Givers help everyone in an organization win/succeed usually at a cost to themselves. When takers win in organization, someone loses. Grant illustrates that givers prefer to give more than they receive and this results in the whole team winning. Givers are willing to provide help, share information and skills, and do the things that nobody wants to do to benefit the team.

Why is the common notion of an alpha a stereotype? The common belief of an alpha is one who is a leader by virtue of their bravado, strength, aggression, and ruthlessness. It is widely believed alphas are dominate because of these qualities.

While it is true in some species, it is a common misunderstanding in many other species. In other species, like wolves, an alpha's strength and power is through their kindness and compassion. Real alpha males and females are compassionate.

People who study wolves in the wild note that an alpha often leads by example. Wolf leaders guide, teach, and care for their pack members.[89] In fact, the stereotypical alpha traits are now used by scientists to describe the behavior of animals who are captive and lonely.[90] An alpha it turns out lives alone in captivity.

Playbook Lesson Sequence 4: Understanding the nature of empathy

Lesson objective: Identify and explain empathy and the empathic response.

Step 1-Guiding Question: What is empathy and why does it matter?

- Empathy is often used interchangeably with sympathy. Sympathy involves feeling sorry for someone (think sympathy card). Empathy can be defined as the ability to understand and share the thoughts or feelings of another. It is a wired biological mechanism. In fact, humans empathize more than they realize. People mirror others constantly. People yawn when they see someone yawning, or laugh when it becomes infectious, mirror facial expressions like a smile, and crowds of people synchronize rhythmic movements with the performers at a Blue Man Group show.

Psychologists categorize empathy in three ways.[91] Cognitive empathy is the innate ability to understand how a person feels and what they might be thinking or experiencing. This is also referred to as theory of mind. It is also explained as stepping into someone else's shoes. Emotional empathy is the innate ability to share the feelings of another person. Whatever the emotion, anguish, sadness, or joy becomes a contagion. We feel what they feel. I cry because you cry. Compassionate empathy is a motivational state moving a person to take action to help based on an intertwined capacity to understand and share the emotions of another. Compassionate action is often, but not universally, the most frequent response to another's suffering.[92]

- Watch Paul Zak explain *The Future of Story Telling* (available via YouTube)
- Watch *The Age of Outrospection* by Roman Krznaric (available via RSA Animate)[93]
- Watch *The Empathic Civilization* by Jeremy Rifkin (available via RSA Animate)[94]
- Discuss some of the questions raised. What is empathy? To what extent would society be better by cultivating empathy? Why does empathy matter?

Step 2-Guiding Question: How is empathy an innate part of human nature?

- Have students take the Emotional Intelligence quiz offered through the Greater Good Center (at UCal-Berkeley) or you can take the quiz as a whole class. Discuss the facial expressions and build consensus on trying to select the correct facial expression.
- Watch the following #MoreThanMean-"Women in Sports 'Face' Harassment" (available via YouTube from Just Not Sports). Discuss as a whole class. Describe the emotions you felt while watching this.
- As a whole class describe the emotions various men demonstrated by reading these tweets. Why did they have difficulty reading them? Why did almost all of them pause before reading them? How many men display compassionate or empathetic facial expressions?

- Describe the emotions the men demonstrated by reading these tweets. Why did they have difficulty reading them? Why couldn't they just read them? Why did almost all of them pause before reading them? What might all of this suggest about empathy?

Step 3-Guiding Question: Why are we emotionally responsive to the actions of others?

- Engage students in the following activity on elevation. Show students a series of videos to elicit an emotional response. Try to include a myriad of videos and media to allow students to experience different emotions. Usually this is done over two classes depending on the length of the class.
It is probably best to view them ahead of time to preview them (and get some tears out). Stop the video and let students reflect and clear their emotional palettes for about 2 minutes between videos. After each video simply respond to what you see on the screen. On a scale of 1–5, rate the intensity of the emotional impact (positive or negative) that you experienced. What did you feel? Did anything that you see make you want to cry? Why? No emotions? Inspired and impressed by the work others do? Compassion? Empathy? A desire to do something? Feel better or worse about the state of the world? Revulsion or disgust? Disillusioned?
- What might this activity illustrate about empathy? Why are we so emotionally responsive to the needs of others?

Step 4-Guiding Question: Why is it that music stimulates and sensitizes us to the emotions of other people? How is it that empathy cultivates musicophilia?

- Watch Andrew Zuckerman's documentary *Music* (available via DVD) or utilize his Zuckerman's website on his film https://andrewzuckerman.com/music/.
- Introduce the following activity. Each student selects and creates the "Greatest Hits" 6 song playlist. One of the songs must reflect in their assessment each of the following:
  1. Sad-what you like to listen to when you are feeling the "blues?"
  2. Happy/Joy-what you like to listen to when you want the good times to keep going?
  3. Pumped up-what do you listen to when you want to get "jacked up" or excited?
  4. 4. Religious/Spirituality/Calming-what do you listen to inspire or reinforce your religious beliefs, foster a mindset of spirituality or a

song that allows you calm your mind and body and soothe yourself? 5/6. 2 other songs that are your favorites for a myriad of reasons.

Part 2 of activity. List the songs, artist, and title. Have copies of lyrics available for classmates to read and examine for each song. (Optional) Have at least multiple paragraph explanations for each of the songs, explaining why, specifically and generally, you selected the songs you did. Students might focus on: How does the music make you feel specifically? Why? How does the music sound? Tone? Emotion of the sound? Do the lyrics match the emotional sound of the music? What experiences are associated with this song? What is it specifically about each of the songs that you enjoy or appreciate? Are any of the lyrics ironic? Contain metaphors? Why should other people appreciate this song(s)?

Part 3 of activity. Have students visit and rotate various stations and listen to the various songs listed by classmates. As they go around the room and read the explanations of other people's songs, determine whether you feel the same emotions from the songs that are described. Do you agree with the descriptions given for each song listened to and that can be from other's explanations and song choices. Do you feel and hear the same things your classmates describe for each of the songs listed? Why?

- What are commonalities between why others like certain songs and why you like certain songs? What are fundamental differences? Out of all of the songs that you examined, which songs best represented each of the various emotions? Why? Did songs have anything in common?
 Assess: Have students write a response to the guiding question for this section. Have students use information from this activity to help support their thinking. In addition, have them address to what extent are song preferences similar to preferences for others that elicit empathy? Why is one person's preference for Madonna different than a person's preference for Miles Davis? Why do we have empathy at times for one person, but not another? What might explain that?

Step 4-Assess student understanding of empathy and the different facets of empathy.

What can be taught & learned about *Human Goodness*?

What is empathy? Empathy is innate, it is an automatic response. We don't need turn empathy on or off. Neuroscientists have identified multiple sections of our brains that help us to understand what others are feeling. Infant and child psychologists have demonstrated that infants, toddlers, and young children are able to take the perspective of another. Overall, empathy is a social-emotional force that provides the foundation for cooperation. Empathy leads to concern and care for others.

Empathy paradoxically can motivate us to turn our heads, looking away from those suffering. This is because empathy is largely context dependent. Not all people experience an empathic response for the same reasons or in the same ways. Empathy is contextually dependent.

Also, individual factors like how stressed we might be, personal preferences, and characteristics of people in need of help can affect empathic responsiveness. As researcher Paul Zak has shown, an individual's oxytocin levels, the neurochemical that has been shown to promote social and familial bonding, can also affect empathic responses in the same way. Lower oxytocin levels lead to more self-centered rather than other-centered behavior.

Are we wired to be inspired? When we witness unexpectedly the best of humanity displayed, someone helping a stranger for example, we often get a warm, pleasant feeling or even tear-up. We feel morally uplifted. Psychologist Jonathan Haidt has called this elevation. Haidt describes elevation "as a warm, uplifting feeling that people experience when they see unexpected acts of human goodness, kindness, courage, or compassion. This feeling often makes a person want to help others and to become a better person himself or herself."[95]

The response to bad deeds is disgust. People have revulsion to acts of racism and cruelty as much as to food that has spoiled. It disgusts us. Elevation is an important facet of human nature. It is evident that observing others doing good for others can in the right circumstances induce us to act with greater kindness, compassion, and benevolence.

How might music illustrate the nature of empathy? As with storytelling, fictional literature, or a movie, music is form of mimesis. Mimesis is an artistic representation or imitation of the real world that involves the reader or listener getting immersed in the art and identifying with characters or music. Musicians carefully craft mechanisms to foster empathic, emotional responses in the listener. Like other forms of art, music engages our emotions, our imaginations, and impacts our mental states.

As world-renowned musicologist Oliver Sachs has noted, for our brain to process music requires the use of multiple parts of our brain working as a symphony. The sounds heard are processed through various brain networks. Music has existed in every culture and musical preferences manifest in the early stages of life.[96] Americans spend more money on music than on prescription drugs and the average American hears more than five hours of music per day.[97] Why? There is an acute emotional reaction to the sounds heard and processed. Many of us subconsciously keep time with the beat, find our feet tapping along, or move our bodies in dance as we become one with the sound.

Music helps to remember past experiences. Music can stir memories of the past via associations. People break into singing a song heard hours or even days after. Songs often form the soundtrack to the various experiences of our lives. What song was playing when you had your first kiss, heartbreak, or invigorating day? Music helps to savor these experiences. Music comforts when people are sad or helps to channel anger. It draws people together in a shared experience. Attending any live concert witnessing tens of thousands of people singing in unison with the musical artist illustrates this beautifully.

People use music to control mental states (e.g., relax, reduce stress) and for mood control (e.g., romantic music). Music is used as a distraction when bored and enhances a spiritual or religious experience (e.g., singing hymns in church). Music amplifies daily activities from exercising to completing mundane tasks. Music stimulates fear (e.g., every horror movie) and suspense (e.g., the Final Jeopardy music). Music creates sounds to mobilize people to fight in wars. Music serves as a vital part of our daily lives.

Playbook Lesson Sequence 6: The Empathy-Altruism Theory

Lesson objective: Identify and explain empathy and empathy's relationship to altruism.

Step 1-Guiding Question: How does empathy motivate altruistic behavior? Introduce C. Daniel Batson's Empathy-Altruism Theory. In a number of experiments over three decades, Batson has sought empirical confirmation to develop his theory of altruism. Batson's theory holds *"that feeling other-oriented emotion elicited by and congruent with the perceived welfare of another person in need (i.e. empathic concern) produces a motivational state with the ultimate goal of increasing the person's welfare by having the empathy-inducing need removed (i.e. altruistic motivation.) The more empathy felt for the person in need, the more motivation to have the need removed."*[98]

> In short, empathic concern produces altruistic motivation. Batson argues that "not all empathic emotion produces altruistic motivation but only empathic concern felt when another is perceived to be in need." Batson claims that two conditions are necessary for the creation of empathy. One must see that a person is in need of help. Second, one must adopt the other's perspective. Empathy then induces altruism because of the compassionate understanding of the pain of another rather than just feeling another's pain.

However, Batson emphasizes that empathic concern is not motivated by a single emotion. Rather empathic concern involves a vast web of feelings like sympathy, compassion, softheartedness, tenderness, sorrow, sadness, upset, distress, concern, and grief. These emotions arouse the physiology of goal-directed behavior to alleviate the perceived pain of another.
- Watch Daniel Batson's talk at the approximate 33-minute talk at the Science of Compassion 2014: Introduction to the Science of Empathy, Altruism, and Compassion (available via the Stanford University Center for Compassion and Altruism Research and Education).
- Watch *Breaking the Wall Between People* by Tania Singer (available via Falling Walls Foundation on YouTube).

What can be taught & learned about *Human Goodness*?

Are our brains wired to produce altruistic behavior? We are social creatures. We need others, as much as others need us. It is apparent that humans have the brain circuitry to understand others, empathize with others, and care about others and interpret this information that motivates us to act altruistically. As researcher Donald Pfaff has described in his book *The Altruistic Brain,* the brain produces altruistic behavior in specific sequences of innate processes.

As Pfaff describes, first our central nervous systems registers an act that you are about to perform toward another person before it is conscious. Next, you picture the person who you will be helping. Often a generic image of a person emerges. The image of that person overlaps with that of one's self. Nerve cells representing the other are firing as the nerve cells representing ourselves fire.[99]

Then you experience a feeling which allows you to evaluate the effects of any potential act. This is when you reason whether the act is good or bad. This takes place between the amygdala and the prefrontal cortex allowing for the neurocognitive ethical switch to be hit.

Lastly, you decide whether to act. If you deem the act to have a good outcome, you act.[100] Then you act. You carry out the sequential cognitive steps to help another because it coincides with the way you would want to be treated yourself. The size of our brains, specifically the prefrontal cortex, the newest part of human brains over millions of years of evolution is what separates us from our primate cousins. This part of the brain allows us to engage in problem-solving, rationalizations, and perspective taking. This ability to be social, that is to get along and work with others, became a crucial part of human evolution.

What does a monkey in Parma, Italy illustrate about the neurobiology of empathy? Our brains constantly mirror our perceptions of the world and other people around us. In 1990 in a research lab in Parma, Italy a team of researchers led by Giacomo Rizzolatti accidentally discovered the existence of what neuroscientists have called mirror neurons.

A macaque monkey's brain was being studied to see what parts of the monkey's brain became active when doing different movements. Before the monkey picked up a peanut and ate it, Rizzolatti noticed that a region of the frontal cortex became activated. Then, by utter surprise the researchers noticed that when the same monkey watched the researchers grab for a peanut the same region lit up even though the monkey didn't move. They discovered mirror neurons which appear to be evidence of the neurobiological basis of empathy.

Mirror neurons fire when we engage in perspective taking.[101] No one knows for sure what a person is thinking or what their brain is doing when acting altruistically. When researchers ask people after the fact what motivated them to help another, these testimonies are subject to a whole host of inaccuracies in reporting and interpretation.

Empathy can become an aversive sensation. Avoidance is a way to lessen the emotional contagion experienced. Pain serves as an important function for human survival. There is physical pain and social pain.

Famed empathy researcher Tania Singer examined the brains of people receiving an electric shock or watching someone else receive it. Singer in a famous 2004 paper has shown that people literally feel the pain of loved ones. Male and female couples participated in the experiment.

In one version of the experiment women watched their boyfriend's arm being shocked. Singer found that in these women's brains watching activated the pain distress network in their brain both when they were being shocked and when watching their loved ones being shocked. These women could feel the pain of their boyfriends even though they weren't actually being shocked.[102]

- Assess student understanding of the empathy-altruism theory.

Playbook Lesson Sequence 7: The Ugly side of empathy

Lesson objective: Identify and explain empathy's impact on us vs. them and tribalistic thinking and behavior.

Step 1-Guiding Question: Humans have an aversion to violence but why haven't humans been able to reduce the curve of military and civilian death rate during wars?

The Heart of Altruism

- Examine the following chart on global deaths since the year 1400 by Max Rosa (via vox.com *600 years of war and peace, in one amazing chart*).
- Debate. Is it ever appropriate to target civilians during war?
- Read *Hope on the Battlefield-Military leaders know a secret: The vast majority of people are overwhelmingly reluctant to take a human life* by Lt. Col. Dave Grossman (June 2010, available Greater Good Magazine).

Step 2-Guiding Question: Why does empathy seem to produce tribal thinking and behavior?

- Show famous photograph of Elizabeth Eckford in 1957. What emotions are being conveyed in the photograph?
- Read *The Story Behind the Famous Little Rock Nine 'Scream Image': It didn't end when Central High School was integrated* by Erin Blakemore (history.com).
- Watch *Eyes on the Prize: Episode 2 Fighting Back (1957–1962)* about the Little Rock 9 and school integration at Central High School in Little Rock, Arkansas in 1957.
- Discuss in small groups and as a whole class. What made integration so difficult? What was the problem? Why couldn't anyone empathize with the students, especially Elizabeth Eckford? As students integrated the school, to what extent did attitudes of white students change? Did integration and daily contact minimize bias and racist attitudes for some students? (Stop at interviews with white female students who say, "the problem is the parents I can get used to going to school. . .").
- Examine Norman Rockwell's painting *The problem we all live with* (created in 1964). What images are being conveyed in the painting?
- Read *Empathy is Tearing Us Apart* by Robert Wright (available via wired.com). The article investigates the ugly side of empathy, us vs. them thinking, in-group and out-group, just world phenomenon.
- Watch any Saturday Night Live of Kristen Wiig playing the character of Sue preparing for a surprise birthday party. The character of Sue can be considered an empath. She is overwhelmed with the emotional contagion she experiences simply thinking about surprising someone on their birthday. She experiences the excitement of the surprise as she imagines the effect on another. One of the aspects of empathy is that we are not empathetic all the time. We would not be able to function. We would be paralyzed by the emotional toll other people's emotions had on us.

Step 3-Guiding Question: How might contact and interactions with others be the antidote to tribalistic and parochialism associated with empathy?

- Read C. P. Ellis *"Why I Quit the Klan"* (Ellis an ardent segregationist and a high-ranking member of the Klu Klux Klan in North Carolina. He later quit the KKK and became a civil rights activist and trade union organizer. The reason for this transformation supports the contact thesis).
- Watch *Invictus* (one story of post-apartheid and reconciliation of South Africa). How did South Africa's national rugby team become a catalyst for reducing intergroup tensions in South Africa?

What can be taught & learned about *Human Goodness*?

What is the ugly side of empathy? We categorize, discriminate, hold biases, and make pre-judgements to classify people. It is easier to be empathetic toward those that are part of our group. The ugly side of empathy is that it is more difficult for empathy to be extended to those deemed outside of one's group. This distinction of us vs. them manifests along racial, ethnic, socioeconomic, nationalistic, and religious lines.

An interesting study that tested the tendency to not help someone outside of one's group was based on the superficial difference of soccer team fandom in England. European football allegiances and rivalries are ingrained at a young age. These team loyalties become part of individual as well as community identity.

In the experiment the person in need of help was a fan of a rival soccer team. Researchers tested whether that distinction would be enough to deter helping especially after witnessing the jogger falling and yelling out in pain. The research study showed that participants were more likely to help a fallen jogger when the jogger was a fellow fan of the same soccer team than when the jogger was a fan of a rival team based on the shirt they were wearing.[103]

But when participants were reminded of that they shared a common identity with the rival fan, that is, they were reminded they were both simply soccer fans, they were more likely to help. Shared similarity produced helping behavior.

Good empathy leads to positive connections with others building trust, cooperation, and community. Bad empathy can lead to hostility, mistrust, scapegoating, and violence. Tribalism appears to be wired. The same neurotransmitters and circuitry involved with empathic concern helps to foster tribalism. Oxytocin, the neurotransmitter that advances our ability to connect, love, and trust others also influences us to be less caring of people outside of our group.[104]

How might exposure to others deemed "different" and repeated intergroup contact be the antidote to the ugly side of empathy? Tribalism is wired. Humans prefer things that are familiar. Familiarity breeds likability. Unknown things, faces, and places tend to generate greater amygdala activation as threatening stimuli. This bias usually generates cautiousness. This often leads to fear and avoidance of the stimuli.

However, there is a difference between wired and hardwired. Human brain circuitry is not entirely hardwired. Our brains can be rewired during our lifetimes. Traveling to new places, meeting new people, learning to speak a foreign language or play an instrument contributes to this.

Tribalism and parochial inclinations can be rewired through repeated experience, exposure, and active learning. The mere exposure effect asserts that the more you see or hear something, you more you like it.

Contact theory holds that contact between two groups can promote tolerance and acceptance. In order for contact to work we have to get to know something or someone. Research shows that exposure and contact don't even need to be positive to foster compatibility or understanding. Only contact is needed. Even indirect contact reduces prejudice.[105] The more familiar something becomes, the more we like it. Inclusivity leads to repeated contact which breeds familiarity and greater likability.

Playbook Lesson Sequence 9: Assess Understanding and Learning

Concept check, quiz-Do you understand the research, the theories, the data, and philosophical considerations behind the various ideas. (Points subject to assessment.) Traditionally designed quizzes along with using scenes from films by which students must demonstrate application of their knowledge based on what is seen in the film. Students can select any film and identify and explain scenes from the film that illustrate each of the assessed concepts.

Reflection journal-students explain what they have learned about the various lesson steps. Explain what they agree with or disagree with.

Draw what you've learned-Explain the applicability of the information to your life. Also explain what you have drawn, how it represents what you've learned. Summarize why you chose to express your understanding in this way.

Analogy concept paper-explain how what has been learned is like a _____ (e.g., an acorn). Make specific connections between assessed concepts and whatever the object may be.

Life Maps-A summation of what students learned in a unit, mapped with images, quotes, and multi-page reflection that explains the map and how if followed, helps one to attain a good life. This should also critically analyze rather than merely summarize what students learned or found applicable to understanding well-being.

Bibliography

Barasch, Marc Ian. *The Compassionate Life: Walking the Path of Kindness*. Healing Path Books, 2017.
Batson, Daniel. *Altruism in Humans*. 1st ed., Oxford University Press, 2011.
Bays, Jan Chozen. *How to Train a Wild Elephant*. Shambhala, 2011.
Ben-Shahar, Tal. *Happier: Learn the Secrets to Daily Joy and Lasting Fulfillment*. 1st ed., McGraw-Hill Education, 2007.
Blankson, Amy, and Shawn Achor. *The Future of Happiness: 5 Modern Strategies for Balancing Productivity and Well-Being in the Digital Era*. BenBella Books, 2017.
Bloom, Paul. *Just Babies: The Origins of Good and Evil*. Reprint, Crown, 2014.
Boehm, Christopher. *Moral Origins: The Evolution of Virtue, Altruism, and Shame*. 1st ed., Basic Books, 2012.
Bok, Sissela. *Exploring Happiness: From Aristotle to Brain Science*. 1st ed., Yale University Press, 2011.
Botton, De Alain. *Status Anxiety*. Vintage, 2005.
Brackett, Marc. *Permission to Feel: Unlocking the Power of Emotions to Help Our Kids, Ourselves, and Our Society Thrive*. Celadon Books, 2019.
Bregman, Rutger. *Humankind: A Hopeful History*. Little, Brown and Company, 2020.
Bregman, Rutger. *Utopia for Realists: How We Can Build the Ideal World*. Reprint, Back Bay Books, 2018.
Brown, Brené. *I Thought It Was Just Me (but It Isn't): Making the Journey from "What Will People Think?" To "I Am Enough."* 1st ed., Avery, 2007.
Brown, Brené. *The Gifts of Imperfection: Let Go of Who You Think You're Supposed to Be and Embrace Who You Are*. 1st ed., Hazelden Publishing, 2010.
Bruni, Frank. *Where You Go Is Not Who You'll Be: An Antidote to the College Admissions Mania*. Grand Central Publishing, 2015.
Burns, David. *Feeling Good: The New Mood Therapy*. Harper, 2012.
Buscaglia, Leo. *Loving Each Other: The Challenge of Human Relationships*. Ballantine Books, 1986.
Carr, Nicholas. *The Big Switch: Rewiring the World, from Edison to Google by Nicholas Carr (2008-01-17)*. W. W. Norton & Company, 2008.
Carr, Nicholas. *The Shallows: What the Internet Is Doing to Our Brains*. W. W. Norton & Company, 2011.

Chouinard, Yvon, and Naomi Klein. *Let My People Go Surfing: The Education of a Reluctant Businessman—Including 10 More Years of Business Unusual.* Updated 2nd ed., Penguin Books, 2016.

Christakis Nicholas, PhD. *Blueprint: The Evolutionary Origins of a Good Society.* Reprint, Little, Brown Spark, 2020.

Churchland, Patricia. *Braintrust: What Neuroscience Tells Us about Morality Publisher: Princeton University Press.* Princeton University Press, 2011.

Boehm, Christopher. *Moral Origins: The Evolution of Virtue, Altruism, and Shame.* 1st ed., Basic Books, 2012.

Csikszentmihalyi, Mihaly. *Flow: The Psychology of Optimal Experience.* 1st ed., Harper & Row, 1990.

Damon, William. *The Path to Purpose: How Young People Find Their Calling in Life.* Reprint, Free Press, 2009.

Davidson, Richard, and Sharon Begley. *The Emotional Life of Your Brain: How Its Unique Patterns Affect the Way You Think, Feel, and Live—and How You Can Change Them.* Avery, 2012.

Disalvo, David. *What Makes Your Brain Happy and Why You Should Do the Opposite.* Amsterdam, Netherlands, Prometheus, 2011.

Siegel Daniel. *Brainstorm: The Power and Purpose of the Teenage Brain.* Illustrated, TarcherPerigee, 2015.

Easterbrook, Gregg. *It's Better Than It Looks: Reasons for Optimism in an Age of Fear.* Illustrated, PublicAffairs, 2019.

Easterbrook, Gregg. *The Progress Paradox: How Life Gets Better While People Feel Worse.* 42180th ed., Random House Trade Paperbacks, 2004.

Emmons, Robert. *Thanks!: How the New Science of Gratitude Can Make You Happier.* Annotated ed., Houghton Mifflin Harcourt, 2007.

Fernandez, Luke, and Susan Matt. *Bored, Lonely, Angry, Stupid: Changing Feelings about Technology, from the Telegraph to Twitter.* Reprint, Harvard University Press, 2020.

Flescher, Andrew Michael, and Daniel Worthen. *The Altruistic Species: Scientific, Philosophical, and Religious Perspectives of Human Benevolence.* 1st ed., Templeton Press, 2007.

Frankl, Viktor. *Man's Search for Meaning.* Beacon Press, 2006.

Fredrickson, Barbara. *Positivity: Top-Notch Research Reveals the Upward Spiral That Will Change Your Life by Fredrickson, Barbara (2009) Paperback.* Harmony, 2009.

Gates, Melinda. *The Moment of Lift.* Adfo Books, 2019.

Gladwell, Malcolm. *Outliers: The Story of Success.* Back Bay Books, 2011.

Goldstein Elisha. *The Now Effect: How a Mindful Moment Can Change the Rest of Your Life.* Reprint, Atria Books, 2013.

Graham, Carol. *Happiness Around the World: The Paradox of Happy Peasants and Miserable Millionaires.* Reprint, Oxford University Press, 2012.

Grant, Adam. *Give and Take: Why Helping Others Drives Our Success.* Reprint, Penguin Books, 2014.

Greene, Joshua. *Moral Tribes: Emotion, Reason, and the Gap Between Us and Them.* Reprint, Penguin Books, 2014.
Gunatillake, Rohan. *Modern Mindfulness.* Griffin, 2017.
Haidt, Jonathan. *The Happiness Hypothesis: Finding Modern Truth in Ancient Wisdom.* 1st ed., Basic Books, 2006.
Hanson, Rick, and Richard Mendius. *Buddha's Brain: The Practical Neuroscience of Happiness, Love, and Wisdom.* 1st ed., New Harbinger Publications, 2009.
Harari, Yuval Noah. *Sapiens: A Brief History of Humankind.* Reprint, Harper Perennial, 2018.
Harman, Oren. *The Price of Altruism: George Price and the Search for the Origins of Kindness.* Illustrated, W. W. Norton & Company, 2010.
Havrilesky, Heather. *What If This Were Enough?* Doubleday, 2018.
Hoff, Benjamin. *The Te of Piglet.* Penguin Books, 1993.
Holiday, Ryan. *Stillness Is the Key.* Adfo Books, 2020.
hooks, bell. *All About Love: New Visions.* 765th ed., William Morrow Paperbacks, 2018.
Housel, Morgan. *The Psychology of Money: Timeless Lessons on Wealth, Greed, and Happiness.* Harriman House, 2020.
Jay, Meg. *The Defining Decade: Why Your Twenties Matter—And How to Make the Most of Them Now.* Twelve, 2012.
Kabat-Zinn, Jon. *Wherever You Go, There You Are: Mindfulness Meditation in Everyday Life.* 10th ed., Hachette Books, 2005.
Kahneman, Daniel. *Thinking, Fast and Slow.* 1st ed., Farrar, Straus and Giroux, 2013.
Keltner, Dacher. *Born to Be Good: The Science of a Meaningful Life.* W. W. Norton, 2009.
Keltner, Dacher, et al. *The Compassionate Instinct: The Science of Human Goodness.* Illustrated, W. W. Norton & Company, 2010.
Kerr, Margee. *Scream: Chilling Adventures in the Science of Fear.* Reprint, PublicAffairs, 2017.
Klein, Stefan. *Survival of the Nicest: How Altruism Made Us Human and Why It Pays to Get Along.* The Experiment, 2014.
Kristof, Nicholas, and Sheryl WuDunn. *A Path Appears: Transforming Lives, Creating Opportunity.* Reprint, Vintage, 2015.
Krznaric, Roman. *How Should We Live? Great Ideas from the Past for Everyday Life.* Reprint, BlueBridge, 2015.
Krnaric, Roman. *The Good Ancestor: A Radical Prescription for Long-Term Thinking.* The Experiment, 2020.
Krznaric, Roman. *Empathy.* Zaltbommel, Netherlands, Van Haren Publishing, 2015.
Lamott, Anne. *Almost Everything: Notes on Hope.* 1st ed., 1st Printing, Riverhead Books, 2018.
Layard, Richard. *Happiness: Lessons from a New Science.* Annotated, Penguin Books, 2006.
Lieberman, Matthew. *Social: Why Our Brains Are Wired to Connect.* Illustrated, Crown, 2014.

Lopez, Shane, and C. Snyder. *The Oxford Handbook of Positive Psychology (Oxford Library of Psychology)*. 2nd ed., Oxford University Press, 2009.

Lyubomirsky, Sonja. *The How of Happiness: A New Approach to Getting the Life You Want*. Illustrated, Penguin Books, 2008.

Lyubomirsky, Sonja. *The Myths of Happiness: What Should Make You Happy, but Doesn't, What Shouldn't Make You Happy, but Does*. Penguin Books, 2014.

MacAskill, William. *Doing Good Better: How Effective Altruism Can Help You Help Others, Do Work That Matters, and Make Smarter Choices about Giving Back*. Reprint, Avery, 2016.

McMahon, Darrin. *Happiness: A History*. First Trade Paper, Grove Press, 2006.

Monroe, Kristen Renwick. *The Heart of Altruism*. Edition Unstated, Princeton University Press, 1998.

Mumford, George. *The Mindful Athlete: Secrets to Pure Performance*. Reprint, Parallax Press, 2016.

Neff, Kristin. *Self-Compassion*. Amsterdam, Netherlands, Adfo Books, 2011.

Novogratz, Jacqueline. *Manifesto for a Moral Revolution*. Griffin, 2021.

Nowak, Martin, and Roger Highfield. *SuperCooperators: Altruism, Evolution, and Why We Need Each Other to Succeed*. Reprint, Free Press, 2012.

Odell, Jenny. *How to Do Nothing: Resisting the Attention Economy*. Melville House, 2020.

Oliner, Samuel. *Do Unto Others: Extraordinary Acts Of Ordinary People*. Basic Books, 2004.

Peterson, Christopher. *A Primer in Positive Psychology (Oxford Positive Psychology Series)*. 1st ed., Oxford University Press, 2006.

Peterson, Christopher. *Pursuing the Good Life: 100 Reflections on Positive Psychology*. Illustrated, Oxford University Press, 2012.

Pfaff, Donald. *The Altruistic Brain: How We Are Naturally Good*. 1st ed., Oxford University Press, 2015.

Post, Stephen. *Unlimited Love*. 1st ed., Templeton Press, 2003.

Prinstein, Mitch. *Popular: Finding Happiness and Success in a World That Cares Too Much About the Wrong Kinds of Relationships*. Reprint, Penguin Books, 2018.

Ricard, Matthieu. *Happiness: A Guide to Developing Life's Most Important Skill*. Reprint, Little, Brown and Company, 2007.

Ridley, Matt. *The Rational Optimist: How Prosperity Evolves (P.S.)*. Illustrated, Harper Perennial, 2011.

Rifkin, Jeremy. *The Empathic Civilization: The Race to Global Consciousness in a World in Crisis*. 1st ed., TarcherPerigee, 2009.

Robinson, Paula. *Practising Positive Education: A Guide to Improve Wellbeing Literacy in Schools*. Positive Psychology Institute Pty Ltd, 2016.

Rosling, Hans, et al. *Factfulness: Ten Reasons We're Wrong About the World—and Why Things Are Better Than You Think*. Reprint, Flatiron Books, 2020.

Rubin, Gretchen. *The Happiness Project*. 25th Printing, HarperCollins Publishers, 2012.

Sachs, Jeffrey. *The Price of Civilization: Reawakening American Virtue and Prosperity*. Random House, 2011.

Sacks, Oliver. *Musicophilia: Tales of Music and the Brain, Revised and Expanded Edition*. Vintage, 2008.
Salwen, Hannah, and Kevin Salwen. *The Power of Half: One Family's Decision to Stop Taking and Start Giving Back*. Reprint, Mariner Books, 2011.
Salzberg, Sharon. *Real Happiness, 10th Anniversary Edition: A 28-Day Program to Realize the Power of Meditation*. 2nd ed., Revised, Workman Publishing Company, 2019.
Sandel, Michael. *What Money Can't Buy: The Moral Limits of Markets*. Farrar, Straus and Giroux, 2012.
Sapolsky, Robert. *Behave: The Biology of Humans at Our Best and Worst*. Illustrated, Penguin Books, 2018.
Sapolsky, Robert. *Why Zebras Don't Get Ulcers: The Acclaimed Guide to Stress, Stress-Related Diseases, and Coping, 3rd Edition*. 3rd ed., Holt Paperbacks, 2004.
Seligman, Martin. *Flourish (A Visionary New Understanding of Happiness and Well-Being)*. 1st ed., Atria Books, 2012.
Selingo, Jeffrey. *There Is Life After College: What Parents and Students Should Know About Navigating School to Prepare for the Jobs of Tomorrow*. Reprint, William Morrow Paperbacks, 2017.
Seppala, Emma. *The Happiness Track: How to Apply the Science of Happiness to Accelerate Your Success*. Reprint, HarperOne, 2017.
Seppala, Emma. *The Oxford Handbook of Compassionate Science*. Oxford University Press, 2017.
Siegel, Daniel. *Brainstorm: The Power and Purpose of the Teenage Brain*. Illustrated, TarcherPerigee, 2015.
Siegel, Daniel. *Aware: The Science and Practice of Presence—The Groundbreaking Meditation Practice*. Tarcher Perigee, 2020.
Singer, Michael. *The Untethered Soul: The Journey Beyond Yourself*. 1st ed., New Harbinger Publications/ Noetic Books, 2007.
Singer, Peter. *The Most Good You Can Do: How Effective Altruism Is Changing Ideas About Living Ethically*. Illustrated, Yale University Press, 2016.
Smith, Christian, and Hilary Davidson. *The Paradox of Generosity: Giving We Receive, Grasping We Lose*. 1st ed., Oxford University Press, 2014.
Sober, Elliott, and David Sloan Wilson. *Unto Others: The Evolution and Psychology of Unselfish Behavior*. New ed., Harvard University Press, 1999.

Soble, Alan. *Eros, Agape and Philia: Readings in the Philosophy of Love*. 1st ed., Paragon House, 1998.
Solnit, Rebecca. *A Paradise Built in Hell: The Extraordinary Communities That Arise in Disaster*. Reprint, Penguin (Non-Classics), 2010.
Solnit, Rebecca. *Hope in the Dark: Untold Histories, Wild Possibilities*. 2nd ed., Haymarket Books, 2016.
Stewart-Williams, Steve. *The Ape That Understood the Universe*. Revised, Cambridge University Press, 2019.
Stone, Deborah. *The Samaritan's Dilemma: Should Government Help Your Neighbor?* 1st ed., Bold Type Books, 2008.

Svoboda, Elizabeth. *What Makes a Hero?: The Surprising Science of Selflessness (Hardback) - 2013 Edition*. Penguin Putnam Inc, 2013.

Tomasello, Michael, et al. *Why We Cooperate (Boston Review Books)*. 1st ed., The MIT Press, 2009.

Trilling, Lionel. *Sincerity and Authenticity (The Charles Eliot Norton Lectures)*. 1st ed., Harvard University Press, 1973.

Twenge Jean. *IGen: Why Today's Super-Connected Kids Are Growing Up Less Rebellious, More Tolerant, Less Happy—and Completely Unprepared for Adulthood—and What That Means for the Rest of Us*. Reprint, Atria Books, 2018.

Waal, De Frans. *The Age of Empathy: Nature's Lessons for a Kinder Society*. 1st ed., Crown, 2010.

Waal, Frans de. *The Bonobo and the Atheist: In Search of Humanism Among the Primates*. W. W. Norton, 2013.

Weiner, Eric. *The Geography of Bliss: One Grump's Search for the Happiest Places in the World*. Reprint, Twelve, 2009.

Weiner, Eric. *The Socrates Express: In Search of Life Lessons from Dead Philosophers*. Avid Reader Press / Simon & Schuster, 2020.

Whillans, Ashley. *Time Smart: How to Reclaim Your Time and Live a Happier Life*. Harvard Business Review Press, 2020.

Wilson, David Sloan. *Does Altruism Exist? Culture, Genes, and the Welfare of Others (Foundational Questions in Science)*. Reprint, Yale University Press, 2016.

Wiseman, Rosalind. *Masterminds and Wingmen: Helping Our Boys Cope with Schoolyard Power, Locker-Room Tests, Girlfriends, and the New Rules of Boy World*. Reprint, Harmony, 2014.

Williams, Florence. *The Nature Fix: Why Nature Makes Us Happier, Healthier, and More Creative*. Illustrated, W. W. Norton & Company, 2018.

Wiseman, Rosalind. *Queen Bees and Wannabees*. 1st ed., Piatkus Books, 2003.

Wrangham, Richard. *The Goodness Paradox: The Strange Relationship Between Virtue and Violence in Human Evolution*. Reprint, Vintage, 2019.

Wright, Robert. *Nonzero: The Logic of Human Destiny*. Reprint, Vintage, 2001.

Zaki, Jamil. *The War for Kindness: Building Empathy in a Fractured World*. Illustrated, Crown, 2020.

Notes

INTRODUCTION

1. Buscaglia, Leo. *Loving Each Other: The Challenge of Human Relationships.* Ballantine Books, 1986. p. 11
2. Percy, Walker. *The Second Coming: A Novel.* Picador, 1999.
3. Barasch, Marc Ian. "Practicing 'Green Compassion': How Do You Stack Up?" *HuffPost*, 17 Nov. 2011, www.huffpost.com/entry/practicing-green-compassi_b_611700.
4. Seligman, Martin. *Flourish (A Visionary New Understanding of Happiness and Well-Being).* 1st ed., Atria Books, 2012. p. 16.
5. Kennelly, Stacey. "How to Be Happy: The Fine Print." *Greater Good*, 8 Aug. 2012, greatergood.berkeley.edu/article/item/how_to_be_happy_fine_print.

CHAPTER 1

1. Mineo, Liz. "Over Nearly 80 Years, Harvard Study Has Been Showing How to Live a Healthy and Happy Life." *Harvard Gazette*, 11 Apr. 2017, news.harvard.edu/gazette/story/2017/04/over-nearly-80-years-harvard-study-has-been-showing-how-to-live-a-healthy-and-happy-life.
2. Mineo, Liz. "Over Nearly 80 Years, Harvard Study Has Been Showing How to Live a Healthy and Happy Life." *Harvard Gazette*, 11 Apr. 2017, news.harvard.edu/gazette/story/2017/04/over-nearly-80-years-harvard-study-has-been-showing-how-to-live-a-healthy-and-happy-life.
3. Waldinger, Robert. "What Makes a Good Life? Lessons from the Longest Study on Happiness." *TED Talks*, Nov. 2015, www.ted.com/talks/robert_waldinger_what_makes_a_good_life_lessons_from_the_longest_study_on_happiness/transcript?language=en.
4. Lyubomirsky, Sonja, et al. "The Benefits of Frequent Positive Affect: Does Happiness Lead to Success?" *Psychological Bulletin*, vol. 131, no. 6, 2005, pp. 803–55. *Crossref*, doi:10.1037/0033-2909.131.6.803.

5. Seligman, Martin E. P., et al. "Positive Education: Positive Psychology and Classroom Interventions." *Oxford Review of Education*, vol. 35, no. 3, 2009, pp. 293–311. *Crossref*, doi:10.1080/03054980902934563.

6. Rose, T., & Ogas, O. (2018). Dark Horse: Achieving success through the pursuit of fulfillment. New York, Harper Collins. https://lsi.gse.harvard.edu/publications/dark-horse-achieving-success-through-pursuit-fulfillment

7. Jung, H., Seo, E., Han, E., Henderson, M. D., & Patall, E. A. (2020). Prosocial modeling: A meta-analytic review and synthesis. *Psychological Bulletin, 146*(8), 635–63. https://doi.org/10.1037/bul0000235

8. "National Commission on Social, Emotional, and Academic Development." *The Aspen Institute*, 19 Mar. 2020, www.aspeninstitute.org/programs/national-commission-on-social-emotional-and-academic-development.

9. "What Is SEL?" *CASEL*, casel.org/what-is-sel. Accessed 21 July 2019.

10. Lyubomirsky, Sonja, Laura King, et al. "The Benefits of Frequent Positive Affect: Does Happiness Lead to Success?" *Psychological Bulletin*, vol. 131, no. 6, 2005, pp. 803–55. *Crossref*, doi:10.1037/0033-2909.131.6.803.

11. Lyubomirsky, Sonja, Laura King, et al. "The Benefits of Frequent Positive Affect: Does Happiness Lead to Success?" *Psychological Bulletin*, vol. 131, no. 6, 2005, pp. 803–55. *Crossref*, doi:10.1037/0033-2909.131.6.803.

12. "Benefits of SEL." *Collaborative for Academic, Social, and Emotional Learning*, casel.org/impact. Accessed 21 July 2020.

13. Yaden, David B., et al. "Teaching Well-Being at Scale: An Intervention Study." PLOS ONE, edited by Daniel Vigo, vol. 16, no. 4, 2021, p. e0249193. Crossref, doi:10.1371/journal.pone.0249193.

14. "UNESCO MGIEP | Building Social and Emotional Learning for Education 2030." *UNESCO MGIEP*, mgiep.unesco.org. Accessed 2 July 2020.

15. David, Clifford. "Transformation Isn't What You Think It Is." *NeuroLeadership Institute*, 12 March. 2019, neuroleadership.com/your-brain-at-work/what-is-transformation?utm_campaign=Your%20Brain%20at%20Work%20-%20Blog&utm_content=87106443&utm_medium=social&utm_source=twitter&hss_channel=tw-19886347.

16. "Chapter 2: Recommendations for Action." *A Nation At Hope*, 9 Jan. 2019, nationathope.org/report-from-the-nation/chapter-2-recommendations-for-action.

17. Anderson, Jenny. "Schools Are Finally Teaching What Kids Need to Be Successful in Life." *Quartz*, 13 Apr. 2016, qz.com/656900/schools-are-finally-teaching-what-kids-need-to-be-successful-in-life.

18. Durlak, Joseph A., et al. "The Impact of Enhancing Students' Social and Emotional Learning: A Meta-Analysis of School-Based Universal Interventions." *Child Development*, vol. 82, no. 1, 2011, pp. 405–32. *Crossref*, doi:10.1111/j.1467-8624.2010.01564.x.

19. Kliff, Sarah, et al. "Today's Teens Are Better than You, and We Can Prove It." *Vox.Com*, 9 June 2016, www.vox.com/a/teens.

20. Martin E. P. Seligman, and James O. Pawelski. "Positive Psychology: FAQs." *Psychological Inquiry*, vol. 14, no. 2, 2003, pp. 159–63. *JSTOR*, www.jstor.org/stable/1449825. Accessed 21 July 2021.

21. Seligman, Martin. *Flourish (A Visionary New Understanding of Happiness and Well-Being)*. 1st ed., Atria Books, 2012. p. 26.

22. Robinson, Paula. *Practising Positive Education: A Guide to Improve well-being Literacy in Schools*. Positive Psychology Institute Pty Ltd, 2016. p. 32.

23. Robinson, Paula. *Practising Positive Education: A Guide to Improve well-being Literacy in Schools*. Positive Psychology Institute Pty Ltd, 2016. p. 22

24. Lyubomirsky, Sonja, Kennon M. Sheldon, et al. "Pursuing Happiness: The Architecture of Sustainable Change." *Review of General Psychology*, vol. 9, no. 2, 2005, pp. 111–31. *Crossref*, doi:10.1037/1089-2680.9.2.111.

25. Sheldon, Kennon M., and Sonja Lyubomirsky. "Revisiting the Sustainable Happiness Model and Pie Chart: Can Happiness Be Successfully Pursued?" *The Journal of Positive Psychology*, vol. 16, no. 2, 2019, pp. 145–54. *Crossref*, doi:10.1080/17439760.2019.1689421.

26. Sheldon, Kennon M., and Sonja Lyubomirsky. "Revisiting the Sustainable Happiness Model and Pie Chart: Can Happiness Be Successfully Pursued?" *The Journal of Positive Psychology*, vol. 16, no. 2, 2019, pp. 145–54. *Crossref*, doi:10.1080/17439760.2019.1689421.

27. Sheldon, Kennon M., and Sonja Lyubomirsky. "Revisiting the Sustainable Happiness Model and Pie Chart: Can Happiness Be Successfully Pursued?" *The Journal of Positive Psychology*, vol. 16, no. 2, 2019, pp. 145–54. *Crossref*, doi:10.1080/17439760.2019.1689421.

28. Flynn, Mariah. "How Long Do the Benefits of SEL Programs Last?" *Greater Good*, 30 Aug. 2017, greatergood.berkeley.edu/article/item/how_long_do_the_benefits_of_sel_programs_last.

29. "Minnesota Center for Twin and Family Research." *Minnesota Center for Twin and Family Research The University of Minnesota*, mctfr.psych.umn.edu/research/happiness.html. Accessed 21 July 2020.

30. Sheldon, Kennon M., and Sonja Lyubomirsky. "Is It Possible to Become Happier? (And If So, How?)" *Social and Personality Psychology Compass*, vol. 1, no. 1, 2007, pp. 129–45. *Crossref*, doi:10.1111/j.1751-9004.2007.00002.x.

31. Hanson, Rick, and Richard Mendius. *Buddha's Brain: The Practical Neuroscience of Happiness, Love, and Wisdom*. 1st ed., New Harbinger Publications, 2009. p. 6.

32. Schwartz, Katrina. "Harnessing the Incredible Learning Potential of the Adolescent Brain." *KQED*, 21 Dec. 2015, www.kqed.org/mindshift/43020/harnessing-the-incredible-learning-potential-of-the-adolescent-brain.

33. Barok, Shahilla. "Did You Know. . .You Have Between 50,000 And 70,000 Thoughts Per Day. . ." *HuffPost UK*, 2 Sept. 2017, www.huffingtonpost.co.uk/shahilla-barok/did-you-knowyou-have-betw_b_11819532.html?guccounter=1.

34. "Understanding the Stress Response." *Harvard Health*, 6 July 2020, www.health.harvard.edu/staying-healthy/understanding-the-stress-response.

35. Sapolsky, Robert. *Why Zebras Don't Get Ulcers: The Acclaimed Guide to Stress, Stress-Related Diseases, and Coping, 3rd Edition*. Holt Paperbacks, 2004.

36. Gilbert, D. T., and Wilson, T. D. (2000). "Miswanting: Some problems in the forecasting of future emotional states." In J. Forgas (ed.), *Thinking and feeling: The*

role of affect in social cognition (pp. 178–97). Cambridge: Cambridge University Press.

CHAPTER 2

1. Lyubomirsky, Sonja. *The Myths of Happiness: What Should Make You Happy, but Doesn't, What Shouldn't Make You Happy, but Does*. Penguin Books, 2014. p. 3.
2. https://ggia.berkeley.edu/practice/best_possible_self.
3. Gilbert, Daniel, and Wilson, Timothy. (2012). "Miswanting: Some problems in the forecasting of future affective states."
4. Poulsen, Bruce. "On the End of History Illusion." *Psychology Today*, 13 Jan. 2013, www.psychologytoday.com/us/blog/reality-play/201301/the-end-history-illusion.
5. Levine, Linda J., et al. "Accuracy and Artifact: Reexamining the Intensity Bias in Affective Forecasting." *Journal of Personality and Social Psychology*, vol. 103, no. 4, 2012, pp. 584–605. *Crossref*, doi:10.1037/a0029544.
6. Sheldon, Kennon M., and Sonja Lyubomirsky. "How to Increase and Sustain Positive Emotion: The Effects of Expressing Gratitude and Visualizing Best Possible Selves." *The Journal of Positive Psychology*, vol. 1, no. 2, 2006, pp. 73–82. *Crossref*, doi:10.1080/17439760500510676.
7. Seligman, Martin. Flourish *A Visionary New Understanding of Happiness and Well-Being*. 1st ed., Atria Books, 2012., p. 2
8. Kaufman, Scott Barry. "What Does It Mean to Be Self-Actualized in the 21st Century?" *Scientific American Blog Network*, 7 Nov. 2018, blogs.scientificamerican.com/beautiful-minds/what-does-it-mean-to-be-self-actualized-in-the-21st-century.
9. "Self-Actualization." *Wikipedia*, en.wikipedia.org/wiki/Self-actualization.
10. U.S. Census Bureau. "Was Household Income the Highest Ever in 2019?" *The United States Census Bureau*, 15 Sept. 2020, www.census.gov/library/stories/2020/09/was-household-income-the-highest-ever-in-2019.html.
11. Statista. "Advertising Spending in the U.S. 2015–2022." *Statista*, 28 Mar. 2019, www.statista.com/statistics/272314/advertising-spending-in-the-us.
12. "Income Inequality." *Inequality.org*, 9 July 2021, inequality.org/facts/income-inequality.
13. Shapiro, Leslie, and Heather Long. "Where Do You Fit on the Global Income Spectrum?" *Washington Post*, 20 Aug. 2020, www.washingtonpost.com/graphics/2018/business/global-income-calculator.
14. Wolff-Mann, Ethan. "What the New Nobel Prize Winner Has to Say About Money and Happiness." *Money*, 13 Oct. 2015, money.com/angus-deaton-nobel-winner-money-happiness.
15. Oishi, Shigehiro, et al. "Income Inequality and Happiness." *Psychological Science*, vol. 22, no. 9, 2011, pp. 1095–100. *Crossref*, doi:10.1177/0956797611417262.
16. "Money Matters to Happiness—Perhaps More than Previously Thought." *Penn Today*, 18 Jan. 2021, penntoday.upenn.edu/news/money-matters-to-happiness-perhaps-more-than-previously-thought.

17. Cowles, Charlotte. "One in Ten Americans Is a Shopaholic, Says Survey." *The Cut*, 31 May 2013, www.thecut.com/2013/05/1-in-10-americans-is-a-shopaholic-says-survey.html.

18. Bryant, Kelly. "You Won't Believe How Much Clothing the U.S. Throws Away in a Year." *TakePart*, 29 May 2015, www.takepart.com/video/2015/05/29/clothes-trash-landfill.

19. Fung, Brian. "'Addicted' to Shopping?" *The Atlantic*, 2 Sept. 2012, www.theatlantic.com/health/archive/2012/09/addicted-to-shopping/261845.

20. Grant, Jon E., et al. "Shopping Problems among High School Students." *Comprehensive Psychiatry*, vol. 52, no. 3, 2011, pp. 247–52. *Crossref*, doi:10.1016/j.comppsych.2010.06.006.

21. DeAngelis, Tori. "Consumerism and Its Discontents." *American Psychological Association*, June 2004, www.apa.org/monitor/jun04/discontents.

22. Aknin, Lara B., et al. "From Wealth to Well-Being? Money Matters, but Less than People Think." *The Journal of Positive Psychology*, vol. 4, no. 6, 2009, pp. 523–27. *Crossref*, doi:10.1080/17439760903271421.

23. Dur, Robert, and Max Lent. "Socially Useless Jobs." *Industrial Relations: A Journal of Economy and Society*, vol. 58, no. 1, 2018, pp. 3–16. *Crossref*, doi:10.1111/irel.12227.

24. https://www.thehappymovie.com/.

25. Krznaric, Roman. *How Should We Live?: Great Ideas from the Past for Everyday Life*. Reprint, BlueBridge, 2015. p. 137

26. Dunn, Elizabeth, and Chris Courtney. "Does More Money Really Make Us More Happy?" *Harvard Business Review*, 22 Apr. 2021, hbr.org/2020/09/does-more-money-really-makes-us-more-happy.

27. Osili, Una, and Sasha Zarins. "Fewer Americans Are Giving Money to Charity but Total Donations Are at Record Levels Anyway." *The Conversation*, 3 July 2018, theconversation.com/fewer-americans-are-giving-money-to-charity-but-total-donations-are-at-record-levels-anyway-98291.

28. Scott, Elizabeth. "10 Tell tale Signs You May Be a Perfectionist." *Verywell Mind*, 22 Feb. 2020, www.verywellmind.com/signs-you-may-be-a-perfectionist-3145233.

29. Harter, Susan, chapter 27, "Authenticity," *Handbook of Positive Psychology*, p. 382 C. R. Snyder, Shane J. Lopez · 2001

30. "VIA Character Strengths Survey & Character Reports." *VIA Institute*, 2021, www.viacharacter.org.

31. Cherif, L., Wood, V. M., and Watier, C. (2020). Testing the effectiveness of a strengths-based intervention targeting all 24 strengths: Results from a randomized controlled trial. *Psychological Reports*. http://doi.org/10.1177/0033294120937441 Niemiec, R. M., and McGrath, R. E. (2019). *The power of character strengths: Appreciate and ignite your positive personality*. Cincinnati, OH: VIA Institute on Character.

32. Kashdan, Todd. "Is It a Good Idea To Build on Signature Strengths?" *Psychology Today*, 1 Feb. 2016, www.psychologytoday.com/us/blog/curious/201602/is-it-good-idea-build-signature-strengths.

33. Lyubomirsky, Sonja. *The How of Happiness: A New Approach to Getting the Life You Want*. Illustrated, Penguin Books, 2008. pp. 208–13.

CHAPTER 3

1. Bok, Sissela. *Exploring Happiness: From Aristotle to Brain Science*. 1st ed., Yale University Press, 2011. p. 63.
2. Moeller, Julia, et al. "High School Students' Feelings: Discoveries from a Large National Survey and an Experience Sampling Study." *Learning and Instruction*, vol. 66, 2020, p. 101301. *Crossref*, doi:10.1016/j.learninstruc.2019.101301.
3. Horowitz, Juliana Menasce, and Nikki Graf. "Most U.S. Teens See Anxiety and Depression as a Major Problem Among Their Peers." *Pew Research Center's Social & Demographic Trends Project*, 30 May 2020, www.pewresearch.org/social-trends/2019/02/20/most-u-s-teens-see-anxiety-and-depression-as-a-major-problem-among-their-peers.
4. Flannery, Mary Ellen. "The Epidemic of Anxiety Among Today's Students | NEA." *National Education Association (NEA)*, 28 Mar. 2018, www.nea.org/advocating-for-change/new-from-nea/epidemic-anxiety-among-todays-students.
5. American Psychological Association. (11 Feb. 2014). *American Psychological Association survey shows teen stress rivals that of adults* [Press release]. http://www.apa.org/news/press/releases/2014/02/teen-stress.
6. Geiger, A. W. "18 Striking Findings from 2018." *Pew Research Center*, 13 Dec. 2018, www.pewresearch.org/fact-tank/2018/12/13/18-striking-findings-from-2018.
7. Gallup, Inc. "Confidence in Institutions | Gallup Historical Trends." *Gallup.Com*, 20 July 2021, news.gallup.com/poll/1597/confidence-institutions.aspx.
8. Sanger-Katz, Margot, and Aaron Carroll. "The 'Euphoria' Teenagers Are Wild. But Most Real Teenagers Are Tame." *The New York Times*, 28 June 2019, www.nytimes.com/2019/06/23/upshot/euphoria-hbo-teens-sex-drugs.html.
9. Emmons, Robert. "How Gratitude Can Help You Through Hard Times." *Greater Good Magazine*, 13 May 2013, greatergood.berkeley.edu/article/item/how_gratitude_can_help_you_through_hard_times.
10. Moeller, Julia, et al. "High School Students' Feelings: Discoveries from a Large National Survey and an Experience Sampling Study." *Learning and Instruction*, vol. 66, 2020, p. 101301. *Crossref*, doi:10.1016/j.learninstruc.2019.101301.
11. "NIMH » Post-Traumatic Stress Disorder (PTSD)." *National Institute of Mental Health*, 1 Nov. 2017, www.nimh.nih.gov/health/statistics/post-traumatic-stress-disorder-ptsd.
12. Baumeister, R. F., Bratslavsky, E., Finkenauer, C., and Vohs, K. D. (2001). Bad is stronger than good. Review of General Psychology, 5(4), 323–70. https://doi.org/10.1037/1089-2680.5.4.323
13. American Psychological Association (2019). *Stress in America: Stress and Current Events. Stress in America TM Survey.*
14. Burns, David D. Feeling Good: The New Mood Therapy. New York, NY: Penguin Books, 1981.
15. Danner, Deborah D., et al. "Positive Emotions in Early Life and Longevity: Findings from the Nun Study." *Journal of Personality and Social Psychology*, vol. 80, no. 5, 2001, pp. 804–13. *Crossref*, doi:10.1037/0022-3514.80.5.804.

16. Seligman, Martin. *Flourish (A Visionary New Understanding of Happiness and Well-Being)*. 1st ed., Atria Books, 2012. p. 189.
17. Hamblin, James. "When Upward Mobility Becomes a Health Hazard." *The Atlantic*, 16 July 2015, www.theatlantic.com/health/archive/2015/07/the-health-cost-of-upward-mobility/398486.
18. Neff, Kristin D. "Self-Compassion, Self-Esteem, and Well-Being." *Social and Personality Psychology Compass*, vol. 5, no. 1, 2011, pp. 1–12. *Crossref*, doi:10.1111/j.1751-9004.2010.00330.x.
19. Beaton, Caroline. "Humans Are Bad at Predicting Futures That Don't Benefit Them." *The Atlantic*, 13 Nov. 2017, www.theatlantic.com/science/archive/2017/11/humans-are-bad-at-predicting-futures-that-dont-benefit-them/544709.
20. Collier, L. (2016, November). Growth after trauma. Monitor on Psychology, 47(10). http://www.apa.org/monitor/2016/11/growth-trauma.
21. Kaufman, Scott Barry. "Post-Traumatic Growth: Finding Meaning and Creativity in Adversity." *Scientific American Blog Network*, 20 Apr. 2020, blogs.scientificamerican.com/beautiful-minds/post-traumatic-growth-finding-meaning-and-creativity-in-adversity.
22. https://en.wikipedia.org/wiki/The_Myth_of_Sisyphus.
23. Harvard Health. "Optimism and Your Health." *Harvard Health*, 1 May 2008, www.health.harvard.edu/heart-health/optimism-and-your-health.
24. Conversano, Ciro, et al. "Optimism and Its Impact on Mental and Physical Well-Being." *Clinical Practice & Epidemiology in Mental Health*, vol. 1, no. 1, 2010, pp. 25–29. *Crossref*, doi:10.2174/17450179010060100025.
25. Seligman, Martin *The Optimistic Child: A proven program to safeguard children against depression and build lifelong resilience* with Karen Reivich, Lisa Jaycox, and Jane Gilliam. Houghton Mifflin (paperback), 1995.
26. Carter, Christine. "The Benefits of Optimism." *Greater Good*, 7 Apr. 2008, greatergood.berkeley.edu/article/item/the_benefits_of_optimism.
27. Fredrickson, Barbara. *Positivity: Top-Notch Research Reveals the Upward Spiral That Will Change Your Life by Fredrickson, Barbara (2009) Paperback*. Harmony, 2009. pp. 21–22.
28. Fredrickson, Barbara. *Positivity: Top-Notch Research Reveals the Upward Spiral That Will Change Your Life*. Harmony, 2009. pp. 32–33.
29. Emmons, Robert. *Thanks!: How the New Science of Gratitude Can Make You Happier*. Annotated ed., Houghton Mifflin Harcourt, 2007. pp. 27–29.
30. Abel, Ernest L., and Michael L. Kruger. "Smile Intensity in Photographs Predicts Longevity." *Psychological Science*, vol. 21, no. 4, Apr. 2010, pp. 542–44, doi:10.1177/0956797610363775.
31. Emmons, Robert. *Thanks!: How the New Science of Gratitude Can Make You Happier*. Annotated ed., Houghton Mifflin Harcourt, 2007. pp. 48–50.
32. Emmons, Robert A. *Thanks!: How the New Science of Gratitude Can Make You Happier*. Boston: Houghton Mifflin Co, 2007.
33. Emmons, R. A., and McCullough, M. E. (2003). Counting blessings versus burdens: An experimental investigation of gratitude and subjective well-being in

daily life. *Journal of Personality and Social Psychology*, 84(2), 377–89. https://doi.org/10.1037/0022-3514.84.2.377

34. Goldman, Jason. "Why Bronze Medalists Are Happier Than Silver Winners." Scientific American, 9 Aug. 2012, blogs.scientificamerican.com/thoughtful-animal/why-bronze-medalists-are-happier-than-silver-winners.

CHAPTER 4

1. Iyer, Pico. "Opinion | The Joy of Quiet." *The New York Times*, 31 Dec. 2011, www.nytimes.com/2012/01/01/opinion/sunday/the-joy-of-quiet.html.

2. Roberts, Nicole. "How Much Time Americans Spend In Front Of Screens Will Terrify You." *Forbes*, 23 Apr. 2019, www.forbes.com/sites/nicolefisher/2019/01/24/how-much-time-americans-spend-in-front-of-screens-will-terrify-you/?sh=756635e91c67.

3. "Charlie Chaplin: The Final Speech from The Great Dictator." *Charlie Chaplin.Com*, www.charliechaplin.com/en/articles/29-The-Final-Speech-from-The-Great-Dictator. Accessed 25 July 2020.

4. Whillans, Ashley. *Time Smart: How to Reclaim Your Time and Live a Happier Life*. Harvard Business Review Press, 2020. p. 15.

5. Tim Urban. "The Experience Machine Thought Experiment." *Wait But Why*, 6 Feb. 2017, waitbutwhy.com/table/the-experience-machine.

6. Zimbardo, Philip & Boyd, John. (1999). "Putting Time in Perspective: A Valid, Reliable Individual-Differences Metric". *Journal of Personality and Social Psychology*. 77. 1271–88. 10.1037/0022-3514.77.6.1271.

7. Boniwell, Ilona. *Positive Psychology In A Nutshell: The Science Of Happiness*. 3rd ed., Open University Press, 2012. p. 76–77.

8. Boniwell, Ilona. *Positive Psychology In A Nutshell: The Science Of Happiness*. 3rd ed., Open University Press, 2012. p. 78.

9. Wilson, Timothy D., et al. "Just Think: The Challenges of the Disengaged Mind." *Science*, vol. 345, no. 6192, 2014, pp. 75–77. *Crossref*, doi:10.1126/science.1250830.

10. Wilson, Timothy D., et al. "Just Think: The Challenges of the Disengaged Mind." *Science*, vol. 345, no. 6192, 2014, pp. 75–77. *Crossref*, doi:10.1126/science.1250830.

11. "Who's Feeling Rushed?" *Pew Research Center's Social & Demographic Trends Project*, 28 February 2006, www.pewresearch.org/social-trends/2006/02/28/whos-feeling-rushed.

12. Whillans, Ashley. *Time Smart: How to Reclaim Your Time and Live a Happier Life*. Harvard Business Review Press, 2020. p. 14

13. "Japanese Calendar." *Wikipedia*, 3 July 2021, en.wikipedia.org/wiki/Japanese_calendar.

14. Paradiso, Gaia. "The Importance of Otium & Thermae, Cultural (s)Places for Socialization & Body Caring." *HuffPost*, 30 Dec. 2017, www.huffpost.com/entry/the-importance-of-otium-thermae-cultural-splaces_b_5a478d1de4b0d86c803c76f0.

15. Hayes, Julian, II. "A Study of 35,375 Americans Found the Perfect Amount of Free Time: 2.5 Hours Per Day." *Inc.com*, 5 Jan. 2021, www.inc.com/

julian-hayes-ii/a-study-of-35375-americans-found-perfect-amount-of-free-time-25-hours-per-day.html.

16. https://news.gallup.com/poll/187982/americans-perceived-time-crunch-no-worse-past.aspx.

17. Whillans, Ashley. *Time Smart: How to Reclaim Your Time and Live a Happier Life.* Harvard Business Review Press, 2020. p. 15.

18. Kasser, Tim, and Kennon M. Sheldon. "Time Affluence as a Path toward Personal Happiness and Ethical Business Practice: Empirical Evidence from Four Studies." *Journal of Business Ethics*, vol. 84, no. S2, 2008, pp. 243–55. *Crossref*, doi:10.1007/s10551-008-9696-1.

19. Carle, Eric. *"Slowly, Slowly, Slowly," Said the Sloth.* Reprint, World of Eric Carle, 2007.

20. Levine, Robert. *A Geography Of Time: The Temporal Misadventures of a Social Psychologist.* Revised ed., Basic Books, 1998. p. 9–10

21. Levine, Robert. *A Geography Of Time: The Temporal Misadventures of a Social Psychologist.* Revised ed., Basic Books, 1998. p. 187

22. Fernandez, Luke, and Susan Matt. *Bored, Lonely, Angry, Stupid: Changing Feelings about Technology, from the Telegraph to Twitter.* Reprint, Harvard University Press, 2020. pp. 358–59.

23. Fernandez, Luke, and Susan Matt. *Bored, Lonely, Angry, Stupid: Changing Feelings about Technology, from the Telegraph to Twitter.* Reprint, Harvard University Press, 2020. pp. 358–59.

24. Blum-Ross, A., and S. Livingstone (2016) *Families and screen time: Current advice and emerging research.* Media Policy Brief 17. London: Media Policy Project. London School of Economics and Political Science.

25. "Men Spent 5.5 Hours per Day in Leisure Activities, Women 4.9 Hours, in 2019: The Economics Daily: U.S. Bureau of Labor Statistics." *U.S. Bureau of Labor Statistics*, 2 July 2020, www.bls.gov/opub/ted/2020/men-spent-5-point-5-hours-per-day-in-leisure-activities-women-4-point-9-hours-in-2019.htm.

26. Perrin, Andrew, and Sara Atske. "About Three-in-Ten U.S. Adults Say They Are 'Almost Constantly' Online." *Pew Research Center*, 26 Mar. 2021, www.pewresearch.org/fact-tank/2021/03/26/about-three-in-ten-u-s-adults-say-they-are-almost-constantly-online.

27. Richter, Felix. "The Generation Gap in TV Consumption." *Statista Infographics*, 20 Nov. 2020, www.statista.com/chart/15224/daily-tv-consumption-by-us-adults.

28. Molla, Rani. "Mary Meeker's Most Important Trends on the Internet." *Vox*, 11 June 2019, www.vox.com/recode/2019/6/11/18651010/mary-meeker-internet-trends-report-slides-2019.

29. Blankson, Amy, and Shawn Achor. *The Future of Happiness: 5 Modern Strategies for Balancing Productivity and Well-Being in the Digital Era.* BenBella Books, 2017. p. 11.

30. Goodin, Tanya. "7 Reasons Your Smartphone Is a Weapon of Mass Distraction." *Time to Log Off*, 22 June 2018, www.itstimetologoff.com/2016/03/04/7-reasons-your-phone-is-a-weapon-of-mass-distraction.

31. Blankson, Amy, and Shawn Achor. *The Future of Happiness: 5 Modern Strategies for Balancing Productivity and Well-Being in the Digital Era.* BenBella Books, 2017. pp. 20–21.

32. Vuorre, Matti, et al. "There Is No Evidence That Associations Between Adolescents' Digital Technology Engagement and Mental Health Problems Have Increased." *Clinical Psychological Science*, 2021, p. 216770262199454. *Crossref*, doi:10.1177/2167702621994549.

33. "A 'Goldilocks Amount of Screen Time' Might Be Good for Teenagers' Wellbeing | University of Oxford." *University of Oxford*, 13 Jan. 2017, www.ox.ac.uk/news/2017-01-13-%E2%80%98goldilocks-amount-screen-time%E2%80%99-might-be-good-teenagers%E2%80%99-wellbeing.

34. Lombardi, Esther. "Themes and Related Quotes From 'Waiting for Godot.'" ThoughtCo, Aug. 29, 2020, thoughtco.com/waiting-for-godot-quotes-741824.

35. Bradt, Steve. "Wandering Mind Not a Happy Mind." *Harvard Gazette*, 11 Nov. 2010, news.harvard.edu/gazette/story/2010/11/wandering-mind-not-a-happy-mind.

36. Brewer, J. A., et al. "Meditation Experience Is Associated with Differences in Default Mode Network Activity and Connectivity." *Proceedings of the National Academy of Sciences*, vol. 108, no. 50, 2011, pp. 20254–59. *Crossref*, doi:10.1073/pnas.1112029108.

37. Kabat-Zinn, Jon. *Wherever You Go, There You Are: Mindfulness Meditation in Everyday Life.* 10th ed., Hachette Books, 2005. p. 4.

38. Hölzel, Britta K., et al. "How Does Mindfulness Meditation Work? Proposing Mechanisms of Action From a Conceptual and Neural Perspective." *Perspectives on Psychological Science*, vol. 6, no. 6, 2011, pp. 537–59. *Crossref*, doi:10.1177/1745691611419671.

39. Torre, Jared B., and Matthew D. Lieberman. "Putting Feelings Into Words: Affect Labeling as Implicit Emotion Regulation." *Emotion Review*, vol. 10, no. 2, 2018, pp. 116–24. *Crossref*, doi:10.1177/1754073917742706.

40. Goldstein, Elisha PhD. *The Now Effect: How a Mindful Moment Can Change the Rest of Your Life.* Reprint, Atria Books, 2013. pp. xiii, introduction.

41. Hölzel, Britta K., James Carmody, et al. "Mindfulness Practice Leads to Increases in Regional Brain Gray Matter Density." *Psychiatry Research: Neuroimaging*, vol. 191, no. 1, 2011, pp. 36–43. *Crossref*, doi:10.1016/j.pscychresns.2010.08.006.

42. Davidson, Richard, and Sharon Begley. *The Emotional Life of Your Brain: How Its Unique Patterns Affect the Way You Think, Feel, and Live—and How You Can Change Them.* Illustrated, Avery, 2012. pp. 222–24.

43. Center for Investigating Healthy Minds. "Meditation Affects Brain Networks Differently in Meditators and Novices - Center for Healthy Minds." *Center for Healthy Minds-University of Wisconsin-Madison*, 23 July 2018, centerhealthyminds.org/news/meditation-affects-brain-networks-differently-in-long-term-meditators-and-novices.

44. "Two Studies Reveal Benefits of Mindfulness for Middle School Students." *MIT News | Massachusetts Institute of Technology*, 26 Aug. 2019, news.mit.edu/2019/mindfulness-mental-health-benefits-students-0826.

45. Sapolsky, Robert. *Why Zebras Don't Get Ulcers: The Acclaimed Guide to Stress, Stress-Related Diseases, and Coping* 3rd ed., Holt Paperbacks, 2004. p. 395.

46. Batchelor, Stephen. "Responding to Life, Instead of Reacting to It." *Ten Percent Happier*, 9 July 2021, www.tenpercent.com/meditationweeklyblog/the-practice-of-being-human.

47. Layous, Kristin, et al. "Reframing the Ordinary: Imagining Time as Scarce Increases Well-Being." *The Journal of Positive Psychology*, vol. 13, no. 3, 2017, pp. 301–8. *Crossref*, doi:10.1080/17439760.2017.1279210.

48. Smith, Jennifer L., and Fred B. Bryant. "The Benefits of Savoring Life." *The International Journal of Aging and Human Development*, vol. 84, no. 1, 2016, pp. 3–23. *Crossref*, doi:10.1177/0091415016669146.

49. Bryant, Fred B., et al. "Understanding the Processes That Regulate Positive Emotional Experience: Unsolved Problems and Future Directions for Theory and Research on Savoring." *International Journal of Wellbeing*, vol. 1, no. 1, 2011. *Crossref*, doi:10.5502/ijw.v1i1.18.

50. "Anticipation: The Psychology of Waiting in Line." *Association for Psychological Science - APS*, 2014, www.psychologicalscience.org/news/were-only-human/anticipation-the-psychology-of-waiting-in-line.html.

51. Gable, Shelly L., et al. "What Do You Do When Things Go Right? The Intrapersonal and Interpersonal Benefits of Sharing Positive Events." *Journal of Personality and Social Psychology*, vol. 87, no. 2, 2004, pp. 228–45. *Crossref*, doi:10.1037/0022-3514.87.2.228.

52. Ibid.

53. Kennelly, Stacey. "10 Steps to Savoring the Good Things in Life." *Greater Good*, 23 July 2012, greatergood.berkeley.edu/article/item/10_steps_to_savoring_the_good_things_in_life.

54. Mumford, George. *The Mindful Athlete: Secrets to Pure Performance*. Reprint, Parallax Press, 2016. p. 119

55. Csikszentmihalyi, Mihaly. *Flow: The Psychology of Optimal Experience*. Book Club Edition (BCE)., Harper & Row, 1990. p. 3

56. Walker, Charles J. "Experiencing Flow: Is Doing It Together Better than Doing It Alone?" *The Journal of Positive Psychology*, vol. 5, no. 1, 2010, pp. 3–11. *Crossref*, doi:10.1080/17439760903271116.

CHAPTER 5

1. "Josephson Institute of Ethics Releases Study on High School Character and Adult Conduct—Josephson Institute of Ethics: Training, Consulting, Keynote Speaking." *Josephson Institute*, 9 Oct. 2009, josephsoninstitute.org/surveys.

2. "Josephson Institute of Ethics Releases Study on High School Character and Adult Conduct—Josephson Institute of Ethics: Training, Consulting, Keynote Speaking." *Josephson Institute*, 9 Oct. 2009, josephsoninstitute.org/surveys.

3. "Education and the Future." *Facing History and Ourselves*, www.facinghistory.org/holocaust-human-behavior/education-and-future. Accessed 25 July 2019.

4. Cherry, Kendra. "The Key Characteristics of Heroes." *Verywell Mind*, 14 May 2020, www.verywellmind.com/characteristics-of-heroism-2795943.

5. Sachs, Jeffrey. *The Price of Civilization: Reawakening American Virtue and Prosperity*. Random House, 2011.

6. *Facing History and Ourselves*, www.facinghistory.org/holocaust-and-human-behavior/chapter-12/analysis-reflection. Accessed 19 Feb. 2020.

7. Kennedy, Robert. "Day of Affirmation Address, University of Capetown, Capetown, South Africa, June 6, 1966 | JFK Library." *John F. Kennedy Presidential Library*, www.jfklibrary.org/learn/about-jfk/the-kennedy-family/robert-f-kennedy/robert-f-kennedy-speeches/day-of-affirmation-address-university-of-capetown-cape-town-south-africa-june-6-1966. Accessed 4 Aug. 2019.

8. https://www.youtube.com/watch?v=21FdpfVZyUo.

9. Rosling, Hans, Ola Rosling, and Anna Rosling Ronnlund. Factfulness: Then Reasons We're Wrong About the World-And Why Things Are Better Than You Think. p. 9

10. Everyone Thinks Americans Are Selfish: They're Wrong. Abigail Marsh, May 26, 2021. *The New York Times* Guest Essay.

11. https://www.facinghistory.org/holocaust-and-human-behavior/chapter-2/universe-obligation.

12. Krznaric, Roman The Good Ancestor The Experiment Publishing, 2020 pp. 238–39.

13. "Values." *Haudenosaunee Confederacy*, www.haudenosauneeconfederacy.com/values. Accessed 28 June 2021.

14. "Garrett Hardin." *Southern Poverty Law Center*, www.splcenter.org/fighting-hate/extremist-files/individual/garrett-hardin. Accessed 19 July 2020.

15. "The Tragedy of the Commons." *www.MrAscience.com*, 19 Oct. 2018, mrascience.com/2017/05/04/the-tragedy-of-the-commons-3.

16. Harden, Garrett. The Tragedy of the Commons Dec. 1968: 1243–48

17. Bregman, Rutger. *Humankind*. Bloomsbury Publishing PLC, 2020. pp. 5–6.

18. Solnit, Rebecca. *A Paradise Built in Hell: The Extraordinary Communities That Arise in Disaster*. Reprint, Penguin (Non-Classics), 2010.

19. Bregman, Rutger. *Humankind*. Bloomsbury Publishing PLC, 2020. pp. 311–12.

20. Editor's Note. "37 Who Saw Murder Didn't Call the Police; Apathy at Stabbing of Queens Woman Shocks Inspector." *The New York Times*, 27 Mar. 1964, www.nytimes.com/1964/03/27/archives/37-who-saw-murder-didnt-call-the-police-apathy-at-stabbing-of.html.

21. Dunlap, David W. 1964 | How Many Witnessed the Murder of Kitty Genovese? April 6, 2016 https://www.nytimes.com/2016/04/06/insider/1964-how-many-witnessed-the-murder-of-kitty-genovese.html.

22. Roberts, Sam. "Sophia Farrar Dies at 92; Belied Indifference to Kitty Genovese Attack." *The New York Times*, 3 Sept. 2020, www.nytimes.com/2020/09/02/nyregion/sophia-farrar-dead.html.

23. Jeff Pearlman, Tribune Newspapers. Newsday. "Infamous '64 Murder Lives in Heart of Woman's 'friend.'" *Chicagotribune.com*, 26 Aug. 2018, www.chicagotribune.com/news/ct-xpm-2004-03-12-0403120260-story.html.

24. Darley, J. M., and Batson, C. D., "From Jerusalem to Jericho: A study of Situational and Dispositional Variables in Helping Behavior." JPSP, 1973, 27, 100–108. http://faculty.babson.edu/krollag/org_site/soc_psych/darley_samarit.html.

25. Darley, J. M., and Batson, C. D., "From Jerusalem to Jericho: A study of Situational and Dispositional Variables in Helping Behavior." JPSP, 1973, 27, 100–108. http://faculty.babson.edu/krollag/org_site/soc_psych/darley_samarit.html.

26. Darley, J. M., and Batson, C. D., "From Jerusalem to Jericho: A study of Situational and Dispositional Variables in Helping Behavior." JPSP, 1973, 27, 100–108. http://faculty.babson.edu/krollag/org_site/soc_psych/darley_samarit.html.

27. Darley, J. M., and Batson, C. D., "From Jerusalem to Jericho: A study of Situational and Dispositional Variables in Helping Behavior." JPSP, 1973, 27, 100–108. http://faculty.babson.edu/krollag/org_site/soc_psych/darley_samarit.html.

28. Ibid.

29. Darley, J. M., and Batson, C. D., "From Jerusalem to Jericho: A study of Situational and Dispositional Variables in Helping Behavior." JPSP, 1973, 27, 100–108. http://faculty.babson.edu/krollag/org_site/soc_psych/darley_samarit.html.

30. Milgram, S. (1974). *Obedience to Authority: An Experimental View*. New York: Harper and Row. https://nature.berkeley.edu/ucce50/ag-labor/7article/article35.htm.

31. Sapolsky, Robert. *Behave: The Biology of Humans at Our Best and Worst*. Illustrated, Penguin Books, 2018. p. 95

32. Svoboda, Elizabeth. "If You're in Danger, Will Bystanders Help?" *Greater Good Magazine*, 2 Oct. 2019, greatergood.berkeley.edu/article/item/if_youre_in_danger_will_bystanders_help.

33. "Analysis & Reflection." *Facing History and Ourselves*, www.facinghistory.org/holocaust-and-human-behavior/chapter-12/analysis-reflection. Accessed 19 July 2020.

34. Marsh, Jason, and Dacher Keltner. "We Are All Bystanders." *Greater Good Magazine*, 1 Sept. 2006, greatergood.berkeley.edu/article/item/we_are_all_bystanders.

35. Marsh, Jason, and Dacher Keltner. "We Are All Bystanders." *Greater Good Magazine*, 1 Sept. 2006, greatergood.berkeley.edu/article/item/we_are_all_bystanders.

36. Marsh, Jason, and Dacher Keltner. "We Are All Bystanders." *Greater Good Magazine*, 1 Sept. 2006, greatergood.berkeley.edu/article/item/we_are_all_bystanders.

37. The Nobel Acceptance Speech delivered by Elie Wiesel in Oslo on December 10, 1986 https://eliewieselfoundation.org/elie-wiesel/nobelprizespeech/.

38. Jarrett, Christian. "Social Psychology Textbooks Ignore All Modern Criticisms of Milgram's 'Obedience Experiments.'" *Research Digest*, 9 Mar. 2018, digest.bps.org.uk/2015/10/13/social-psychology-textbooks-ignore-all-modern-criticisms-of-milgrams-obedience-experiments.

39. https://en.wikipedia.org/wiki/Milgram_experiment.

40. "What Can We Learn from the Milgram Experiment." *Khan Academy*, www.khanacademy.org/test-prep/mcat/behavior/social-psychology/v/what-can-we-learn-from-the-milgram-experiment. Accessed 19 July 2020.

41. Khan Academy, "What can we learn from the Milgram experiment" https://www.khanacademy.org/test-prep/mcat/behavior/social-psychology/v/what-can-we-learn-from-the-milgram-experiment.

42. Adam Smith, Jeremy. "Mindfulness Helps You Feel Good about Helping." *Greater Good Magazine*, 2015, greatergood.berkeley.edu/article/item/mindfulness_helping.

43. Frano, Zeno, and Philip Zimbardo. "The Banality of Heroism." *Greater Good*, 1 Sept. 2006, greatergood.berkeley.edu/article/item/the_banality_of_heroism.

44. Svoboda, Elizabeth. *What Makes a Hero?: The Surprising Science of Selflessness 2013 Edition*. Penguin Putnam Inc, 2013. pp. 8–9.

45. Oliner, Samuel. *Do Unto Others: Extraordinary Acts Of Ordinary People*. Basic Books, 2004. p. 95

46. Monroe, Kristen Renwick. "The Political Psychology of Genocide." *Ethics in an Age of Terror and Genocide: Identity and Moral Choice*, Princeton University Press, 2012, pp. 189–247. JSTOR, www.jstor.org/stable/j.ctt7rtff.11.

47. https://www.facinghistory.org/resource-library/rescuers-holocaust-taking-stand

48. Monroe, Kristen Renwick. *The Heart of Altruism*. Edition Unstated, Princeton University Press, 1998.

p. 6

49. Monroe, Kristen Renwick. *The Heart of Altruism*. Edition Unstated, Princeton University Press, 1998.

p. 198.

50. Paxson, Maggie. "What We Can Learn About Being Good From a Village That Saved Thousands During the Holocaust." *Time*, 19 Sept. 2019, time.com/5680342/french-village-rescued-jews.

51. Keneally, Thomas. "How Good People Got That Way." *The New York Times*, 4 Sept. 1988, www.nytimes.com/1988/09/04/books/how-good-people-got-that-way.html.

52. Fogelman, Eva. *Conscience and Courage: Rescuers of Jews During the Holocaust*. Anchor, 1995. p. 254.

53. Fogelman, Eva. Conscience and Courage: Rescuers of Jews During the Holocaust. Anchor, 1995. pp. 158–59

54. Harman, Oren. *The Price of Altruism: George Price and the Search for the Origins of Kindness*. Illustrated, W. W. Norton & Company, 2010.

55. Hudson, et al. "Altruism, Cheating, and Anticheater Adaptations in Cellular Slime Molds." *The American Naturalist*, vol. 160, no. 1, 2002, p. 31. *Crossref*, doi:10.2307/3078996.

56. Mulholland, John. "Earthquakes, Tsunamis and a Naked Tribe. It's Chile—and Not Just the Galápagos—That Inspired Darwin." *The Guardian*, 22 Feb. 2017, www.theguardian.com/science/2015/jan/11/chile-biocultural-centre-charles-darwin-scientific-research.

57. Hilts, Philip. "Fossil Shows Ants Evolved Much Earlier Than Thought." *The New York Times*, 29 Jan. 1998, www.nytimes.com/1998/01/29/us/fossil-shows-ants-evolved-much-earlier-than-thought.html.

58. Brian Hare, Victoria Wobber, and Richard Wrangham, "The self-domestication hypothesis: Evolution of bonobo psychology is due to selection against aggression," *Animal Behaviour*, Volume 83, Issue 3, 2012, https://doi.org/10.1016/j.anbehav.2011.12.007.

59. Waal, Frans de, and de Waal. *The Bonobo and the Atheist: In Search of Humanism Among the Primates*. W. W. Norton, 2013. p. 63.

60. Tan, J., Ariely, D., and Hare, B. Bonobos respond prosocially toward members of other groups. *Sci Rep* 7, 14733 (2017). https://doi.org/10.1038/s41598-017-15320-w.

61. Dreher, Diane. "Survival, Aggression—and Compassion What We Can Learn from the Rhesus Monkeys." *Psychology Today*, 25 Aug. 2016, www.psychologytoday.com/us/blog/your-personal-renaissance/201608/survival-aggression-and-compassion.

62. Little, Becky. "How Did Humans Evolve." *History*, 2021, www.history.com/news/humans-evolution-neanderthals-denisovans.

63. Boehm, C. The natural selection of altruistic traits. Hum Nat 10, 205–52 (1999). https://doi.org/10.1007/s12110-999-1003-z.

64. Churchland, Patricia. *Braintrust: What Neuroscience Tells Us about Morality*. Princeton University Press, 2011.

65. McNerney, Samuel. "Jonathan Haidt and the Moral Matrix: Breaking Out of Our Righteous Minds." *Scientific American Blog Network*, 8 Dec. 2011, blogs.scientificamerican.com/guest-blog/jonathan-haidt-the-moral-matrix-breaking-out-of-our-righteous-minds.

66. Kimball, Roger, et al. "James Q. Wilson on the Moral Sense." *The New Criterion*, 1993, newcriterion.com/issues/1993/9/james-q-wilson-on-the-moral-sense.

67. Generousity p. 204–5

68. Churchland, Patricia. *Braintrust: What Neuroscience Tells Us about Morality*. Princeton University Press, 2011.

69. Saletan, William. "'The Righteous Mind,' by Jonathan Haidt." *The New York Times*, 22 Mar. 2012, www.nytimes.com/2012/03/25/books/review/the-righteous-mind-by-jonathan-haidt.html.

70. Behne, Tanya, et al. "One-Year-Olds Comprehend the Communicative Intentions behind Gestures in a Hiding Game." *Developmental Science*, vol. 8, no. 6, 2005, pp. 492–99. *Crossref*, doi:10.1111/j.1467-7687.2005.00440.x.

71. Weir, K. (2014, April). Not-so blank slates. *Monitor on Psychology*, 45(4). http://www.apa.org/monitor/2014/04/blank-slates.

72. Weir, K. (2014, April). Not-so blank slates. *Monitor on Psychology*, 45(4). http://www.apa.org/monitor/2014/04/blank-slates.

73. Denworth, Lydia. "Two Channels of Empathy." *Psychology Today*, 2017, www.psychologytoday.com/us/blog/brain-waves/201712/the-two-channels-empathy.

74. Zahn-Waxler, C., Radke-Yarrow, M., Wagner, E., and Chapman, M. (1992). Development of concern for others. *Developmental Psychology*, 28(1), 126–36. https://doi.org/10.1037/0012-1649.28.1.126.

75. Hamlin, J. Kiley, and Karen Wynn. "Young Infants Prefer Prosocial to Antisocial Others." *Cognitive Development*, vol. 26, no. 1, 2011, pp. 30–39. *Crossref*, doi:10.1016/j.cogdev.2010.09.001.

76. Hamlin, J Kiley et al. "Social evaluation by preverbal infants." *Nature* vol. 450,7169 (2007): 557–59. doi:10.1038/nature06288.

77. Greene, Joshua. *Moral Tribes: Emotion, Reason, and the Gap Between Us and Them*. Reprint, Penguin Books, 2014. pp. 46–46.

78. "What Is Epigenetics? | CDC." *Centers for Disease Control and Prevention*, 3 Aug. 2020, www.cdc.gov/genomics/disease/epigenetics.htm.

79. Rogers, Kara. "Group selection." *Encyclopedia Britannica*, 21 Jul. 2016, https://www.britannica.com/science/group-selection. Accessed 29 June 2021.

80. Trivers, Robert L. "The Evolution of Reciprocal Altruism." *The Quarterly Review of Biology*, vol. 46, no. 1, 1971, pp. 35–57. *Crossref*, doi:10.1086/406755.

81. Keltner, Dacher. *Born to Be Good: The Science of a Meaningful Life*. W. W. Norton & Company, 2009. (Preface XI).

82. Madison, Lucy. "Elizabeth Warren: 'There Is Nobody in This Country Who Got Rich on His Own.'" *CBS News*, 22 Sept. 2011, www.cbsnews.com/news/elizabeth-warren-there-is-nobody-in-this-country-who-got-rich-on-his-own.

83. "Game Theory." *Wikipedia*, 27 June 2021, en.wikipedia.org/wiki/Game_theory.

84. Inspired by Nicole Le Roux and her demonstration as a guest lecturer in class.

85. Clear, James. "How to Be Happy: A Lesson on Happiness From an African Tribe." *James Clear*, 7 Aug. 2018, jamesclear.com/how-can-i-be-happy-if-you-are-sad.

86. Seltzer, Leon. "The Prisoner's Dilemma and the 'Virtues' of Tit for Tat." *Psychology Today*, 2016, www.psychologytoday.com/us/blog/evolution-the-self/201607/the-prisoner-s-dilemma-and-the-virtues-tit-tat.

87. Dash, Mike. "The Story of the WWI Christmas Truce." *Smithsonian Magazine*, 23 Dec. 2011, www.smithsonianmag.com/history/the-story-of-the-wwi-christmas-truce-11972213.

88. Krnaric, Roman. *The Good Ancestor: A Radical Prescription for Long-Term Thinking*. The Experiment, 2020. pp. 61–62.

89. Mech, L. David. "Whatever Happened to the Term 'Alpha Wolf'?" *International Wolf Center*, 2008, www.wolf.org.

90. Letzter, Rafi. "There's No Such Thing As An Alpha Male." *Business Insider*, 2016, www.businessinsider.com/no-such-thing-alpha-male-2016-10.

91. Krznaric, Roman. *Empathy*. Amsterdam, Netherlands, Adfo Books, 2014. pp. 10–11

92. Suttie, Jill. "Why the World Needs an Empathy Revolution." *Greater Good Magazine*, 1 Feb. 2019, greatergood.berkeley.edu/article/%E2%80%8Bitem/why_the_world_needs_an_empathy_revolution.

93. Krznaric, Roman. "RSA ANIMATE: The Power of Outrospection." *YouTube*, 3 Dec. 2012, www.youtube.com/watch?v=BG46IwVfSu8.

94. Rifkin, Jeremy. "Empathic Civilization." *RSA Animate*, 2010, www.thersa.org/comment/2010/05/rsa-animate-empathic-civilisation.

95. Haidt, Jonathan. "The Positive Emotion of Elevation." *Prevention & Treatment*, vol. 3, no. 1, 2000. *Crossref*, doi:10.1037/1522-3736.3.1.33c.

96. Sacks, Oliver. *Musicophilia: Tales of Music and the Brain*. Twelfth Printing, Vintage, 2008. (preface).

97. Levitin, Daniel. *The World in Six Songs: How the Musical Brain Created Human Nature.* Dutton, 2009. p. 3.

98. Batson, Daniel. *Altruism in Humans.* 1st ed., Oxford University Press, 2011. p. 29.

99. Pfaff, Donald. *The Altruistic Brain: How We Are Naturally Good.* 1st ed., Oxford University Press, 2015. p. 58.

100. Pfaff, Donald. *The Altruistic Brain: How We Are Naturally Good.* 1st ed., Oxford University Press, 2015. pp. 9–10.

101. Rifkin, Jeremy. *The Empathic Civilization: The Race to Global Consciousness in a World in Crisis.* 1st ed., TarcherPerigee, 2009. pp. 82–83.

102. Munoz, Lisa. *"Feeling Others' Pain: Transforming Empathy into Compassion."* Cognitive Neuroscience Society, 21 Aug. 2015, www.cogneurosociety.org/empathy_pain.

103. Levine, Mark, et al. "Identity and Emergency Intervention: How Social Group Membership and Inclusiveness of Group Boundaries Shape Helping Behavior." *Personality and Social Psychology Bulletin*, vol. 31, no. 4, 2005, pp. 443–53. *Crossref*, doi:10.1177/0146167204271651.

104. Rathore, Ajay. "Empathy & Tribalism - Ajay Rathore." *Medium*, 13 Aug. 2019, medium.com/@ajay.rathore_49409/empathy-tribalism-f6afa2c717e2.

105. Pettigrew, Thomas F., et al. "Recent Advances in Intergroup Contact Theory." *International Journal of Intercultural Relations*, vol. 35, no. 3, 2011, pp. 271–80. *Crossref*, doi:10.1016/j.ijintrel.2011.03.001.

About the Author

Stephen A. Banno Jr. is an award-winning social studies educator and creator of the widely popular high school course that explores the science of happiness, kindness, and altruism, which he has taught over his twenty-five-year career. Banno has been a presenter and tennis coach, served as an advisor to many student clubs, and assumed leadership roles collaborating to promote civil rights, racial equity in education, homework innovation, and service learning. He lives near Cape Cod, Massachusetts, with his wife, son, and their dog.

www.ingramcontent.com/pod-product-compliance
Lightning Source LLC
Chambersburg PA
CBHW020654230426
43665CB00008B/429